Public Policy toward Corporations

Public Policy toward Corporations

edited by
Arnold A. Heggestad

UNIVERSITY PRESSES OF FLORIDA
University of Florida Press
Gainesville

UNIVERSITY PRESSES OF FLORIDA is the central agency for scholarly publishing of the State of Florida's university system, producing books selected for publication by the faculty editorial committees of Florida's nine public universities: Florida A&M University (Tallahassee), Florida Atlantic University (Boca Raton), Florida International University (Miami), Florida State University (Tallahassee), University of Central Florida (Orlando), University of Florida (Gainesville), University of North Florida (Jacksonville), University of South Florida (Tampa), University of West Florida (Pensacola).

Orders for books published by all member presses should be addressed to University Presses of Florida, 15 NW 15th Street, Gainesville, FL 32603.

Library of Congress Cataloging-in-Publication Data
Public policy toward corporations / edited by Arnold A. Heggestad.
p. cm.
ISBN 0-8130-0880-8
1. Industry and state—United States.   I. Heggestad, Arnold A., 1943–.
HD3616.U47P82   1987   87-21324
338.973—dc19

Copyright © 1988 by the Board of Regents
of the State of Florida

Printed in the U.S.A. on acid-free paper

This book is dedicated by the contributing authors to
Robert F. Lanzillotti
in recognition of his service as Dean of the College of
Business Administration of the University of Florida
from 1969 to 1986.

Contents

Contributors ix
Introduction xi
I. Current Antitrust Enforcement
  1. Mr. Reagan and Antitrust
    Walter Adams and James W. Brock 3
  2. Antitrust in the Current Economic Environment
    William A. Lovett 17
  3. The New Attack on Antitrust
    Willard F. Mueller 53
II. Antitrust Economics
  4. Vertical Integration of a Monopolist: *Paschall v. Kansas City Star*
    Roger D. Blair and James M. Fesmire 83
  5. A Note on Delivered Pricing Systems
    Yoram C. Peles 102
  6. Quality of Service, Contestable Markets, and the Effectiveness of Motor Carrier Rate Bureaus as Cartels
    Arthur DeVany and Thomas R. Saving 108
III. Regulation and the Theory of the Firm
  7. Deregulation, Competition, and Risk in Commercial Banking
    Arnold A. Heggestad and Stephen D. Smith 129
  8. The Economics of Regulation: Theory and Policy in the Postdivestiture Telecommunications Industry
    David L. Kaserman and John W. Mayo 141
  9. Pricing Achievements in Large Companies
    Kenneth G. Elzinga 166
  10. The Goal of the Firm: Revisited
    Haim Levy 180

Contributors

Walter Adams	Distinguished University Professor (Economics), Past President, Michigan State University
Roger D. Blair	Professor of Economics University of Florida
James W. Brock	Associate Professor of Economics Miami University (Ohio)
Arthur DeVany	Professor of Economics University of California—Irvine
Kenneth G. Elzinga	Professor of Economics University of Virginia
James M. Fesmire	Professor of Economics University of Tampa
Arnold A. Heggestad	William H. Dial Professor of Banking University of Florida
David L. Kaserman	Professor of Economics Auburn University
Haim Levy	Professor of Finance Hebrew University and University of Florida
William A. Lovett	Professor of Law and Economics Tulane University Law School

John W. Mayo	Assistant Professor of Economics University of Tennessee
Willard F. Mueller	William F. Vilas Research Professor of Agricultural Economics, Economics, and Law University of Wisconsin—Madison
Yoram C. Peles	Professor of Economics Hebrew University
Thomas R. Saving	Professor of Economics Texas A&M University
Stephen D. Smith	Associate Professor of Finance Georgia Tech University

Introduction

THE American economic system has entered perhaps one of the most turbulent periods of its history. Deregulation, foreign competition, and the increasing role of financial markets in the decisions of American corporations all pose major challenges to American industry.

Deregulation of American industry has been the centerpiece of the Reagan administration's economic policy. Banking, telecommunications, airlines, and trucking have been transformed as the result of legislation and public policy decisions in recent years. In most cases these decisions have been appropriate and correct, but they have triggered strong reactions from the affected industries and generated unintended stress.

Corporations in many industries are facing extreme competition from an increasingly aggressive, and successful, array of foreign industries. Market shares of some of the strongest U.S. firms have fallen, the trade deficit has risen to record levels, and increasingly economists and business leaders are questioned as to whether American industry, in its present environment, can compete with emerging industries in Europe and Asia.

The combination of stresses inherent in these forces and the increasing role of financial markets in firm decision processes have led to a major restructuring of American industry, including massive consolidation movements in some industries. This trend has been facilitated by an apparent relaxation of antitrust standards, especially regarding mergers. In other industries, subsidiaries of conglomerate firms have been spun off, sold, or liquidated. Finally, hostile takeovers and tender offers, encouraged by an increasingly sophisticated financial community, have led to great pressure on corporate management to keep profitability high.

This book contains original research papers addressed to the foregoing issues and related topics by experts in the field of public policy toward industry. It has three main sections: current policy toward antitrust enforcement, and antitrust law as an effective vehicle for controlling consolidations and mergers; antitrust policy, especially the effectiveness of the Robinson-Patman and Sherman acts in controlling firm behavior; and regulated industries, the impact of deregulation on them, and the theory of the firm in the current economic environment.

Contemporary antitrust enforcement policy is considered, first, by Walter Adams and James Brock, who argue that the Reagan administration's permissive policies have effectively and completely undermined the effect of the antitrust laws in controlling mergers. William A. Lovett takes a longer view of antitrust policy in the United States and concludes that in a dynamic sense and over time, antitrust policy has been used to confront the problems of the period. He argues that the current challenge is for the United States to develop national strategy and policy to make American industry more competitive internationally. Willard Mueller strongly criticizes the Reagan administration for its lack of enforcement of legislation and expresses deep concern whether antitrust policy will continue to be an effective device to ensure that the behavior of corporations works in the public interest in a competitive economy.

In the section on antitrust economics, Roger Blair and James Fesmire analyze the problem of pricing in a situation with vertically successive monopolies, specifically a monopoly newspaper distributing through exclusive dealerships. They prove that it would be in the public interest if the newspapers were vertically integrated, and in this context they consider the recent Eighth Circuit Court decision in *Paschall v. Kansas City Star.*

Yoram Peles revisits the issue of delivered price systems, which is extremely important in international trade and cartels. He concludes that the system is more efficient than a system based on price at the factory and that its use can be justified.

Arthur DeVany and Thomas Saving consider another pricing issue as it applies to the trucking industry. They analyze the effectiveness of rate bureaus that may set general rate increases and broad rate structures in the context of a competitive trucking industry and strong antitrust scrutiny of cartel behavior.

Arnold A. Heggestad and Stephen Smith examine the impact on financial institutions of deregulation of deposits. They demonstrate that the removal of deposit rate ceilings could lead to increased risk taking in the banking sector with an increased failure rate for financial intermediaries.

David Kaserman and John Mayo discuss deregulation of the telecommunications industry and argue that technological change has made desirable even greater deregulation than is currently in place.

Kenneth Elzinga examines the effects of firm pricing strategies on financial performance. He builds on the 1958 Lanzillotti study of pricing behavior in major corporations and considers the ability of companies that had set specific goals to achieve their objectives such as a target rate of return. This paper is provocative in demonstrating that firms were not able to obtain and meet their pricing goals.

Haim Levy provides an analysis of the agency problem that is inherent in a world of asymmetric information and the resulting conflict that develops between management and owners of corporations. He demonstrates that the effect of this conflict is that management will reject risky projects with positive value in the interests of job security.

All of the distinguished scholars represented in this volume have attacked current problems and issues facing the corporation in the current economic environment. The studies are rigorous and timely and it is hoped that they will be of interest to other economists, corporate executives, and policy makers.

Part I. Current Antitrust Enforcement

1. Mr. Reagan and Antitrust

Walter Adams and James W. Brock

UNDER THE Reagan administration, antitrust bashing has once again become a fashionable sport in Washington. While the enforcement agencies have been diligent in their crackdown on hard-core price fixing and bid rigging (primarily in the construction industry) and have opposed some of the more egregiously anticompetitive proclivities of various regulatory commissions, the antimonopoly and antimerger laws have been largely ignored. The merger guidelines were rewritten in 1982 and again in 1984, so that the Justice Department (according to a recent count) has seen fit to challenge only twenty-six of the ten thousand merger applications filed during the 1980s, while at the same time approving some of the largest consolidations in American industrial history. Most significant, however, is the administration's current effort to implement a legislative overhaul of antitrust.

In this paper we shall examine the administration's allegation that antitrust is a nineteenth-century anachronism which blocks efficiency-enhancing mergers and joint ventures, which undermines U.S. competitiveness in world markets, and which therefore contributes to record foreign trade deficits and the decline of American industry on the world scene. In short, we shall inquire whether the proposed euthanasia of our antimerger laws has any empirical validity and any social justification.

Merger Trends

The United States is once again in the midst of a major merger movement. New records are being set not only in the *number* of mergers but also in the *size* of mergers. In 1986, for example, mergers and acquisitions totaled 4,022

Table 1.1. Selected acquisitions and mergers involving major oil companies, 1955–1984 (assets in millions of dollars)

Year	Acquiring Company	Assets	Acquired Company	Assets
1955	Sunray Oil	$ 300.0	Mid Continent Pet.	$ 186.3
1956	Gulf Oil	2,160.0	Warren Pet.	163.9
1960	Standard (N.J.)	9,894.7	Monterey Oil	102.2
1961	Standard (Cal.)	2,782.3	Standard (Ky)	141.9
1963	Gulf Oil	4,243.6	Spencer Chem.	123.3
1963	Cities Service	1,505.8	Tennessee Corp.	100.0
1965	Union Oil	916.5	Pure Oil	766.1
1966	Conoco	1,679.5	Consolidation Coal	446.1
1966	Atlantic Ref.	960.4	Richfield Oil	499.6
1967	Kerr McGee	383.3	Amer. Potash	117.7
1967	Tenneco	3,756.8	Kern County Land	435.3
1967	Signal Oil	678.1	Mack Trucks	303.0
1967	Diamond Alkali	275.6	Shamrock Oil	173.7
1968	Occidental Pet.	779.1	Hooker Chem.	366.5
1968	Occidental Pet.	779.1	Island Creek Coal	115.2
1968	Tenneco	1,911.4	Newport News Ship.	139.3
1968	Sun Oil	1,598.5	Sunray DX Oil	749.0
1969	Atlantic-Richfield	2,450.9	Sinclair Oil	1,851.3
1970	Standard (Ohio)	772.7	British Pet.	657.3
1974	Burmah Oil	2,590.9	Signal Oil	340.1
1976	Marathon Oil	2,005.4	Pan Ocean Oil	139.5
1976	Mobil	18,767.5	Montgomery Ward	1,500.0*
1977	Atlantic-Richfield	8,853.3	Anaconda	2,050.9
1977	Gulf Oil	13,449.0	Kewanee Ind.	389.0
1977	Union Oil	4,226.8	Molycorp Inc.	163.6
1977	Tenneco	7,177.1	Monroe Auto Equip.	190.3
1979	Standard (Ind.)	14,109.3	Cyprus Mines	733.9
1979	Exxon	41,530.8	Reliance Elect.	613.3
1979	Shell Oil	16,127.0	Belridge Oil	3,660.0*
1979	Getty Oil	6,031.9	ESPN	
1979	Mobil Oil	27,505.8	General Crude Oil	792.0*
1980	Mobil Oil	32,705.0	Vickers Energy/Transocean	715.0*
1980	Getty Oil	8,266.7	Reserve Oil & Gas	628.0*
1980	Getty Oil	8,266.7	ERC Corp	536.0*
1981	Occidental Pet.	8.074.5	Iowa Beef Proc.	795.0*
1981	Standard (Ohio)	15,743.3	Kennecott	1,800.0*
1981	Gulf Oil	20,429.0	Kemmerer Coal	325.0*
1981	DuPont	23,829.0	Conoco	7,600.0*
1981	Tenneco	16,808.0	Houston Oil & Min.	400.0*
1981	U.S. Steel	13,316.0	Marathon	6,500.0*
1982	Occidental Pet.	15,772.5	Cities Service	4,000.0*
1984	Texaco	27,100.0	Getty Oil	10,100.0*
1984	Socal	23,500.0	Gulf	13,200.0*
1984	Mobil	36,400.0	Superior	5,700.0*
1986	U.S. Steel/Marathon	18,989.0	Texas Oil & Gas	2,930.0*
1986	Occidental Pet.	12,273.1	Midcon	3,000.0*

*Reported purchase price.

—the highest count since 1974. The total value of all acquisitions reached a record of $125.23 billion in 1984 and new records of $139.13 billion in 1985 and $190 billion in 1986. Combinations valued at $1 billion (or more) have increased steadily—from 3 in 1980, to 34 in 1986.

Beyond these aggregate statistics, at least three significant trends are discernible:

First, the two hundred largest industrial firms in the United States have been in the forefront of this activity. Not only have they bought "small" and "medium-sized" companies, but more and more frequently, they have merged with each other. In recent years, for example, DuPont (fifteenth-largest in the nation) has acquired Conoco (fourteenth-largest in the nation); U.S. Steel (nineteenth-largest) has acquired Marathon Oil (thirty-ninth-largest); Occidental Petroleum (twentieth-largest) has acquired Iowa Beef Processors (eighty-first-largest); Allied Corporation (fifty-fifth-largest) has acquired Bendix (eighty-sixth-largest); and most recently, Allied (now the twenty-sixth-largest industrial firm) has agreed to merge with Signal Companies (sixty-first-largest in the nation). As a result of these and similar megamergers, aggregate control over more and more economic activity is being steadily concentrated into fewer and vastly more powerful hands.

Second, and particularly dramatic, is the merger spree in the petroleum industry, which is summarized in table 1.1. Note, for example, the recent megamergers between the integrated majors—Occidental and Cities Service, Texaco and Getty, Standard Oil of California (Socal) and Gulf—which represent consolidations between the industry's eleventh- and eighteenth-largest, third- and twelfth-largest, and fifth- and sixth-largest firms, respectively. Note also the merger in 1984 between Mobil (the second-largest integrated producer) with Superior, the nation's largest independent explorer for and producer of oil and natural gas. Finally, note the sizable conglomerate mergers involving the major oil companies: Mobil and Montgomery Ward, Exxon and Reliance Electric, Occidental and Iowa Beef Processors, Standard Oil of Ohio and Kennecott Copper, DuPont and Conoco, U.S. Steel and Marathon, etc. All told, the top twenty oil companies spent $26.6 billion on mergers and acquisitions in the short period 1978–81; for the years 1981–83, oil and gas company acquisitions totaled an additional $44.2 billion. It is significant that none of these mergers has been challenged by the U.S. antitrust authorities.

A third aspect of the current merger movement deserves special attention, i.e., "joint ventures." Such arrangements are, in effect, partial consolidations that eliminate competition in those sectors in which the participating companies choose to cooperate rather than to compete. They are analogous to horizontal mergers, in spite of the fact that joint ventures are not counted in official merger statistics. A prime example is the joint venture between General Motors and Toyota—the first- and third-largest auto companies in the

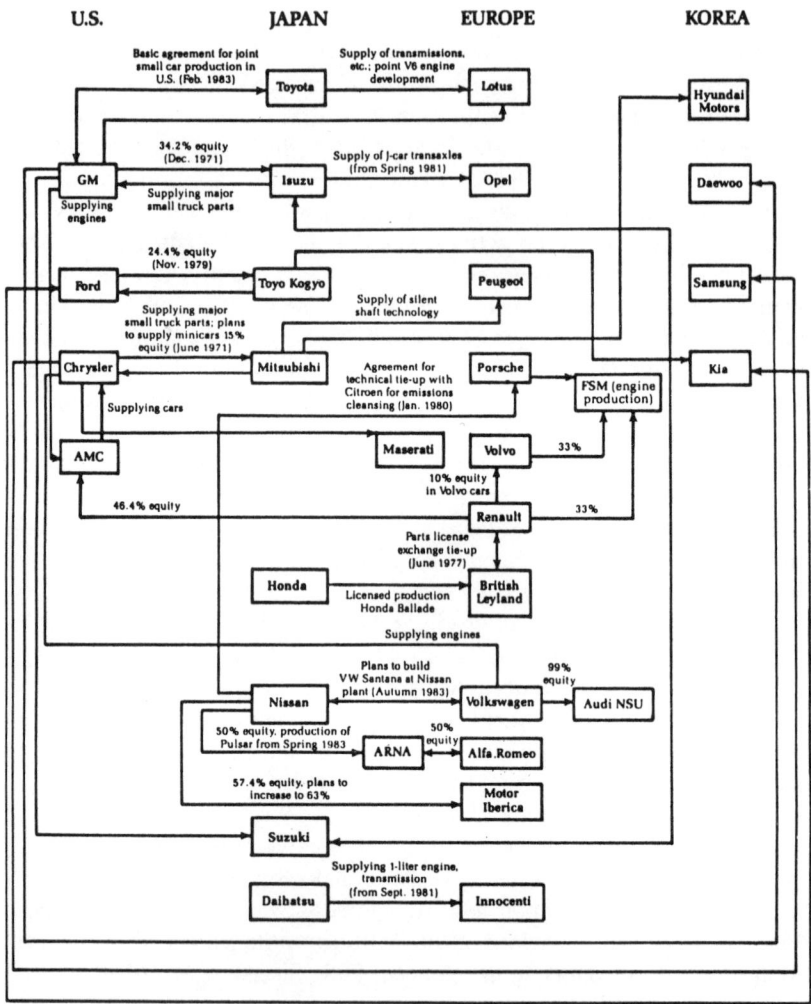

Fig. 1.1. Interlocking relationships among the world's major auto producers. Source: adapted from *Ward's Automotive Yearbook* 1984, p. 52, and various issues of the *Wall Street Journal*.

world. The effects of the arrangement on the U.S. market seem obvious: (1) it eliminates the direct competition that would have occurred between GM and Toyota had they not collaborated; (2) it eliminates the product and production innovations that GM would have been forced to make in order to compete in this important field; (3) it prevents the more vigorous competition that would have taken place if instead of collaborating Toyota had constructed a new manufacturing facility (as Honda and Nissan have done) in the large, lucrative U.S. market; (4) it facilitates an intimate familiarity between the firms through the sharing of information regarding their pricing and product plans, strategies, and tactics, thereby reducing the measure of uncertainty that has made foreign producers like Toyota potent sources of competition for the domestic oligopoly; and (5) it acts as an inducement to additional joint ventures involving other leading producers and thereby encourages further concentration (and less competition) in an already overconcentrated field. (See figure 1.1 for the interlocking relationships that already exist among the world's major auto producers.)

Rationalizations of the Merger Movement

The antitrust laws regarding mergers are abundantly clear. Section 7 of the Clayton Act of 1914 (as amended by the Celler-Kefauver Act of 1950) prohibits all mergers and acquisitions that "may tend to substantially lessen competition" or that "may tend to create a monopoly." The law was to apply to all mergers, horizontal, vertical, and conglomerate, that had the specified anticompetitive effects.

Nevertheless, the Reagan administration has chosen to ignore the law and the obligation to enforce it. Its failure to prosecute megamergers rests primarily on three rationalizations:

(1) The Reagan administration—like its academic apostles of the Chicago School—believes that mergers are designed to achieve efficiency and economies of scale and that mergers rarely have anticompetitive consequences. Moreover, it considers a trend toward economic concentration as "prima facie evidence that greater concentration is socially desirable. The trend indicates that there are emerging efficiencies or economies of scale—whether due to engineering and production developments or to new control and management techniques—that make larger size more efficient. This increased efficiency is valuable to the society at large, for it means that fewer of our available resources are being used to accomplish the same amount of production and distribution." Striking at such trends "prevents the realization of those very efficiencies that competition is supposed to encourage."[1] Therefore, the Reaganites argue, horizontal mergers affecting up to 70 percent of any market should automatically be permitted.[2] Vertical and conglomerate mergers should be ignored altogether because, by definition, they do not involve direct competitors and thus can pose no competitive threat.[3] Vertical and conglomerate power, in this view, are optical illusions.

(2) The Reagan administration believes that mergers (especially, takeovers)

are a valuable instrument for forcing corporate managements to perform in the best interest of the stockholders. According to the President's Council of Economic Advisors, for example, the separation of management from ownership in the modern corporation and the delegation of authority by stockholders to management create "a possibility that management will operate the corporation in management's best interests, and not in the best interests of the corporation's stockholders." The adverse consequences of this practice are serious, the Council warns, "because, if unchecked, it can deter socially beneficial mergers, keep assets from being allocated to higher valued uses, impede adoption of more profitable capitalization plans, and otherwise prevent publicly traded corporations from making the largest possible contribution to aggregate economic performance." Takeovers and the generalized "market for corporate control," according to this view, prevent a divergence of interests by forcing incumbent management to "demonstrate that its performance is competitive with the performances of other potential managers. . . . In this fashion, the external market for corporate control disciplines managers who believe they have maximized the value of the corporation's shares when, in fact, they have not." Upon this (undocumented) belief that mergers improve efficiency and transfer resources to higher valued uses the Council bases its warning that restraints on takeover activity would only protect inefficient managers from the discipline of the merger market for corporate control.[4]

(3) The Reagan administration—following the teachings of Oliver Williamson—apparently believes that capital markets are an imperfect method for optimizing society's investment decisions; that decentralized decision making by myriads of lenders and borrowers is based on inadequate information and involves wasteful transaction costs; and, therefore, that superior results can be obtained by entrusting to giant conglomerates the responsibility for centralized generation, control, and allocation of capital. The Reaganites believe that centralized planning by conglomerates is superior to decentralized planning by the capital market for three reasons: "First, it is an internal rather than external control mechanism with the constitutional authority and expertise to make detailed evaluations of the performance of each of its operating parts. Second, it can make fine-tuning as well as discrete adjustments. This permits it both to intervene early in a selective, preventative way (a capability that the capital market lacks altogether), as well as to perform ex post facto corrective adjustments, in response to evidence of performance failure, with a surgical precision that the capital market lacks. . . . Finally, the costs of intervention by the general office are relatively low." In this view, conglomerates are "capitalism's creative response to the evident limits which the capital market experiences in its relation to the firm."[5]

Armed with these rationalizations, the Reagan administration sees no reason to take action on the merger front. If, for example, the second-largest and third-largest automobile companies (i.e., Ford and Chrysler) were to merge, the Reaganites would perceive the result to be nothing more than increased competition for General Motors. If the two largest steel companies (i.e., U.S. Steel and LTV) were to merge, the Reaganites would rely on ferocious import competition to protect American consumers. If the largest airline (United) were to merge with the largest aircraft manufacturer (Boeing), this would be dismissed as a vertical merger and considered to have no anticompetitive consequences. If Exxon were to combine with IBM, this would be applauded as a mechanism for improving the allocation of capital resources. Above all, since economic concentration is viewed as prima facie evidence of enhanced efficiency, all these mergers would be seen as a contribution to economic welfare. Potentially adverse consequences, we would be told, are a mirage unlikely to be encountered in a smoothly functioning "market economy."

Reality versus Ideology

The foregoing rationalizations of mergers, in particular, and giantism, in general, are not supported by empirical evidence. Indeed, when subjected to dispassionate, clinical analysis, these rationalizations are found to be rooted in ideology rather than reality.

Industrial giantism is not a prerequisite for efficiency.—In his classic 1956 study of twenty representative industries, Joe S. Bain found that, in eleven of twenty cases, the least-cost, most efficient plant would account for less than 2½ percent of the industry's total national sales; in fifteen of twenty cases, for less than 7½ percent; and in only one case, for more than 15 percent. Moreover, in estimating economies obtained by a single firm operating multiple plants, Bain concluded that in six of twenty industries, the cost advantages of multiplant firms "were either negligible or totally absent"; in another six industries, the advantages were "perceptible" but "fairly small;" and in the remaining eight industries, no estimates could be obtained.[6]

A more recent study of twelve industries in seven nations carried out by economist F. M. Scherer generally corroborates Bain's earlier findings. After analyzing minimum optimal scale (MOS) plants required for least-cost production, Scherer reports three key findings: First, with only one exception, "the optimum plant sizes tend to be quite small relative to the national market—too small to warrant high levels of concentration, assuming that each leading firm is large enough to operate only one MOS plant."[7] Second, the loss of production efficiencies in plants vastly smaller than those of optimal scale is surprisingly small; for half of the industries studied, a plant one-third the scale at which unit costs are minimized would suffer cost disadvantages of only 5 percent or less.[8] Third, even after explicitly allowing for production efficiencies that might be achieved by a single firm operating multiple plants, actual firm sizes and market concentration levels significantly exceed those required by economies of scale: market shares held by the top three producers exceeded scale-dictated shares by a factor of ten in two industries; by four to six times in four industries; and by two to three times in three industries.[9] Thus, Scherer's analysis revealed that "actual concentration in U.S. manfacturing industry appears to be considerably higher than the imperatives of scale economies require;"[10] and, further, "that in more than half the industries covered by our research, substantial deconcentration could be effected while forcing at most slight scale economy sacrifices."[11]

Countless other studies and analyses, for specific industries as well as for the manufacturing sector generally, for specialized firms as well as for conglomerates, have demonstrated that giant firm size and extreme industry concentration are *not* technologically determined by the dictates of large-scale economies. As Nobel-laureate George Stigler observed long ago: "One can be opposed to economic bigness and in favor of technological bigness in most basic industries without inconsistency, because our economy is so large that we can have companies large enough to operate efficient plants and numerous enough to be competitive."[12]

In retrospect, Stigler's observation has proved to be prophetic. Today, as *Business Week* notes: "In a rebellion against the conventional wisdom, dozens of manufacturers—including AT&T, FMC, and General Electric—are embracing a new philosophy. Their managers are suddenly talking about 'diseconomies of scale.' They are replacing huge manufacturing complexes with new, smaller plants.... From telecommunications to steel, companies are turning away from bigness to find efficiency"[13] (see fig. 1.2).

Industrial giantism is not a prerequisite for technological progress.—Industrial giantism is not the Prometheus of our high-tech civilization. It is neither a prerequisite for technological progress nor a felicitous instrument for promoting innovation efficiency. It is not the beneficent institution portrayed by corporate propagandists and their academic handmaidens.

This conclusion is based on more than anecdotal and episodic evidence. For example, after surveying a plethora of statistical cross-section studies, F. M. Scherer concluded that "very high concentration has a favorable effect only in rare cases, and more often it is apt to retard progress by restricting the number of independent sources of initiative and by dampening firms' incentive to gain market position through accelerated research and development."[14] Nor is high industry concentration conducive to greater risk taking in research; according to Mansfield, cross-industry results "provide little or no indication that very concentrated industries tend to devote a relatively large percentage of R&D to basic research and to long-term, ambitious, and risky projects."[15]

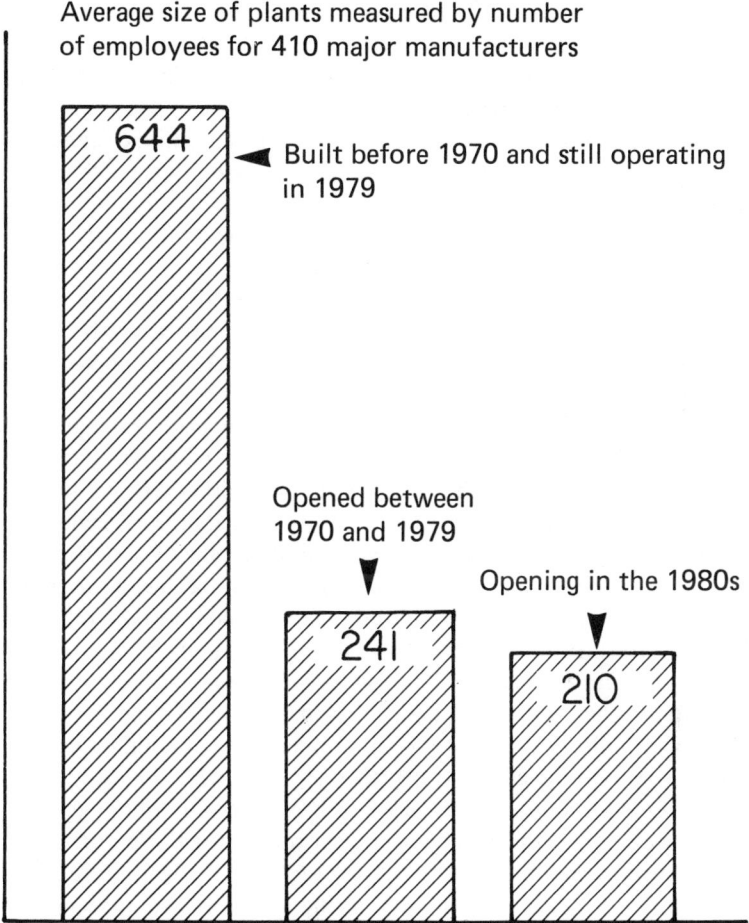

Fig. 1.2. How plant size is shrinking. Source: *Business Week*, 22 October 1984.

Some business leaders are beginning to recognize as much. In their managerial planning, they are beginning to transcend the bigness mystique that so long dominated their corporate belief system. They are beginning to abjure what they once accepted without question as the conventional wisdom. For example, when he was questioned on 19 March 1985 by the *Detroit Free Press* regarding innovative information processing systems for the Saturn small-car project, the chairman of General Motors, Roger B. Smith, confided: "Where is all this great stuff coming from? It's not really coming out of IBM . . . but it's coming out of little two and three-man companies, because they're finding out that 40 guys can't do something that three people can do. It's just the law of human nature."[16] Other corporate leaders, increasingly sensitive to the inventive infirmities of giantism, are now launching small, organizationally separate "start-up" subsidiaries that, they anticipate, will be more inventive and entrepreneurial in spirit.[17]

Could it be that some day the *Fortune* 500 will march into the high-tech future under a banner emblazoned with the revolutionary slogan "Small is Beautiful"?

Conglomerates are not an ideal mechanism for guiding society's allocation of capital.—The recent wave of conglomerates' voluntary divestitures of operating companies they had acquired during the 1960s and 1970s casts considerable doubt on the proposition that conglomerate giants are particularly astute controllers and allocators of capital. "In recent years," as Arthur Burck, a specialist in corporate mergers and reorganizations, points out, "35% of acquisition announcements reflected divestitures, almost all companies that had once been acquired."[18] For example, Gulf & Western was a hyperactive conglomerate acquisitor of sixty-seven companies during the short seven-year period 1960–68; now characterized by *Fortune* as "a conceptually messy agglutination," the firm recently disclosed a massive divestiture plan of billion-dollar proportions, which reportedly includes its zinc, movie theater, cigar, mattress, furniture, video game, and Madison Square Garden operations.[19] Between 1961 and 1968, ITT, one of the nation's largest conglomerates, acquired forty-seven firms with assets of $1.5 billion and operating variously in electronics, consumer financing, car rentals, hotels, baking, and lumber; in 1982, however, ITT also disclosed a vast divestiture program involving more than forty subsidiaries—a program described by one Wall Street analyst as "the biggest sell-off of assets in corporate history."[20] And Big Oil is struggling to divest itself of conglomerate acquisitions. Texaco has sold ESPN (the cable TV sports network); Arco has disposed of its ill-fated investment in the giant Anaconda Copper Company; Mobil is attempting to find a buyer for its spectacularly unsuccessful Montgomery Ward subsidiary; Exxon has written off Reliance Electric; Amoco has spun-off Cyprus Mines (an acquired copper mining company); and Standard Oil of Ohio and Sun Oil have also divested nonoil acquisitions. If conglomerates are such astute capital managers, why would they invest so much in so many acquisitions only to later abandon them? Would capital markets have made the same mistakes?[21]

In this connection, it is important to emphasize that despite the current deconglomeration wave, the building of massive conglomerate empires was not a socially harmless and socially costless experiment. The fact that conglomerate managements are now being punished for their erstwhile mistakes—that the market is now making them pay the price for delinquent judgment in the past—does not mean that society has escaped unscathed. For society, as for individuals, there is no such thing as a free lunch. Every action taken in its name (or on its behalf) exacts an "opportunity cost"—i.e., the cost of not having done something else. Two decades of managerial energy devoted to the conglomerate quick-growth game are two decades during which management's attention is diverted from investment in new plants, new products, and improved manufacturing techniques.

Summary

Based on U.S. experience, the following considerations seem relevant to designing a sound merger policy:

(1) Merging two major steel companies saddled with antiquated, inefficient facilities—LTV and Youngstown in the mid-1970s, and LTV and Republic in the mid-1980s—does not solve the efficiency problem. Combining two losers does not make a winner. If the objective is to become competitive in world markets—to compete successfully against Japan, Inc.—what is needed are new, modern, state-of-the-art plants that are cost-effective. Mergers are not the means to that end.

(2) Merging two giant oil companies does not contribute to energy independence for the United States. It results in neither increased exploration and development nor in the production of one additional barrel of oil or cubic foot of natural gas. Such mergers are a species of paper entrepreneurialism—an effort to find oil on the floor of the New York Stock Exchange.

(3) Giant conglomerate mergers do not enhance efficiency. Experience shows that synergy, the notion that 2+2=5, is a fiction—the invention of imaginative conglomerateurs and their propagandists. Conglomerate giants are *imperia in imperio,* enjoying vast discretionary power not subject to public accountability or public control. They are formed to flatter the ego of men who are like those military commanders who measure their worth by the number of stars on their epaulettes.

(4) Megamergers do not result in the replacement of "inferior" managements by "superior" managements. The management of the acquired company is generally protected by some "golden parachute" arrangement. In the recent megamerger between Allied Corp. and Signal Cos., for example, the top officials of the two companies were reported to have received at least $50 million in cash, stock giveaways, and other benefits. According to the 12 August 1985 *Wall Street Journal:*

> The biggest winners in the proposed payout plan are the three executives who engineered the merger. Edward L. Hennessy Jr., Allied chairman

and chief executive officer, who will head the new concern, is slated to receive an estimated $4.2 million through a combination of accelerated cash awards and stock credits. Forrest N. Shumway, Signal chairman and chief executive, and Michael D. Dingman, Signal president, are expected to receive about $4 million each under just one aspect of their existing contracts, a company spokesman said. . . . Messers. Shumway and Dingman are expected to receive millions more through other contract provisions triggered by the merger. Mr. Shumway will serve as vice-chairman and head of Allied-Signal's executive committee, and Mr. Dingman will be president of the new company. . . . As reported, Messrs. Shumway and Dingman also have received guaranteed employment contracts at Allied-Signal. Under a contract clause, Mr. Dingman, who is slated to succeed Mr. Hennessy when he retires in 1990, is guaranteed to receive salary and benefits regardless of whether he works.

(5) Megamergers are typically financed with borrowed funds rather than cash. Aside from the fact that this has macroeconomic effects (by exacerbating the credit crunch), such debt financing places the merging companies in a precarious position. For example, Mobil (the second-largest U.S. oil company) carries a 40 percent debt burden as a result of its purchase of Superior Oil; Phillips Petroleum's debt is 80 percent of its capitalization—the price it paid to turn back corporate raiders; Occidental Petroleum had to sell off its oil reserve in Colombia because of the debt it incurred when it bought Cities Service; and Chevron (Standard Oil of California) had to sell Gulf's prime oil reserves in Canada to reduce the staggering debt it incurred to raise the $13 billion it paid for Gulf Oil.

There is no need to amplify this list. The point is clear. With few exceptions, megamergers do not result in the building of new plants, increased spending on R&D, or the creation of new jobs or capital. More often than not, they constitute a rearrangement of the deck chairs on the Titanic, and this neither strengthens the nation's economy nor enhances its competitiveness in world markets.

Conclusion

If our analysis is correct, a "liberalization" of the antimerger statutes (or their outright repeal) is not in order. Indeed, public policy might well be pointed in the opposite direction. One alternative would be to prohibit the use of borrowed funds, especially the issue of junk bonds, to finance megamergers. Such a policy would substantially decelerate the current merger mania. Another, more stringent, alternative would be to amend Section 7 of the Clayton Act so as to prohibit outright all corporate mergers involving corporations with assets of more than $1 billion, *unless* the acquiring corporation could affirmatively demonstrate—say, before an expert tribunal like the Federal Trade Commission—that the proposed merger would not be likely to lessen competition in any line of commerce; that it would enhance operating efficiency and contribute substantially to the firm's international competitiveness; and that it would promote technological progress in demonstrably specific ways. Such legislation would, of course, permit any firms, *regardless* of size, to grow by internal expansion—i.e., by building rather than buying. It would even permit growth by acquisition, but only on the basis of proven social advantage rather than on the basis of public relations claims and media hype. Its most positive benefit would be to refocus management's attention on creative entrepreneurship and away from unproductive financial shell games.

Notes

1. R. Bork, *The Antitrust Paradox* (New York: Basic Books, 1978), 205–6.
2. Ibid., 221.
3. Ibid., 226–27, 248.
4. Annual Report of the Council of Economic Advisors, 1985, 188–99.
5. O. Williamson, *Markets and Hierarchies* (New York: Free Press, 1975), 158–59.
6. J. Bain, *Barriers to New Competition* (Cambridge: Harvard University Press, 1956), 73, 85–88.
7. F. Scherer, *Industrial Market Structure and Economic Performance*, 2d ed. (Chicago: Rand McNally, 1980), 94.
8. Ibid.
9. F. Scherer et al., *The Economics of Multi-Plant Operation* (Cambridge, Mass.: Harvard University Press, 1975), 339.
10. Scherer, *Industrial Market Structure*, 118.
11. Scherer et al., *Economics of Multi-Plant Operation*, 393.
12. U.S. Congress, House Subcommittee on the Study of Monopoly Power, pt. 4-A, 81st Cong., 2d sess., 1950, 967.
13. *Business Week*, 22 October 1984, 152.
14. Scherer, *Industrial Market Structure*, 438. See also J. M. Blair, *Economic Concentration* (New York: Harcourt Brace Jovanovich, 1972), 199–254; Walter Adams and James W. Brock, *The Bigness Complex* (New York: Pantheon, 1986).
15. Edwin Mansfield, *The Economics of Technological Change* (New York: Norton & Co., 1968).
16. *Detroit Free Press*, 19 March 1985, 9A.
17. *Business Week*, 18 April 1983, 84–89.
18. *Business Week*, 6 December 1982, 14.
19. *Fortune*, 4 April 1983, 141–42; *Wall Street Journal*, 15 August 1983, 3. Detailed analysis of Gulf & Western's conglomerate acquisition spree in the 1960s is contained in Federal Trade Commission, Staff Report, *Economic Report on Corpo-*

rate Mergers, 28 August 1969, reprinted in U.S. Congress, Senate Subcommittee on Antitrust and Monopoly, *Economic Concentration, Hearings,* pt. 8A, 91st Cong., 1st sess., 1969.
20. *Fortune,* 11 January 1982, 34–39; Federal Trade Commission, *Economic Report on Corporate Mergers.*
21. Perhaps mergers are consummated in the heat of the moment, and perhaps this explains why there are inevitable morning-after regrets. Perhaps merger makers could avoid mistakes if they heeded a popular Italian proverb: "L'amore e com'il vino. La sera e buono, la matina e guasto" (Love is like wine. In the evening, it's wonderful. The morning after, it tastes awful).

2. Antitrust in the Current Economic Environment

William A. Lovett

U.S. ANTITRUST law and enforcement is a distinctively American contribution to the economic regulation of modern industrial economies. Its goals have been to promote fairness, competition, efficiency, decentralization, and small business, along with fostering broader economic opportunity and prospects for social mobility.[1] Monopolies and excessive concentrations of economic power (not justified by social efficiency) have been discouraged under this tradition.[2] The result has been a more humane, productive, and resilient industrial society with wider participation and sharing of success. This performance has strengthened a federal democracy and helped transform an agrarian society with limited industry (before the Civil War) into an industrial giant with vigorous entrepreneurship and much higher living standards for the majority.

Successful U.S. antitrust policy has been emulated (to some degree) in an increasing number of industrial societies since World War II.[3] Decartelization policies were imposed on West Germany and Japan immediately after the war and gradually took root in their cultures. Shortly thereafter, Britain, followed by other European nations, implemented decartelization policies (along with Articles 85 and 86 of the European Economic Community [EEC] Treaty). Most of Europe and the EEC now use anticartel and procompetition policies to some degree. Antitrust traditions have also developed in Canada, India, and Australia. More recently, antitrust policies have been established in new industrial countries, including South Korea, Taiwan, Brazil, Argentina, and even Mexico (to a modest degree). Some kind of antitrust policy has become normal for most broadly participative free-enterprise countries (as opposed to Marxist socialism or oligarchic capitalism).[4]

Earlier Background and Development

English Common Law and the New American Republic

The roots of American antitrust can be traced to early common law court decisions encouraging freer access to certain occupations and trades.[5] While England shared in European feudal and guild restrictions that limited freedom for most peasant serfs and many artisans, a limited tradition of case law against trade restraints gradually emerged. By the Tudor period (Edward VI), statutes against "forestalling," "regrating," and "engrossing" were enacted, which outlawed cornering a market, persuading people to enhance prices, or "any of which practices make the market dearer to the fair trader."[6] Although Elizabeth I encouraged some monopolies in new industries, the courts began to limit them (*Davenant v. Hurdis*, 1599; and *Darcy v. Allen*, 1602), and the Statute of Monopolies in 1624 outlawed them generally, except for patents on new inventions, along with printing, saltpeter, gunpowder, great ordnance and shot.[7]

This was the mid-eighteenth-century legal environment. Adam Smith sought further liberalizing toward freer trade and competition.[8] He urged elimination of feudal and guild privileges, trade barriers, and corporate charters of monopoly. This English common law and ideology were transplanted literally through the saddlebags of early American lawyers and publicists to a rapidly growing, frontier Republic, a hospitable home for liberal legal institutions and economic doctrines. Yet not much U.S. litigation drew directly upon the common law precedents against restraint of trade, forestalling, etc. In a big new agricultural country with millions of farms, hundreds of thousands of shops and artisans, and rapidly multiplying factories, not much litigative effort was needed to build institutions of yeomanry. The subdivision of most of the country into family farms and ranches, however, was very important as a competitive discipline, along with rapidly extended federalism and many new states, towns, and cities.[9]

Early Industrial Monopolies, Trusts, and the Sherman Anti-Trust Act.

As some nationwide industrial combines, trusts, and corporations developed in the later nineteenth century, however, government supervision and regulation gradually attempted to limit undue exploitation of their economic power. State public service commissions began to regulate railroad and utility rates, followed by the Interstate Commerce Commission in 1883 (strengthened substantially by the Hepburn Act of 1906).[10] And Congress enacted the Sherman Act in 1890, which outlawed combinations, conspiracies, or agreements in restraint of trade, together with attempts to monopolize trade among the states or with foreign nations.[11]

While initial Sherman enforcement was limited, key decisions (*Trans-Missouri Freight*, 1897; *Joint-Traffic*, 1898; and *Addyston Pipe*, 1898–99) proscribed price fixing and cartel agreements as illegal.[12] Theodore Roosevelt established the Bureau of Corporations in 1903 as an investigative agency to deal with the big "trusts" and industrial combinations, and the Supreme Court in 1904 held a great railroad merger unlawful in *Northern Securities v. United States*.[13] Somewhat later the Court broke up three leading "monopolies" (*Standard Oil, American Tobacco*, and the *Sugar Trust*, 1910–11) under the "rule of reason."[14] While interpreting the Sherman Act more liberally to bar only *unreasonable* restraints of trade, the Court still held that a dominating industrial combine created through mergers and using predatory pricing practices (localized price cuts to eliminate small competitors or disproportionate discounts extracted from suppliers) could be unlawful. And early vertical price-fixing restraints were limited, so that sellers could not force uniform resale prices upon goods already sold into the stream of interstate commerce (*Dr. Miles*, 1911).[15]

Clayton and FTC Acts

But the Supreme Court's new "rule of reason" doctrine (championed by Louisiana's Edward D. White as chief justice) created an obvious ambiguity.[16] Just how much restraint of trade or attempt to monopolize would be "unreasonable" and subject to illegality under the Sherman Act? All major political factions in 1912 (Bull Moose Republicans, Old Guard Republicans, and Democrats) endorsed a Fair Trade Commission to define the law more precisely.[17] The result was the Clayton and Federal Trade Commission Acts of 1914.[18] The Clayton Act outlawed stock acquisitions in corporations (a common form of merger), price discrimination, exclusive dealing and tying arrangements, and interlocking directorates, whenever the effect "may be substantially to lessen competition" in any line of commerce in any section of the country.[19] Labor unions were exempted for the most part from prosecution under the antitrust laws, and new private treble-damage actions (with reasonable attorney's fees) were authorized to mobilize further enforcement of the Sherman and Clayton Acts.[20] In addition, the Federal Trade Commission Act created a new quasi-judicial enforcement body (the FTC) with broad investigative powers and cease-and-desist-order authority to remedy "unfair methods of competition."[21] The Bureau of Corporations' staff was transferred to the FTC, becoming its Bureau of Economics.

Early enforcement efforts in the Wilson administration were promising, but the FTC was distracted with World War I industrial mobilization efforts. Then came the president's illness, controversy over the League of Nations, and a political victory for conservative Republicans under Warren Harding.[22]

Relaxed Antitrust and the Good Trust Era

Prosperity and economic growth with a significant spread of new industries—automobiles, gasoline stations, airplanes, radios, movies, records, and plastics continued through World War I into the 1920s. A proliferation of new appliances and improved machinery and technology changed everyday life. Henry Ford's mass production line efficiency seized the world's imagination, as did chain stores, mass distribution and merchandizing. Many small-town and rural people were flocking to the bigger cities. In these circumstances, with a shift to more conservative faith in free enterprise, there was less populist alarm about the dangers of bigger business.[23]

Furthermore, with Sherman Act enforcement, leading American firms moderated their growth policies, limiting the drive to consolidate entire industries and resulting in less blatant predatory behavior. In three monopolization cases—*American Can*, 1916–21; *U.S. Steel*, 1920; and *International Harvester*, 1927—leading combines had slowed their expansion, accepted less than dominance, and in the Court's words, "resorted to none of the brutalities or tyrannies . . . of other [earlier] combinations."[24] The Court added that "mere size" is no offense and that the "existence of unexerted power" is no abuse.[25]

Nonetheless, the courts still rejected price fixing and cartel agreements. In *Trenton Potteries*, 1927, the Court refused a claim of reasonability for a price-fixing group with 82 percent of the vitreous pottery (bathroom fixtures) industry.

> The aim and result of every price-fixing agreement, if effective, is the elimination of one form of competition. The power to fix prices, whether reasonably exercised or not, involves power to control the market and to fix arbitrary and unreasonable prices. The reasonable price fixed today through economic and business changes may become the unreasonable price of tomorrow. . . . Agreements which create such potential power may well be held to be in themselves unreasonable.[26]

Furthermore, in *American Column and Lumber*, 1921, the Court held unlawful an "Open Competition Plan," in which *detailed* invoice pricing, shipments, and inventory data were shared through a trade association, because this facilitated "tacit understanding that all were to act together" to fix market prices and thus restrict competition by concerted action.[27] But, the Court held in *Maple Flooring*, 1925, that *aggregated* supply, demand, and cost data could be collected and disseminated by trade associations, since this would improve industry efficiency and allow independent competition.[28]

With respect to distribution and vertical restraints, the Court held tying arrangements unlawful when patented machinery was used as leverage to force purchases of other collateral products, e.g., patented film projectors and film sales (*Motion Picture Patents,* 1917), or patented freezing containers and dry ice (*Carbice,* 1931).[29] On the other hand, the law relaxed significantly with respect to resale price maintenance when systematic customer selection to enforce resale prices was allowed (*Colgate,* 1919), and "agency-consignment" contracts to achieve this result on patented light bulbs were held permissible (*General Electric,* 1926).[30] Meanwhile, the Clayton Act provisions (1914) on price discrimination proved weak and unenforceable in practice, and big discounts to chain store buyers become more important in fostering supermarket and other chains.[31]

Depression Strains and Legislation

The Great Depression brought a crisis of unemployment and reduced sales and earnings to many families, farms, and business enterprises.[32] An early New Deal response was the National Recovery Administration (NRA), which promoted codes of industrial conduct and pricing for most manufacturing industries and many distribution sectors. Efforts to improve prices and incomes were made also in the agricultural sector (Agricultral Adjustment Act [AAA]). A system of farm price controls, subsidies, and support for agriculture gradually was established. Labor unions received encouragement, especially under the Wagner Act and from the new National Labor Relations Board (NLRB). The financial sector (banking, securities, and thrift institutions) became more closely regulated. A new Federal Deposit Insurance System (FDIC and FSLIC) and the Securities and Exchange Commission (SEC) helped regulate the stock exchanges and securities markets. Modest federal regulation in the power, communications, and transport sectors were enlarged substantially and made more systematic. The Social Security system was also created, with federal old-age pensions, unemployment compensation, and more complete state workman's compensation (accident insurance coverage).

Initially, though, antitrust law was neglected and even weakened during the New Deal.[33] NRA industrial codes and regulation were favored instead, and the Court relaxed the *Addyston Pipe-Trenton Potteries* rule against price fixing and cartels. In *Appalachian Coals,* 1933, a coal industry market stabilization plan and attempts toward a distress cartel were approved.[34] But NRA codes and price-fixing efforts failed to restore employment and general prosperity. Instead, they aggravated unemployment and surplus strains by tending to keep some prices rigid, which hindered markets from clearing properly at full employment.[35]

When the NRA was declared unconstitutional as an invalid delegation of congressional power, there was renewed pressure for helping small business.

"Fair trade" laws (state and federal) followed that gave manufacturers greater resale price maintenance power in the hope of raising an umbrella of higher retail price margins, under which small retailers, groceries, and drug and liquor stores might survive chain competition.[36] And more significant, in some respects, the Section 2 Clayton Act rule against price discrimination was strengthened. Under new Robinson-Patman Act amendments, the burden of proof for illegal price discrimination was reduced significantly to mere "competitive injury," but the rule's scope was narrowed to "goods of like grade and quality." The FTC was given an enforcement mandate, and it tried to narrow primary and secondary line price differentials through extensive cease-and-desist order enforcement. In this way, deep discounts to chains could be reduced (secondary line "injury") and predatory pricing against isolated smaller firms inhibited (primary line "injury").[37]

Thurman Arnold and Systematic Antitrust Enforcement

In 1937 Thurman Arnold, an imaginative law professor, became head of the Antitrust Division of the U.S. Department of Justice. Arnold's *Folklore of Capitalism* had criticized weak antitrust enforcement and the NRA's promotion of business codes.[38] In particular, he warned of market dominance, trade associations, price leadership, patent pools, and securities manipulation as means toward increased profits, higher prices, and reduced competition. Under Arnold's leadership a larger, more systematic investigative and prosecution effort followed.[39]

Major new decisions emerged, including *Socony Vacuum,* 1940, which outlawed price-fixing cartels as unlawful per se without regard to the reasonability of their pricing.[40] (This restored the anticartel tradition of *Addyston Pipe–Trenton Potteries* and left *Appalachian Coals* ignored.) Close-knit patent pools that restricted competition in significant industries were challenged. Vertical restraints, tying arrangements, and exclusivity practices that might limit competition were attacked.[41] Perhaps most important, the antitrust supervision and enforcement effort was enlarged greatly, made more professional, and combined with some talented economists. Although most of the Antitrust Division and FTC shifted to war mobilization and price control efforts during World War II, expanded antitrust enforcement resumed in both agencies after the war.

In *Alcoa,* 1945; *American Tobacco,* 1946; and *United Shoe Machinery,* 1953; leading industrial firms were subjected to a tougher monopolization rule.[42] Now market leadership or dominance combined with exclusionary practices was sufficient for prosecution, remedial injunctions, or even possible divestiture (where multiple competitors could be established viably to replace a dominant enterprise). (Similar deconcentration and decartelization were pursued to some degree in occupied Germany and Japan under U.S. auspices.)[43]

Basing-point pricing systems were broken up in *Cement Institute,* 1948, although the Court set significant limits upon cartel prosecution by holding that "conscious parallelism" in pricing or conduct would not be sufficient, without more, to constitute an illegal combination or conspiracy in restraint of trade (*Theatre Enterprises,* 1953).[44] On the other hand, blatant conspiracies to fix prices or restrain trade could be dealt with firmly with extensive treble-damage liabilities, as in *Heavy Electrical Equipment,* 1960.[45] And exclusive patent licensing pools that significantly restrained competition were broken up, with reasonable royalty, compulsory licensing declared as relief to ensure easier entry, as in *Imperial Chemical Industries,* 1952.[46]

With respect to statutory development, a major change was amendment of Section 7 of the Clayton Act, 1950, to close the asset-merger loophole.[47] Unfortunately, the original Section 7 merger provision (1914) was emasculated by poor draftsmanship. Although designed to limit mergers generally that "may be substantially to lessen competition," the statute only proscribed mergers involving acquisitions of stock in corporations. Thus, mergers via acquisitions of corporate assets were unregulated, regardless of size or anticompetitive consequences. An FTC Economic Report on Mergers, 1940–47, viewed with alarm an increased rate of corporate mergers during the expansion associated with the war and postwar prosperity. Congress feared a rising tide of economic concentration and accordingly outlawed *all* mergers that might substantially lessen competition with the Celler-Kefauver Act amendments of 1950.

Structuralist Enforcement Policy: Late 1950s to 1970s

Concentration, Entry Barriers, and Oligopolies

Modern industrial organization economics and imperfect competition analysis developed mainly since the 1930s.[48] Most earlier classical and neoclassical economists simply condemned monopolies and supported freer competition. But Adam Smith, for example, saw dangers in business combinations, which anticipated modern concerns. He observed that:

> People of the same trade seldom meet together, even for merriment and diversion, but the conversation ends in a conspiracy against the public or in some contrivance to raise prices. . . .[49]

> [T]he interest of dealers . . . in any . . . branch of trade or manufactures is always in some respects different from, and even opposite to that of the

public. To widen the market and narrow the competition, is always the interest of the dealers. [Thereby dealers may] levy, for their own benefit, an absurb tax upon the rest of their fellow citizens.[50]

Nonetheless, the bulk of older economists had seen monopoly as a special, rather limited, situation so long as freer competition was sustained by law and government. Frank Taussig, a leading American neoclassical economist in the early twentieth century, summed up prevailing views:

Complete and unqualified monopoly is rare. . . . Successful corners are rare. . . . Hence too much stress should not be laid on the theory of monopoly price in explaining the phenomena of actual life.[51]

It was the rise of some concentrated industries (including early trusts and monopolistic combinations around the turn of this century) followed by many "oligopolies" in the 1920s that led to serious questions about the performance of industries with relatively few significant enterprises. Widespread sluggishness, rigid prices, and slow economic recovery in the 1930s accentuated these concerns.

By the later 1950s "structuralist" thinking was becoming predominant in the new speciality of industrial organization economics, and it emphasized the widespread presence of oligopolies.[52] While performance varied among the industries, the new learning suggested that high concentration oligopolies protected by significant entry barriers and sufficient product differentiation would often behave somewhat more monopolistically and less competitively. In special circumstances (e.g., with rapid demand growth, substantial technological progress, or divergent costs of production), concentrated industries might still be vigorously competitive and could perform reasonably well. But in more stable industries, entry-protected, high-concentration oligopolies tended to higher profits, greater sluggishness, and weaker overall performance and often allowed excessive union wage demands to be passed along to the public with cost-push, "structural" inflation pressures.

Accordingly, the following public policies seemed logical. While high-concentration oligopolies were hard to break up, it would be fairly easy to prevent large mergers that could cause significant concentration increases. Entry barriers should be lowered, if possible, and easier access provided to international trade. Big firms enjoying "market power" (i.e., leaders in entry-protected, high-concentration oligopolies) should be closely supervised by antitrust agencies. Such firms were the most likely to exploit their leverage, collaborate with each other to restrict competition, eliminate weaker and small business rivals, and/or exploit the consuming public.[53]

Merger policies.—During the later 1950s a "structuralist" approach to mergers was implemented by the Antitrust Division and the Federal Trade Commission with many antimerger complaints. Lower courts provided support to this policy in early decisions (*Hamilton v. Benrus,* 1953; and *Bethlehem-Youngstown,* 1958).[54] The Warren Court then decisively endorsed this policy with strong opinions in *Brown Shoe,* 1962, and *Philadelphia Bank,* 1963.[55] The Court emphasized a congressional purpose to limit a rising tide of economic concentration.

A tough line was laid down on larger horizontal and vertical mergers.[56] Big companies with hefty market shares were not allowed to make mergers within their own industries or markets nor to buy up their leading customers or suppliers. The only significant exception was the "failing company" doctrine, under which firms in serious financial trouble with doubtful prospects of survival could be acquired. (Obviously, the elimination of already failing firms as independent competitors would represent little loss to competition; a bailout merger would be more likely to save jobs, plants, and assets than to force weak companies into bankruptcy.) This policy still permitted many smaller mergers among medium-sized and lesser firms and even tolerated modest acquisitions by big companies. It meant, however, that the largest industrial corporations were less able to grow by merger than were small or medium-sized rivals. This was considered a desirable result in gradually fostering more decentralized, vigorous competition over the long run.

With respect to diversification or conglomerate mergers, however, a much softer line emerged.[57] Relatively few complaints against conglomerate mergers were filed, despite the fact that such transactions flourished and grew rapidly during the rising bull market of the mid to late 1960s. While large horizontal and vertical mergers were sharply limited, the route to diversification remained open and largely unchecked, except for some of the biggest U.S. corporations (which felt somewhat inhibited from large-scale diversification by merger). (In 1969, three major complaints were filed against "superconglomerate" mergers. Each involved billion dollar acquisitions, and each was blocked substantially by settlement.)[58] Otherwise, the only legal doctrine used much against diversification mergers under Section 7 of the Clayton Act concerned the "elimination of potential entrants." Under this reasoning a conglomerate acquisition could be challenged if a significant reduction in the number of likely entrants into an industry resulted from a merger. But not many acquisitions had this much impact. Often there were many conceivable entrants (and the elimination of one was insignificant) or little entry was likely by direct investment (so an outside acquisition did not much alter an oligopoly's competition). In some situations, though, just a few entrants were available, so that elimination by merger of one strong candidate for independent entry might significantly weaken the force of new competition. The Supreme Court endorsed this theory in *Penn-Olin*, 1964, and *Falstaff-Narraganset*, 1973, but backed away in *Marine Bancorporation*, 1974, as the new Burger Court majority favored a more relaxed rule on diversification mergers.[59]

Meanwhile, the pace of merger activity eased substantially as the economy slowed during the 1970s, and stock prices lost their sustained upward momentum.[60] Merger enforcement relaxed slightly during the mid to late 1970s, but the law did not change significantly. Large horizontal and vertical mergers were still considered unlawful, while most diversification mergers went unchallenged (and only the largest corporations were inhibited from making major diversification acquisitions). But sluggish stock prices slowed merger deal making appreciably.

Cartels and price fixing.—Price fixing and cartel agreements remained unlawful per se (under *Socony-Vacuum*) in the 1960s and 1970s.[61] But antitrust enforcement efforts increased somewhat in this period, and the object lesson of heavy treble-damage liabilities to overcharged customers (even class actions) made business more aware of the costly risks of misbehavior. Many economists, however, observed that highly concentrated oligopolies did not require explicit price-fixing cartels to maintain effective consensus on slightly increased prices and somewhat more generous profit margins. Conscious interdependence, mutual limits to rivalry, and sophisticated price leadership could sustain these outcomes, provided that significant new entry and excess capacity could be avoided.[62]

Concern about this loophole in price-fixing behavior became part of inflation controversy in the late 1960s and the 1970s.[63] Concentrated oligopolies normally offered weaker resistance to strong union wage demands. When general inflationary momentum was launched by fiscal-monetary stimulus or large government deficits (with near full employment), a significant wage-price spiral could be set in motion. This inflationary momentum was hard to stop without a substantial, sustained recession.

Experience of the late 1970s and early 1980s suggested only two major ways to limit serious inflationary pressures in mature economies (with widespread concentrated oligopolies):[64] (1) Some countries (such as Japan) used fairly balanced fiscal-monetary and wage-price discipline. They limited budget deficits, monetary growth, and union wage demands and kept their industries (and export prices) sufficiently competitive by world market standards. (2) Other countries (including the United States during the early to mid-1980s) used a more drastic recession to create ample slack in labor and industrial markets. This slump greatly slowed wage and price increases, though at the cost of some losses in real growth and employment. Obviously, the stronger compromise is more complete discipline with less slump, more growth, and more employment. A third option (followed by many nations) was to accept indexed inflation with less obvious slump and unemployment for the short term and hope things might improve somehow in the future.[65] Unfortunately, sustained inflation normally tended to distort investment, often reduced productivity, encouraged capital flight, and slowed real economic growth. In retrospect, the wisest policy (though not always easy politically), seems to be combined fiscal, monetary, and wage-price discipline.[66]

Distribution restraints and price discrimination.—Distributional restraints and price discrimination can be anticompetitive in some circumstances.[67] Strong firms in concentrated oligopolies (with weak rivalry from little firms and not much discipline from outside entrants) may exploit their "market power" in a number of ways. They can act in concert to boycott or exclude competitors; impose tying or exclusive dealing relationships to "lock in" customers (or suppliers) and make entry more difficult for outsiders; artificially enlarge patent entry barriers (patent "abuse"); or use price discrimination in selected markets to discipline, weaken, cripple, or destroy independent competitors. Or, vertical restraints can be used to exploit consumers by enhancing prices for bigger profit margins, so long as entry is limited by product differentiation, trade restraints, size of market, or other circumstances. And firms with big bulk buying power could insist upon preferential prices well below average costs (i.e., "marginal cost" discounts) not available to ordinary and small business buyers and thus achieve substantial "economies" from bargaining clout (unrelated to operating efficiency economies).

Structuralist enforcement policy found it helpful, therefore, to supplement a strong merger enforcement and price-fixing policy with public prosecution and private litigation against those trade restraints in distribution and price discrimination with significant anticompetitive risks or consequences. In this way small and medium-sized business could prosper more fairly, and the competitive process be more securely maintained and safeguarded. The broad policy could be summarized as follows: While extensive latitude for contracts and distributional freedom was recognized, marketing restraints and price discrimination were limited when they tended to be anticompetitive and lacked redeeming social benefit.

Existing antitrust law provided ample basis for such enforcement efforts. The Sherman Act outlawed "unreasonable restraints of trade," "attempts to monopolize," and "monopolization." The Clayton Act outlawed tying and exclusive dealing arrangements that might substantially lessen competition in any line of commerce or section of the country. And the Robinson-Patman Act amendments (to Section 2 of the Clayton Act) outlawed price differences in goods of like grade and quality where sufficient competitive injury resulted. All these rules were privately enforceable, with access to treble damages and reasonable attorney's fees. In addition, the Antitrust Division of the U.S. Department of Justice enforced the Sherman Act, tying and exclusive dealing rules, while the FTC enforced the Robinson-Patman Act. Intelligent discretion, however, was presumably exercised by the antitrust agencies in selecting vertical restraint and price discrimination cases for prosecution.

During the 1960s antitrust rules in this area became reasonably well defined, with extensive case decisions, ample text materials, and frequent seminars taught by specialists in antitrust practice.[68] The specific rules for each kind of vertical restraint or discrimination were adapted to the likelihood of competitive injury and redeeming benefits (if any) to competition and the public.

Concerted refusals to deal or boycotts.—Concerted refusals to deal or group boycotts tending to exclude competitors were held per se unlawful, with a narrow exception for "good morals" enforcement in the public interest.[69] Thus, professional sports leagues might exclude gamblers or drug abusers, and securities exchanges could remove dishonest brokers and salesmen. But industry trade associations could not legally discourage or punish lower-priced competitors or otherwise limit healthy rivalry in the public interest.

Individual refusals to deal.—Under *Colgate*, 1919, a broad freedom to select individual customers and dealers was recognized.[70] But *Parke Davis*, 1960, and other decisions held that individual refusals to deal could be antitrust violations if undertaken as part of unlawful conspiracies, restraints of trade, or attempts to monopolize.[71] (This included horizontal and vertical price fixing, tying, or significant exclusionary conduct.) But the burden of proof to show such abuses would fall upon complaining parties, cutoff dealers, or government antitrust agencies. And although private complaints were often brought, proof was not easy to establish in many cases. Even so, the availability of such relief did reduce considerably the ruthlessness of many companies in handling small business dealers and franchisees. Dealer protection statutes often requiring good faith and fair treatment for dealers added further safeguards in some industries (or states) and helped improve the customary bargaining status and expectation of smaller dealers and franchisees.

Vertical price fixing.—Resale price maintenance contracts and enforcement through systematic customer selection were unlawful (*Dr. Miles*, 1911; *Parke Davis*, 1960; and *Simpson v. Union Oil*, 1964).[72] However, sellers could refuse to deal with customers that did not respect suggested resale prices (*Colgate*, 1919). This policy greatly encouraged discount chains, lower retail prices to consumers, and more efficient, low-cost marketing. On the other hand, sellers that sought to create premium price, high-quality brands could do so through carefully recruited specialty stores that followed suggested resale prices. But attempts to systematically impose resale prices on mass marketing normally would break down under illegality (without the shelter of "fair trade" laws). (Under the Miller-Tydings Act of 1937 and McGuire Act of 1952 the states had been authorized to enact fair trade laws to legalize resale price maintenance. But this enabling legislation was repealed by Congress in 1975 with very little protest.)[73]

Tying arrangements.—Under *Northern Pacific,* 1958, and *Loews,* 1962, tying arrangements were labeled unreasonable (and presumptively unlawful) whenever a party had sufficient economic power with respect to the tying product to appreciably restrain free competition in the market for the tied product and a substantial amount of commerce was affected.[74] In limited circumstances (e.g., technological quality control and new competitors), somewhat more latitude for tying might be allowed. But in most cases tying was unlawful when used by firms with "market power" or significant economic leverage. This policy helped reduce entry barriers, allowed easier competition from smaller rivals, and tended to prevent "full-line forcing" tactics. This policy was especially significant in limiting oppression and onerous pricing within strong brand distribution and franchiser-franchisee networks. In this way buyers and sellers enjoyed more freedom in selecting optimum purchases at competitive prices. On the other hand, package dealing for convenience and/or discount pricing purposes generally was permitted under this policy. Only where sufficient economic power to appreciably restrain competition was involved could there be any question of illegality for tying arrangements, so that smaller firms and companies with limited market shares could rarely be challenged under this tying rule. Of course, firms with only modest market influence could not successfully impose onerous prices, terms, or conditions upon their customers or dealers. Competition would prevent such "overcharging." In this way, the risk exposure for unlawful tying was confined essentially to companies with substantial market power and the leverage to impose onerous burdens upon customers and the public.

Exclusive dealing.—Exclusive dealing arrangements involve situations where suppliers or dealers agree to limit their transactions to one relationship of supply or marketing (at least for a period of time). Examples include exclusive requirements-supply contracts, where sellers or buyers (or both) agree to confine dealings to a single source, outlet, or relationship; or exclusive franchises under which a franchisee accepts exclusivity as a condition for participating in the benefits of a franchiser's organization and distribution network. Because these arrangements are widespread, involve obvious economies to participants, and need not be onerous or burdensome to participants or the general public, antitrust law is relatively lenient. Although a few decisions held exclusive dealing unlawful where substantial foreclosure from a market resulted (*Standard Stations,* 1949, and *Brown Shoe,* 1966), rather little challenge to requirements contracts or exclusive dealing (franchise) networks actually occurred.[75] Exclusive dealing (in contrast to concerted refusals to deal, vertical price fixing, and tying) was presumed to be lawful under the rule of reason. If, however, a strong franchise organization with significant market power or leverage engages in exclusionary practices, attempts to monopolize, group boycotts, price fixing, or unlawful tying, such misconduct could easily constitute antitrust law violations. But the mere existence or use of exclusive dealing or franchise networks in concentrated industries was never seriously challenged, even if their leading firms enjoyed significant market power or potential leverage.

Price discrimination.—Price discrimination (like exclusive or package dealing) can injure competition in some circumstances, and yet price differences often merely reflect and result from healthy competitive bargaining and rivalry in the marketplace. While early monopoly decisions (*Standard Oil* and *American Tobacco*) found predatory pricing could be unlawful, and Section 2 of the Clayton Act (1914) outlawed price discrimination that might "substantially lessen competition," little real enforcement or constraint upon price discrimination occurred until after the Robinson-Patman Act (Section 2 Clayton) amendments (1936).[76]

Under Robinson-Patman burdens of proof were relaxed, with mere "injury" to competition sufficient for illegality. On the other hand, only price differences in goods or commodities of "like grade and quality" could be challenged. Furthermore, three affirmative defenses were specified: (1) cost justification (generally interpreted in terms of *average* total costs allocable to each class of customers); (2) meeting competition of low-priced competitors; and (3) distress or salvage sales (including perishables). Thus, the act attempted to select only that price discrimination that might be seriously injurious to competition for prosecution by the FTC and private treble-damage litigation.[77]

Initial FTC enforcement was hard-line, and courts accepted "mere diversion" as a sufficient standard for competitive injury. But many criticized this policy as overly zealous, and some structuralist economists warned that "oligopoly consensus" and pricing uniformity could be encouraged. Thus, competition might be weakened for the sake of protecting competitors.

Accordingly, by the early to mid-1960s a significant increase in the burden of proof to "substantial" competitive injury was required.[78] This met most of the objections to overkill in prosecution, and the number of FTC complaints declined greatly (as the Commission placed more emphasis upon merger enforcement and somewhat later upon consumer protection or antideceptive practice efforts). But private small business complaints increased and were approved by the Supreme Court in the leading case of *Utah Pie*, 1967.[79] Most private litigation concentrated upon "primary line" and territorial price discrimination, i.e., potential predatory pricing situations that threatened smaller business survival or competition. Deep discounts to chains and big buyers were hard to detect and litigate (without extensive FTC investigation), so that secondary line enforcement efforts relaxed substantially beginning in the late 1960s. The Robinson-Patman Act still remains on the books, though, with considerable compliance momentum from private counsel to large firms.[80]

Further erosion in Robinson-Patman enforcement was urged by some scholars, who proposed greater latitude for marginal-cost discounting.[81] Although the courts were slow to follow these suggestions in the 1970s, such thinking has become more fashionable in the Reagan era. Small business and plaintiff advocates complain, however, and resist this "emasculation" of the law. If large firms can cover their fixed-cost overhead expenses in higher-concentration, secure-market areas, a broad leeway for marginal-cost discounting will allow for much more predatory pricing and make private complaints much more difficult to litigate. Also, what was left of secondary line compliance momentum could be undercut.[82]

Private Enforcement Expansion

The concept of treble-damage relief against monopolization can be traced back to the English Statute of Monopolies (1624).[83] This was revived under American law as a right to private treble damages and injunctive relief in Section 4 of the Clayton Act, along with a right to reasonable attorney's fees.[84] Such private enforcement applies to all Sherman and Clayton Act violations (though not the FTC Act remedy against "unfair or deceptive acts or practices").[85] Limited use of private antitrust remedies occurred through the succeeding half-century.

But in the late 1950s, one big price-fixing–treble-damage litigation— *United States v. Westinghouse, et al.*, 1960—became an important breakthrough in popularizing private antitrust actions.[86] In this case, a blatant, extended price-fixing and market allocation conspiracy had been exposed through extensive congressional and grand jury investigation. Six heavy electrical equipment manufacturers were allocating contracts and sales and had been fixing prices for years (with secret meetings, bid rigging, and a complicated sharing formula involving phases of the moon—a lunar cycle for concealment) on hundreds of millions of dollars of equipment during the 1950s. The trial judge, shocked at the conspiracy's scale and duration, refused to accept nolo contendere pleas, found the defendants guilty, and sentenced six leading executives to jail terms. This left the companies exposed to easy attack for treble damages by the TVA and most private power companies. The issue of liability was now res judicata, allowing rapid proof of damages. Hundreds of respectable, business-oriented law firms all over the country represented plaintiffs in nearly two thousand related treble-damage suits.

This well-publicized litigation reduced inhibitions against private antitrust lawsuits among conservative counsel and educated many more lawyers to their potential for client damages and attorney's fees. Private antitrust litigation became increasingly common through the 1960s and into the 1970s. Liberalized access to the class action device stimulated more interest in such litigations for consumers, smaller businesses, franchisees, and even some trade groups and associations. By the 1970s, as government prosecution eased off in some areas of antitrust, private enforcement became important in sustaining the credibility and overall effectiveness of the antitrust laws.[87]

This expanded private litigation and discovery unfortunately proved to be a mixed blessing.[88] Antitrust enforcement did increase, especially for distributional restraints, and perhaps also in predatory pricing or primary line discrimination cases. But some of this new litigation was not handled well, and questionable claims were asserted. Relatively inexperienced plaintiffs' attorneys added elements of nuisance litigation and waste to antitrust enforcement. Even when clients had valid complaints under the law (and skillful settlement negotiations may have been productive), inexperienced attorneys often conducted inept, excessive, and incomplete discovery and investigation. Unrealistic claims frequently were pressed, and less than proper representation was common.

Not surprisingly, defense counsel resisted and exploited this increased wave of private antitrust litigation. Far more attorneys (with more billable hours) worked for defendant corporations than for plaintiffs. Defense counsel commonly responded to complaints and plaintiff discovery with aggressive counterdiscovery and motion practice. Dilatory tactics and confusion normally strengthens defendant bargaining power, enhances prospects for successful defense, and adds greatly to billable hours. "Running the meter" became a well-known practice among some lawyers. Antitrust litigation seemed to be profitable for a considerable roster of lawyers but many business executives regarded it as costly boondoggling.

The growing volume of antitrust litigation generated an increasing need for expert witness research and testimony by industrial organization economists. In some respects this improved the rationality of antitrust litigation, but it tended to coopt a substantial number of economists into taking partisan, "hired gun" roles. Because large corporate defendants could normally afford bigger fees for experts than could small business plaintiffs (the latter often used contingent fee contracts for lawyers), more of the best economic talent gravitated into defense work. (Defendants also paid experts promptly, whereas many plaintiffs' counsel were slow and unreliable in compensating experts and offered lower rates.) In time industrial organization economists (as a whole) became somewhat more defense-oriented, although considerable intellectual diversity remains in this field.

International Trade Policies

American trade policy evolved through three major stages: (1) *1792–1860:* Low to moderate revenue tariffs (with only limited sectors of protection) and decreasing tariffs in the late part of the period; (2) *1861–1932:* Substantial and widespread protection with considerable revenue also obtained from tariffs; and (3) *1933–1986:* Steadily reduced tariff and trade barriers with increasing openness to foreign competition, especially since the Kennedy (1963–67) and Tokyo (1974–79) rounds of negotiations under the GATT (General Agreement on Tariffs and Trade).[89]

Foreign industrial competition gradually became more significant after World War II, especially since the late 1960s. By the mid-1980s, 70 percent of U.S. industry confronted substantial import competition.[90] This added greatly to the strength of competitive rivalry within many American industries. In some sectors imports from lower wage and more efficient foreign suppliers were creating serious displacement strains, particularly with an increasingly overvalued dollar between 1983 and 1986.[91] (The dollar became seriously overvalued by 1984–85 due to greatly increased budget deficits, higher interest rates, unequal recoveries from world recession, and big capital flows into the United States.) In these circumstances, protectionist pressures grew, and American trade policy became more controversial.[92] Foreign export subsidies, industrial policies and targeting efforts, and more restricted access to many markets abroad were seen as serious problems in light of the severe U.S. trade deficit. While the dollar declined substantially after February 1985 (its highest value since Nixon's 1971 "devaluation"), experts differed on whether currency realignment and "free trade" would be sufficient to restore U.S. industrial competitiveness.

Free trade believers and multinational lobbyists wanted to contain protectionism and sought another GATT round for this purpose. Some hoped to get somewhat "freer" trade from Japan and new industrial countries (NICs). But the AFL-CIO, many Democratic politicians, and some business interests demanded more "trade equity," stronger unfair trade practice remedies, and more "balanced openness" in world markets. Some urged a new U.S. industrial policy on Japanese lines, with more R&D support, technology sharing, and selective trade restrictions to rejuvenate "sick" industries. Others proposed a revival of revenue tariffs (used earlier in U.S. history) or at least a value-added tax on imports to offset foreign VAT waivers on exports. But most experts agreed that restoring U.S. industrial competitiveness was a serious long-term challenge, even though foreign trade rivalry could be a useful supplement to antitrust policy enforcement.[93]

Recent Antitrust Relaxation

Chicago School and Neoclassical Revival

Structuralist thinking had become dominant by the 1950s in industrial organization economics.[94] This new branch of economic research emphasized oligopoly theory and monopolistic and imperfect competition analysis. It encouraged industry studies and government data collection and stressed the importance of understanding market structure (concentration, entry conditions, and product differentiation), conduct of firms, and industrial performance. From the 1940s to the early 1950s a consensus evolved for "workable competition" as the standard for antitrust and regulatory policy. While "perfect competition" (complete information, mobility, free entry, and atomistic rivalry) would be infrequent in the real world, the practical question was whether antitrust or other government policies could make markets and industries perform better. Where corrective remedies could achieve lower entry barriers, improved competition, and/or stronger industrial performance, they should logically be implemented through antitrust or other policies. But economies of scale, difficult technology, or transport costs often required oligopoly. Even relatively high concentration and entry barriers were hard to reduce in many industries and markets. In such circumstances, limited rivalry might be all that could be achieved, i.e., no antitrust or government policies could improve performance. "Workable competition" would exist when antitrust and government action had done all that was feasible or desirable to improve industrial structure, conduct, or performance. In other words, government and antitrust policy could not achieve "perfect competition" everywhere (an unrealistic goal) but should accept "workable competition" as a practical guideline.[95]

Not surprisingly, economists differed on how much antitrust or other intervention would be helpful or productive. Enthusiasts for stronger action tended to favor tougher merger limits, some deconcentration, and vigorous enforcement of antitrust generally. Some even wanted limits on large-firm advertising and product differentiation. The "hard-liners" complained that 1960s-era antitrust policy was still insufficient.[96]

An opposite, conservative wing led by University of Chicago economists saw less danger in oligopoly generally.[97] They believed entry was not difficult in most industries and that interproduct rivalry helped limit excess pricing. Accordingly, "Chicago School" adherents favored substantial relaxation of antitrust. Only the larger horizontal mergers need be blocked, and anticartel enforcement should continue. Chicago writers urged more freedom for vertical restraints and price discrimination, because they saw new entry and interproduct rivalry as generally effective. The most extreme "free marketeers" insisted that all vertical restrictions and pricing discrimination were really "procompetitive."[98] Even if smaller firms were eliminated and concentration increased, the potential for big-firm entry was sufficient competitive discipline. And most Chicago and revived neoclassical economists viewed big business in a more favorable light; they accepted bigness as warranted by scale and integration economies and as generally good for the economy. In their eyes, smaller businesses deserved no special "protection of competitors" and should take care of themselves.

Moderates took a middle view. They held seminars and symposia in which a full spectrum of structuralist, moderate, and Chicago (revived neoclassical) "experts" were represented.[99] Increasingly, antitrust law scholarship became economically sophisticated and utilized industrial organization economics. Moderates, faced with a spreading divergence on policy (from hard-line structuralists seeking more deconcentration, e.g., Hart bill of the mid-1970s to Chicago free marketeers wanting major relaxation), endorsed continuity in antitrust doctrine and rules with perhaps a mild relaxation of enforcement. The moderate view, in fact, was dominant within the antitrust agencies and the courts from the late 1960s through the late 1970s (representing the administrations of Nixon, Ford, and Carter).

Reagan Administration Policies and Congressional Reaction.

The Reagan administration brought a more conservative, free-market outlook into government. Chicago-oriented leaders took charge of the Antitrust Division (William Baxter) and FTC (James Miller). New *Merger Guidelines* (1982 and 1984) were promulgated by the Justice Department that greatly relaxed previous guidelines and limited only the larger horizontal mergers.[100] Hardly any mergers have been challenged thereafter. Anticartel enforcement continued but was directed almost entirely against small business price fixers. And a new rule-of-reason policy was announced with respect to vertical restraints, and *Vertical Restraint Guidelines* implemented that view in late 1984.[101] While the Senate Republican majority accepted these changes in policy, House Democrats offered substantial opposition, and the House recently voted to condemn the *Vertical Restraint Guidelines*.[102] Although lower court decisions have shifted substantially in the Reagan Administration's direction, the Supreme Court majority has not yet substantially altered most of the leading antitrust law precedents.

In early 1986 the Reagan administration formally proposed further relaxation of antitrust law:[103] (1) *Mergers*—Greatly increased burden of proof for illegality under Section 7 of the Clayton Act to require a "significant probability" of harm to competition, defined as "the ability of one or more firms profitably to maintain prices above competitive levels for a significant period of time." Also, specific economic circumstances are to be considered, including number and size of firms, ease of entry (foreign or domestic), potential for output expansion by small firms if prices are raised, product nature and terms of sale, conduct of firms, and potential efficiencies. In addition, further opportunities for mergers and consolidation would be given under amendments to the Trade Act of 1974. Under a "Promoting Competition in Distressed Industries Act," if the International Trade Commission (ITC) were to find serious competitive injury from foreign competition, the president could order up to five years virtual holiday for mergers, and the law would prohibit any further import relief in the form of duties or restrictions for ten years thereafter. Thus, domestic consolidation could be greatly encouraged as a response to foreign competiton. (2) *Interlocking Directorates*—The original limitations in Section 8 of the Clayton Act on interlocking directorates would be substantially relaxed. (3) *Remedies*—Restrict treble damages to price-fixing cases and generally limit other damages to "actual damages," plus costs and reasonable attorney's fees. But substantially prevailing defendants would be allowed costs plus reasonable attorney's fees if the plaintiff's conduct has been "frivolous, unreasonable, without foundation or in bad faith."

Obviously, these new Reagan administration proposals reflect Chicago-oriented, free-market thinking. Whether much additional "stimulus" to the economy would result (even granting their assumptions) is questionable. A great relaxation of merger, vertical-restraint, and price-discrimination enforcement already has occurred within the last five years. But for structuralist and moderate critics, these initiatives aggravate an alarming emasculation (or at least a serious weakening) of antitrust policy that has gone too far and should be reversed (at least to some extent).

To structuralist enthusiasts for antitrust the Reagan era has brought a window of opportunity for excessive mergers and wasteful "takeover" activity.[104] The new proposals will entrench this emasculation of merger law and would consolidate a tragic transformation of U.S. industry, marketing, and service activities into high-concentration, sluggish oligopolies. The weakening of vertical restraint and price discrimination enforcement will erode the viability of small business competitors in many markets. The fact that price-fixing cartels are still challenged (mostly against unsophisticated price fixers in small business) is not very significant. High-concentration oligopolies have enjoyed for many years a de facto loophole for oligopoly consensus and follow-the-leader pricing. Hence, the cumulative impact of the Reagan era has been to encourage higher levels of concentration, more product differentiation, gradually increasing entry barriers, and more structural inflation momentum. In the view of critics, even though greatly increased unemployment and weakened unions have largely eliminated "wage-push" inflation, the problems of "price-push" inflation have not really been corrected. Reagan-era antitrust policies will only aggravate these high-concentration oligopoly problems over time and help widen income and wealth differentials (already growing due to greater tax relief in higher brackets).[105]

While worldwide recession did reduce the prices of commodities (e.g., feed grains, oil, lumber, metals), along with greatly slowing wage increases, some industrial, distribution, and service prices have increased. Thus, the underlying rate of inflation continued at 2.5–3.5 percent from 1982 to 1985, which reflects a lack of sufficient competition in many sectors and markets.[106]

Foreign imports also added more competition in recent years, especially due to the dollar's overvaluation from 1983 to 1986.[107] But this surge of imports did not bring inflation to a complete halt. Wherever possible domestic and foreign firms (e.g., automobiles, appliances, footwear, clothing, grocery retailing, health care) took advantage of any limits on competition to increase prices slightly even if production costs (including imports) may have declined slightly. From a structuralist viewpoint, the most recent Reagan administration "distressed industry" proposals for a five-year merger holiday would invite widespread consolidation and facilitate private (hard to discover) market-sharing deals between U.S. and big foreign firms.[108] Prices and profit margins can be increased this way, but competition and consumer interests will suffer. In the long run, U.S. industry would have its competitiveness in world markets weakened even further.

For moderate critics there may be more uncertainty and less definite projections of weakened competition. Yet most moderate antitrust experts, lawyers, and economists believe that the relaxation under Reagan has been excessive. Few moderates support any greater weakening of antitrust enforcement, and most prefer somewhat stronger merger limitations and continued action against those vertical restraints and/or price discriminations that might injure competition. While many moderates would accept constraints on nuisance plaintiff suits, most see significant political, social, and economic benefits to a reasonable opportunity for private antitrust relief, at least actual damages, and realistic attorney's fees.[109]

Prospects and Controversy

Antitrust policy has strong roots in American history, ideology, and law. Antitrust enforcement enjoys support from most consumers and small business. Those favoring federalism and liberal democracy share faith in decentralized economic power. The antitrust tradition is hard to suppress over the long run, and it has shown recurrent vitality in politics.[110]

Obviously a neglect of antitrust creates potential for political opposition. And the relaxation under Reagan is highly controversial. Among antitrust experts, lawyers, economists, journalists, and historians, the recent shift in U.S. policy has raised many questions and elicited widespread criticism. From the standpoint of the structuralists and many moderates, a restoration of "mainstream" antitrust enforcement is badly needed now. Delay will only increase distortions and weaken competitive efficiency. Some moderates feel less urgency but still object to many elements of the relaxation under Reagan.

In some ways, however, the economic situation of America today is changing. International competition is much stronger; foreign imports, suppliers, and branch plants now play a more substantial role in U.S. manufacturing. This complicates the task of investigation and analysis. Structure, conduct, and performance appraisals are still essential. But domestic antitrust policy has become entangled, in some respects, with industrial development and international trade–finance policies.

Healthy international trade and competition from abroad are largely beneficial to domestic consumers and efficiency. But recent macroeconomic imbalances, exceptionally large budget deficits, heavy foreign borrowing, huge balance of payments and trade deficits, and a significantly overvalued dollar produce significant distortions in trade. Between 1980 and 1986 U.S. imports surged from $250 billion to $387 billion, while exports held at $220 billion. Although the dollar finally began a substantial decline in the summer of 1985 that continued through the winter of 1986, its further trajectory is not clear. Some believe that a return to U.S. budget balance and exchange-rate realignment will be sufficient to restore American industrial competitiveness. Others remain doubtful.

Many U.S. economists are convinced that a much tougher industrial–trade policy challenge faces the country. The previous long lead the United States had in manufacturing productivity, technology, and scale of operations no longer exists in many markets. The United States must now compete in a more competitive world with many relative equals and a growing roster of hardworking new industrial countries. Foreign industrial development policies, export subsidies and promotion, lower interest rates, targeting strategies, and restricted access to many overseas markets are significant elements of the international trade scene. To some degree, the United States will have to match, respond in kind, or achieve more effective responses to foreign industrial policies. Sentiment in Congress is growing for more trade equity and a better balanced world trade regime.

In any event, U.S. antitrust policy must now incorporate some new goals and possible constraints. While fairness, efficiency, competition, a healthy role for small business, decentralization, and economic opportunity are still important, trade policy objectives must be implemented as well. U.S. industry must compete in a world market with rival industrial policies, sustain viable exports. and achieve a better import-export balance. A healthy industrial base with proper regard for national security must be maintained. All this means that industrial development, market structure, conduct, and performance should be reviewed more carefully than ever. Antitrust policy must become more sophisticated in sectors where international trade impacts. But a more competitive world market does not justify a dismantling or emasculation of sound, carefully developed antitrust rules and enforcement traditions.[111]

Notes

1. U.S. antitrust law has been supported by many constituencies historically: the "public interest," small business and farmers, the "yeomanry" or populists, ordinary consumers, and those fearing excessive concentration of economic power in a federal democratic republic. Antitrust traditionally emphasizes "fair" competition as a process to promote a broad freedom for enterprise with confidence in economic efficiency, expanded output, lower prices, and limits on profit set by the dynamic of competitive rivalry. Most antitrust scholars see multiple goals as interrelated and natural. Other public policies contribute to these goals too, including tax law, education, research and development support, and public utility regulation (for monopolies and industries suffering major constraints on competition). While some writers offer "one-dimensional" or single-objective strategies like "competitive markets" or "microeconomic efficiency," the majority of antitrust law scholars find such views unpersuasive and historically inaccurate. For nearly a century, Congress and the courts have developed general statutory language (for the most part), and more specific case-by-case decision making (with some latitude for shifting emphasis). The courts always wrestle with somewhat conflicting views, economic interests, and priorities in the task of interpretation. But most lawyers accept this responsibility as normal and proper for the courts and administrative agencies. [For an insightful review of antitrust goals, see Eleanor Fox and James Halverson, eds., *Industrial Concentration and the Market System: Legal, Economic, Social and Political Perspectives* (ABA Section of Antitrust Law, 1979), 137–50. See also Harlan Blake and Robert Pitofsky, *Antitrust Law* (Mineola, N.Y.: Foundation, 1967), 1–58.]
2. The dangers of monopoly and concentrated power (economic, political, and social) have been traditional antitrust concerns, although constitutional law, tax law, public utility and media regulation, and government enterprise (in a few sectors) also help deal with these problems.
3. See, for example, *Guide to Legislation on Restrictive Business Practices*, vols. 1– 5, OECD (with 1983 Supplement); D. J. Gilstra, ed., *Competition Law in Western Europe and the U.S.A*, 3 vols. (Netherlands: Kluwer); *World Law of Competition*, 5 vols. (Matthew Bender, 1984); Julian Maitland Walker, *International Anti-Trust Law*, vols. 1–2 (Oxford: ESC Publishing Ltd., 1984); R. J. Radway, "Antitrust,

Technology Transfers and Joint Ventures in Latin America Development," *Law Am.* (University of Miami Law School) 15 (Spring 1983):1; E. White, "La Legislation antimonolica y el control del puder economic en America Latina: recientes tendencias," *Derecho de la Integracion* 11 (November 1978):28, Banco Interamericano de Desarrollo, Instituto para la Integracion de America Latina, Buenos Aires; G. Cabanellas, Jr., *Antitrust and Direct Regulation of International Transfer of Technology Transactions* (Munich: Max Planck Institute for Foreign and International Patent, Copyright, and Competition Law, 1984). See also Corwin D. Edwards, *Trade Regulations Overseas: The National Laws* (Dobbs Ferry, NY: NYU Oceana, 1966); Corwin D. Edwards, *Control of Cartels and Monopolies: An International Comparison* (Dobbs Ferry, NY: NYU Oceana, 1967); Eleanor M. Hadley, *Antitrust in Japan* (Princeton, NJ: Princeton University, 1970); The Monopolies & Restrictive Practices Act, 1969, as amended, 1984 [India], with Rules, as amended (Book Corporation, Calcutta, 1985); A. M. Chakraborti, *MRTP: A Compendium* (New Delhi, Bhargara, Delhi: Centre for Legal Studies, 1982); Meong-cho Yang, "Industrialization, Concentration and Competition Policy: The Korean Antitrust Law, Comparative and International Experience" (S.J.D. diss., Tulane Law School, 1983).

In Taiwan, a newly drafted "Fair Trade Law" (to incoporate some antitrust legislation) has been under serious consideration. If passed by the legislative Yuan, the proposed legislation will impose restrictions on corporate consolidation and other unfair trade practices that have the effect of monopoly or distortion of fair market prices.

4. See references cited in n. 3. Marxists assert that excessive concentration of wealth inherent in capitalist development and profits from private investments are "surplus value" that should belong to the working class. To the extent that capital becomes highly concentrated in new industrial countries, Marxian complaints may seem to be justified. Accordingly, prudent conservatives and liberal reformers alike find merit in antitrust and other policies that broaden wealth and participation in capitalist development. Only the more extreme socialists, Marxians, and selfish capitalists (with short-sighted naïveté) resist such correctives, each preferring to control highly concentrated industries on his own terms. (Some conservatives, though, wonder whether much "corrective reform" is really needed. They contend that capitalist development inherently *broadens* wealth or at least that industrial and wealth concentration are not so worrisome.)

5. For example, "The Schoolmasters Case," Y. B. Henry IV, f. 47, pl. 21 (Ct. of Common Pleas) Hilary Term (1410; reprint, Handler, *Trade Regulation,* 2d ed., Brooklyn: Foundation, 1951), 10–17 (with other cases). See also Hans B. Thorelli, *The Federal Antitrust Policy* (Baltimore: Johns Hopkins University), 9–53; and Donald Dewey, "Common Law Background of Antitrust Policy," *Va. L. Rev.* 41 (1955):759. See also Earl Kintner, *Federal Antitrust Law* (Anderson, 1984), vol. 1, chap. 2; and Walter Adams and Horace M. Gray, *Monopoly in America* (New York: Macmillan, 1955).

6. William Blackstone, *Commentaries on the Law of England* (1765–70), book 4 ("of Public Wrongs"), chap. 12 ("of Offences Against Public Trade"), secs. 175–77, Forestalling, Regrating, and Engrossing. See, for example, the edition of William Carey Jones (Baton Rouge, LA: Claitor's, 1976), xxxi. Ironically, the early statutes against forestalling, regrating, and engrossing finally were repealed by England in 1844. Nonetheless, the principle of common law misdemeanor for trade

Antitrust in the Current Economic Environment 41

restraints was carried into U.S. law to some degree. See Bishop's comment in vol. 2 of the Jones edition, 2345. See also Thorelli, *Federal Antitrust Policy* (see n. 5), chap. 1, 9-53. For the original statutory text, see *Statutes of the Realm,* compiled by K. Geo. III, vol. 4, pt. 5 & 6 Edw. VI, c. XIV (1551-52; reprint, London: Dawsons of Pall Mall, 1963). See also Dewey, "Common Law Background" (see n. 5), 762-65.
7. *Davenant v. Hurdis,* 72 English Reports 769 (1599); *Darcy v. Allen,* 77 English Reports 1260 (1602); Blackstone, *Commentaries* (see n. 6), sec. 178, Monopolies. For text of the Statute of Monopolies, see *Statutes of the Realm,* K. Geo. III (see n. 6), vol. 4, pt. 2, 21 Jac. I c. 3 (1623-24).
8. Adam Smith, *Wealth of Nations* (1776; Modern Library Edition, New York: Random House, 1937).
9. See Thorelli, *Federal Antitrust Policy* (see n. 5), generally. Also, see Richard T. Ely, *Monopolies and Trusts* (New York: Macmillan, 1900); and John D. Hicks, *The Federal Union* (Boston: Houghton Mifflin, 1946) and John D. Hicks, *The American Nation* (Boston: Houghton Mifflin, 1952).
10. See references cited in n. 9. See also Earl Kintner, *Federal Antitrust Law,* vol. 1, chaps. 1-4.
11. Sherman Act, 26 Stat. 209 (1890), as amended, 15 U.S.C. Sections 1-7. Note that Section 7 authorized private rights of action, treble damages, costs and attorney's fees for successful litigants. For a good early summary of case law, see Albert H. Walker, *History of the Sherman Law of the U.S.A.,* (New York: The Equity Press, 1910); and Thorelli, *Federal Antitrust Policy* (see n. 5).
12. *United States v. Trans-Mississippi Freight Ass'n,* 166 U.S. 290 (1897); *United States v. Joint Traffic Ass'n,* 171 U.S. 505 (1898); and *United States v. Addyston Pipe & Steel Co.,* 85 Fed. 271 (6th Cir. 1898), 175 U.S. 211 (1899).

For convenient citations and summaries of leading cases, see the standard antitrust law text materials. Most widely used, perhaps, is the *Attorney General's National Committee Report* (Washington, D.C., 1955), and the updating series published by the Antitrust Section of the American Bar Association (*Antitrust Developments,* 1955-68; *Antitrust Law Developments,* 1975, with supplements in 1977, 1979, and 1981; and *Antitrust Law Developments,* 1984). See also standard casebooks, including Phillip Areeda, *Antitrust Analysis,* 3rd ed. (Little Brown, 1981); S. Chesterfield Oppenheim, Glen Weston, and J. Thomas McCarthy, *Federal Antitrust Laws* (West, 1981); Louis B. Schwartz, John Flynn, and Harry First, *Free Enterprise and Economic Organization: Antitrust,* 6th ed. (1983); Milton Handler, Harlan Blake, Robert Pitofsky, and Harvey Goldschmid, *Trade Regulation,* 2d ed. (Foundation, 1982); Richard Posner and Frank Easterbrook, *Antitrust Cases,* 2d ed. (West, 1980); and E. Thomas Sullivan and Herbert Hovenkamp, *Antitrust Law, Policy and Procedure* (Michie, 1984); Lawrence Anthony Sullivan, *Antitrust* (West Hornbook, 1977); Roger Blair and David Kaserman, *Antitrust Economics* (Homewood, IL: Irwin, 1985); Herbert Hovenkamp, *Economics and Federal Antitrust Law* (West Hornbook, 1985); and larger scale treatises, including Phillip Areeda and Donald Turner, *Antitrust Law,* vols. 1-7 (Little Brown, 1978-86); and Kintner, *Federal Antitrust Law,* (see n. 10), vols. 1-8.
13. *Northern Securities Co. v. United States.,* 193 U.S. 197 (1904).
14. *Standard Oil Co. of New Jersey v. United States,* 221 U.S. 1 (1911); *United States v. American Tobacco Co.,* 221 U.S. 106 (1911); and *In re. American Sugar Refining Co.,* 223 U.S. 743 (1911), dismissing appeal from 178 F. 109 (S.D.N.Y. 1910).

15. *Dr. Miles Medical Co. v. John D. Park & Sons Co.*, 220 U.S. 373 (1911).
16. See White's opinion, *Standard Oil* (see n. 14); and White's earlier dissenting opinions in *Trans-Missouri Freight* (see n. 12); and *Northern Securities* (see n. 13). For a biographical sketch, see Cynthia Brosio, "Edward Douglas White: Splendid Survivor of the Lost Cause" (Tulane Law School, December 1985, Photocopy).
17. See Hicks, *American Nation* (see n. 9), 415–54. See also Paolo E. Colleta, *The Presidency of William Howard Taft* (Lawrence: University of Kansas, 1973), esp. 217–48.
18. See references cited in n. 17. Clayton Act, 38 Stat. 730 (1914), as amended, 15 U.S.C. Sections 12–27, and Federal Trade Commission Act, 38 Stat. 717 (1914), as amended, 15 U.S.C. Sections 41–58.
19. Clayton Act, Sections 7, 2, 3, and 8, respectively.
20. Clayton Act, Sections 10 and 4, respectively.
21. Federal Trade Commission Act, Sections 5, 6, 9, 10 and 16. For the early development of the FTC see T. C. Blaisdell, *The Federal Trade Commission* (New York: Columbia University, 1932).
22. See Hicks, *American Nation* (see n. 9), 540–64.
23. See, for example, Hicks, *American Nation* (see n. 9), 545–94, esp. 582–86.
24. *United States v. American Can Co.*, 230 Fed. 859, (D.Md. 1916), *appeal dismissed*, 256 U.S. 706 (1921); *United States v. U.S. Steel Corporation*, 251 U.S. 417 (1919); and *International Harvester Co. of America v. Kentucky*, 234 U.S. 216 (1927). The quoted language appears in *U.S. Steel*, 251 U.S. at 441–42, 455–57. But compare Day's dissent, 251 U.S. at 457–66.
25. *U.S. Steel*, 251 U.S. at 451.
26. *United States v. Trenton Potteries Co.*, 273 U.S. 392, 397, (1927).
27. *American Column & Lumber Co. v. United States*, 257 U.S. 377 (1921).
28. *Maple Flooring Manufacturers Ass'n v. United States*, 268 U.S. 563 (1925).
29. *Motion Picture Patents Co. v. Universal Film Manufacturing Co.*, 243 U.S. 502 (1917); and *Carbice Corp. of America v. American Patents Development Corp.*, 283 U.S. 27 (1931).
30. *United States v. General Electric Co.*, 272 U.S. 476 (1926).
31. See references cited in n. 37.
32. See Hicks, *American Nation* (see n. 9), 595–618; and Arthur M. Schlesinger, Jr., *The Crisis of the Old Order, 1919–1933* (Boston: Houghton Mifflin, 1957); and Arthur M. Schlesinger, Jr., *The Coming of the New Deal* (Boston: Houghton Mifflin, 1959).
33. See Schlesinger, *New Deal* (see n. 32), esp. 87–194. See also Benjamin Kirsh, *The National Industrial Recovery Act* (New York: Central Book Co., 1933); Leverette Lyon, et al., *The National Recovery Administration: An Analysis and Appraisal* (Washington, D.C.: Brookings, 1935).
34. *Appalachian Coals, Inc. v. United States*, 288 U.S. 344 (1933).
35. See Lyon, *National Recovery Administration* (see n. 33); and Thurman Arnold, *Folklore of Capitalism* (New Haven: Yale University, 1937).
36. The Miller Tydings Act, 50 Stat. 693 (1937), and the McGuire Fair Trade Act, 66 Stat. 631 (1952) enabled state laws authorizing (or even mandating, in some circumstances) resale price maintenance. See James Angell McLaughlin, "Fair Trade Acts," *U.P.a. L. Rev.* 86 (June 1938):803 and Ollie R. Arens, "The Fair Trade Acts—The Latest Attack on the Loss Leader Problem," *Wash. Univ. Quart. Rev.* 22 (June 1937):549. The Federal Fair Trade Laws were repealed in 1975, 89 Stat. 801 (1975).

37. Robinson-Patman Act, 49 Stat. 1526 (1936), amending Section 2 Clayton Act, codified at 15 U.S.C. Sections 13, 21. See William A. Lovett, "A Crossroads for the Robinson-Patman Act," *Tulane L. Rev.* 45 (December 1970): 1; Fred Rowe, *Price Discrimination Under the Robinson-Patman Act* (Little Brown, 1962); Kintner, *Federal Antitrust Law* (see n. 12), vol. 3, *The Robinson-Patman Act,* 1983, with 1986 Supplement; and ABA Antitrust Section, *The Robinson-Patman Act: Policy and Law,* vol. 1 and 2, monograph no. 4 (Chicago, IL: American Bar Assoc., 1980).
38. Thurman Arnold, *Folklore of Capitalism* (New Haven, CT: Yale University, 1937).
39. See, for example, Thurman Arnold, *Bottlenecks of Business* (New York: Reynal & Hitchcock, 1940).
40. *United States v. Socony-Vacuum Oil Co.,* 310 U.S. 150 (1940).
41. See Arnold, *Bottlenecks of Business* (see note 39). See also Investigation of Concentration of Economic Power, Final Report and Recommendations of the Temporary National Economic Committee (TNEC), purusant to Public Resolution No. 113 (75th Congress), Senate, 77th Cong., 1st sess., Doc. 35 (Washington, D.C.: GPO, 1941). For an early economic guide to antitrust policy, see Corwin D. Edwards, *Maintaining Competition: Requisites of a Governmental Policy* (New York: McGraw-Hill, 1949).
42. *United States v. Aluminum Co. of America,* 148 F.2d 416 (2nd Cir. 1945); *American Tobacco Co. v. United States,* 328 U.S. 781 (1946); and *United States v. United Shoe Machinery Corp.,* 110 F.Supp 295 (D. Mass. 1953), *aff'd,* 347 U.S. 521 (1954).
43. See Edwards, *Trade Regulations Overseas* and *Control of Cartels and Monopolies* (see n. 3); Edwards, *Maintaining Competition* (see n. 41); and Hadley, *Antitrust in Japan* (see n. 3).
44. *Federal Trade Commission v. Cement Institute,* 333 U.S. 683 (1948); and *Theatre Enterprises, Inc. v. Paramount Film Distributing Corp.,* 346 U.S. 537 (1954).
45. See, for example, John G. Fuller, *The Gentlemen Conspirators: The Story of the Price-Fixers in the Electrical Industry* (New York: Grove Press, 1962). See also *Time,* 18 January 1960, 78; *Business Week,* 18 April 1961, 176; and *Time,* 10 September 1965, 82.
46. *United States v. Imperial Chemical Industries,* 105 F.Supp. 215 (S.D.N.Y. 1952).
47. Celler-Kefauver Act, 64 Stat. 1125 (1950).
48. Leading works include: Edward H. Chamberlin, *Monopolistic Competition* (Cambridge, MA: Harvard University, 1933); Joan Robinson, *Imperfect Competition* (London: Macmillan, 1933), William Fellner, *Competition Among the Few* (New York: Knopf, 1949); Edwards, *Maintaining Competition* (see n. 41); George Stocking, *Workable Competition and Antitrust Policy* (Nashville, TN: Vanderbilt University, 1952); Edward S. Mason, *Economic Concentration and the Monopoly Problem* (Cambridge, MA: Harvard University, 1957); Carl Kaysen and Donald Turner, *Antitrust Policy* (Cambridge, MA: Harvard University, 1959); Joe S. Bain, *Barriers to New Competition* (Cambridge, MA: Harvard University, 1965); Joe S. Bain, *Industrial Organization* (New York: Wiley, 1959); George Stigler, *The Organization of Industry* (Homewood, IL: Irwin, 1968); Willard F. Mueller, *A Primer on Monopoly and Competition* (New York: Random House, 1970); H. J. Goldschmid, H. M. Mann, and J. F. Weston, *Industrial Concentration: The New Learning* (Boston: Columbia–Little Brown, 1974); and Frederick M. Scherer, *Industrial Market Structure and Economic Performance* (Chicago: Rand McNally, 1970, 1979). A rich literature of specific industries, articles, monographs, hear-

ings, statistical data, and extensive controversy has blossomed since the late 1930s. (Few recent scholars, in fact, are entirely familiar with all this learning, and a tendency toward ideological polarization and unbalanced awareness was becoming evident in the 1970s.)

49. Adam Smith, *Wealth of Nations*, Modern Library Edition (New York: Random House, 1937), 128.
50. Ibid., 250.
51. Frank Taussig, *Principles of Economics*, 4th ed. (New York: Macmillan, 1930), 208, 212.
52. See references cited in n. 48
53. See, for example, Edwards, *Maintaining Competition;* Kaysen and Turner, *Antitrust Policy;* Bain, *Barriers to New Competition;* Mueller, *Monopoly and Competition;* and Scherer, *Industrial Market Structure* (see n. 48).
54. *Hamilton Watch Co. v. Benrus Watch Co.*, 114 F.Supp. 307 (D. Conn). *aff'd*, 206 F.2d 738 (2nd Cir. 1953); *United States v. Bethlehem Steel*, 168 F.Supp. 576 (S.D.N.Y. 1958).
55. *Brown Shoe Co. v. United States*, 370 U.S. 294 (1962); and *United States v. Philadelphia National Bank*, 374 U.S. 321 (1963).
56. For a convenient summary, see U.S. Congress, House Antitrust Subcommittee, Committee on the Judiciary, *The Celler-Kefauver Act: Sixteen Years of Enforcement*, Staff Report, 90th Cong., 1st sess., 1967; and W. F. Mueller, *The Celler-Kefauver Act: The First 27 Years*, U.S. Congress, House Subcommittee on Antitrust and Commercial Law, Committee on the Judiciary, Staff Report, 96th Cong., 1st sess., 1979. For leading cases, see ABA Antitrust Section, *Antitrust Developments*, 1955–68; and ABA Antitrust Section, *Antitrust Developments*, 1975, 1977, 1979, and 1981 (see n. 12). The 1968 Justice Department *Merger Guidelines* represented the highwater mark of Section 7 Clayton Act enforcement against horizontal and vertical mergers. For a brief analytical summary of the 1968 Justice Department *Merger Guidelines*, see Kenneth Clarkson and Roger Leroy Miller, *Industrial Organization: Theory, Evidence, and Public Policy* (New York: McGraw-Hill, 1982), 343.
57. See references cited in n. 56. For alternative views on conglomerate merger policy in the late 1960s, see FTC Staff Economic Report on Conglomerate Mergers, 3 November 1969; Report of the White House Task Force Report on Antitrust Policy, 5 July 1968 (the Neal Report); and Report of the Task Force on Productivity and Competition, 18 February 1969 (the Stigler Report).
58. *United States v. Ling-Temco-Vought, Inc.* (Ling, Temco-Vought-Jones & Laughlin Steel), a strong settlement was approved, 315 F.Supp. 130 (W.D.Pa. 1970); *United States v. Northwest Industries*, (Northwest Industries–B. F. Goodrich), preliminary injunction issued, 301 F.Supp. 1066 (1969) [merger later abandoned]; and *United States v. ITT* (D. Conn. 1969), and related cases. The ultimate settlement was summarized, *Antitrust & Trade Regulation Report*, 3 August 1971. While some antitrusters condemned the settlement, many approved it in view of the government's unsuccessful efforts in lower court decisions. Whether a stronger litigation and appellate argument might have been mounted is an open question that remains controversial.
59. *United States v. Penn-Olin Chemical Co.*, 378 U.S. 158 (1964); *United States v. Falstaff Brewing Corporation*, 410 U.S. 526 (1973); and *United States v. Marine Bancorporation, Inc.*, 418 U.S. 602 (1974).

Antitrust in the Current Economic Environment 45

60. Merger activity increased substantially in the 1960s, reaching a peak in the "go-go" mid- to late 1960s, but larger transactions were mostly conglomerate. A considerable slump in merger numbers and assets followed in the 1970s (which should be further discounted for the impact of inflation). See William G. Shepherd, *The Economics of Industrial Organization* (Englewood Cliffs, NJ: Prentice-Hall, 1979), 161–71; and James V. Koch, *Industrial Organization and Prices*, (Englewood Cliffs, NJ: Prentice-Hall, 1980), 254–60. (Nonetheless, some critics of the merger movement still insist that excessive numbers of independent medium-sized companies were allowed to be acquired in the 1970s. See Mueller, *The Celler-Kefauver Act* [see n. 56].) More recently, however, in the Reagan "boom" years (with more permissive regulation and a more bullish stock market), merger activity soared to new highs—$116.7 billion in 1984 and $175 billion in 1985 (*N.Y. Times*, 16 March 1986, Business section, 1). (For alternative recent data on merger activity, see Preston Martin, Statement before Senate Subcommittee on Securities, Committee on Banking, Housing, and Urban Affairs, 4 April 1985, Appendix Attachment Tables 1 and 2. The strong recent surge is also indicated.)
61. *United States v. Socony-Vacuum Oil Co.*, 310 U.S. 150 (1940). See, for example, ABA Antitrust Section, *Antitrust Developments*, and other standard texts (see n. 12).
62. For a good discussion, see William G. Shepherd, *Economics of Industrial Organization* (see n. 60), 301–15.
63. Highlights of this literature included: U.S. Congress, Senate Subcommittee on Antitrust and Monopoly, Committee on the Judiciary, *Administered Prices: A Compendium on Public Policy*, 88th Cong., 1st sess., 1963; U.S. Congress, Joint Economic Committee, Study Papers Nos. 10 and 11 ("Potential Public Policies to Deal with Inflation Caused by Market Power," Emmette S. Redford; "A Brief Interpretive Survey of Wage-Price Problems in Europe," Mark W. Leiserson) in *Study of Employment, Growth, and Price Levels*, 86th Cong., 1st sess., 11 December 1959; Alfred Buehler, ed., "Inflation," *The Annals* 326 (November 1959); Thomas Wilson, *Inflation* (Cambridge, MA: Harvard University, 1961); F. W. Paish, *Rise and Fall of Incomes Policy*, 2d ed., Hobart Paper No. 47 (London: Inst. Econ. Affairs, 1971); Lloyd Ulman and Robert J. Flanagan, *Wage Restraint: A Study of Incomes Policies in Western Europe* (Berkeley: University of California, 1971); Robert Lekachman, *Inflation: The Permanent Problem of Boom and Bust* (New York: Vintage–Random House, 1973); Arnold R. Weber, *In Pursuit of Price Stability: The Wage-Price Freeze of 1971* (Washington, D.C.: Brookings, 1973); Robert F. Lanzillotti, Mary Hamilton, and R. B. Roberts, *Phase II in Review* (Washington, D.C.: Brookings, 1975); Arnold Weber and Daniel Mitchell, *The Pay Board's Progress* (Washington, D.C.: Brookings, 1978); Walter Galenson, *Incomes Policy; What Can We Learn From Europe?* (Ithaca, NY: Cornell University, 1973); Lawrence Krause and Walter Salant, eds., *Worldwide Inflation: Theory and Recent Experience* (Washington, D.C.: Brookings, 1977); Thomas J. Dougherty, *Controlling the New Inflation* (Lexington, MA: Lexington-D.C. Heath, 1981); Samuel A. Morley, *Inflation and Unemployment*, 2d ed., (Hinsdale, IL: Dryden, 1979); William A. Lovett, *Inflation and Politics: Fiscal, Monetary, and Wage-Price Discipline* (Lexington, MA: Lexington-D.C. Heath, 1982); Leland B. Yeager, *Experiences with Stopping Inflation* (Washington, D.C.: Amer. Enterprise Inst., 1981); Arthur Okun, *Prices and Quantities: A Macroeconomic*

Analysis (Washington, D.C.: Brookings, 1981); Wayne Vroman, *Wage Inflation: Prospects for Deceleration* (Washington, D.C.: Urban Institute, 1983); and Robert Flanagan, David Soskice, and Lloyd Ulman, *Unionism, Economic Stabilization, and Incomes Policies: European Experience* (Washington, D.C.: Brookings, 1983).

64. See, for example, in n. 63, Lovett, *Inflation and Politics;* Krause and Salant, *Worldwide Inflation;* Morley, *Inflation and Unemployment;* Yeager, *Experiences with Stopping Inflation;* Okun, *Prices and Quantities;* and Flanagan, Soskice, and Ulman, *Unionism, Economic Stabilization, and Incomes Policies.*

65. For a critical review of the indexation literature, see Lovett, *Inflation and Politics* (see n. 63), esp. 33–35 and notes on pp. 51–56. See also John Williamson, *Inflation and Indexation: Argentina, Brazil, and Israel* (Washington, D.C.: Inst. for Int'l. Econ., 1985).

66. See Lovett, *Inflation and Politics* (see n. 63), more generally. The United States experimented with wage-price "discipline" in many forms. World War II controls (1942–45) and more limited Korean War controls (1950–52) were followed by Kennedy-Johnson-era "jawboning"—guidelines and guideposts (1961–68); Nixon's Phase I–IV wage-price controls (1971–73); Ford's wage-price monitoring (1974–76); and Carter's "voluntary controls" (1978–80). For review and comparison with other leading countries, see Lovett, *Inflation and Politics.* The ultimate lessons were that wage-price restraints could not keep the lid on serious fiscal-monetary inflation pressure. But selective guidance could be somewhat helpful in limiting excessive union wage demands and upward price momentum in concentrated industries, provided that reasonably firm fiscal and monetary discipline was maintained (i.e., only modest government deficits and money supply expansion kept in line with economic growth potential).

67. See, for example, Bain, *Barriers to New Competition,* 317–39; and Scherer, *Industrial Market Structure,* 571–94 (see n. 48); together with Shepherd, *Economics of Industrial Organization,* 316–38 (see n. 60).

68. The best summary is found in successive editions and supplements of the ABA Antitrust Section's *Antitrust Developments* (see n. 12), and most recently, *Antitrust Law Developments* (Second). The most important services are the *Antitrust & Trade Regulation Report,* BNA, weekly, together with the multivolume looseleaf, *Trade Regulation Reporter,* CCH, along with the *Antitrust Law Journal,* ABA Section of Antitrust Law, quarterly. See also *Antitrust Bulletin;* and *Journals of Antitrust Law & Economics,* for professional articles by active practitioners and experts.

69. ABA Antitrust Section, *Antitrust Law Developments* (Second) (see n. 12), 6–11; and Areeda, *Antitrust Analysis* (see n. 12), 495–540.

70. *United States v. Colgate & Co.,* 250 U.S. 300 (1919).

71. *United States v. Parke, Davis & Co.,* 362 U.S. 29 (1960); ABA Antitrust Section, *Antitrust Law Developments* (Second) (see n. 12), 55–65, 99–109, 6–11.

72. See references cited in n. 71. *Simpson v. Union Oil Co.,* 377 U.S. 13 (1964); *Dr. Miles Medical Co. v. John D. Park & Sons,* 220 U.S. 373 (1911). For more recent controversy, see William S. Comanor, "Vertical Price Fixing, Vertical Market Restrictions, and the New Antitrust Policy," *Harv. L. Rev.* 98 (1985):982.

73. See references cited in n. 36.

74. *Northern Pacific Ry. Co. v. United States* 1 (1958); *United States v. Loews,* 371 U.S. 38 (1962). ABA Antitrust Section, *Antitrust Law Developments* (Second) (see n. 12), 75–94. See also. W. David Slawson, "A New Concept of Compe-

tition: Reanalyzing Tie-in Doctrine After Hyde," *Antitrust Bull.* 30 (Summer 1985):257.
75. *Standard Oil Co. of Calif. (Standard Stations) v. United States,* 337 U.S. 293 (1949); *Federal Trade Commission v. Brown Shoe Co.,* 384 U.S. 316 (1966). ABA Antitrust Section, *Antitrust Law Developments* (Second) (see n. 12), 95–99.
76. *Standard Oil Co. v. United States,* 221 U.S. 1 (1911); *United States v. American Tobacco Co.,* 221 U.S. 106 (1911). See also references cited in n. 37.
77. See references cited in n. 76.
78. See references cited in n. 76. Lovett, "Robinson-Patman Act" (see n. 37), 14–40. For more recent cases, see ABA Antitrust Section, *Antitrust Law Developments* (Second), 230–38.
79. *Utah Pie Co. v. Continental Baking Co.,* 386 U.S. 687 (1967). See Lovett, "Robinson-Patman Act" (see n. 37), 20–29. See also the opinion of Commissioner Phillip Elman, *Dean Milk Co.,* (1965), cited by Lovett, "Robinson-Patman Act" (see n. 37), 22–24 for an excellent guideline on proof of competitive injury in primary line cases.

> A seller violated the statute if, by virtue of operating in a number of geographical markets, he has the power to lower his price in one market while maintaining higher prices elsewhere, and does so in circumstances where, as a matter of reasonable business probability, the effect may be to eliminate, impair or lessen competition substantially, to tend to create a monopoly in any market, to destroy unfairly or cripple other sellers' capacity to compete, to block the entry of new competitors into the market, or to punish, discipline or intimidate a competitor who has not held the price line or has otherwise shown competitive independence.

80. Even though Reagan administration officials are largely unsympathetic to Robinson-Patman enforcement, the law remains in force. Counselors to private plaintiffs and defendants frequently advise something in the way of precautionary compliance, particularly since somewhat more vigorous enforcement could emerge in the future (at least in private antitrust cases and court decisions).
81. The most extreme critics insist that price discrimination of a predatory or anticompetitive nature would be irrational, or at least rare or unlikely. Robert Bork, *The Antitrust Paradox* (New York: Basic, 1978), 149–55; Frank Easterbrook, "Predatory Strategies and Counterstrategies," *U. Chicago L. Rev.* 48 (1981):263; and John McGhee, "Predatory Pricing Revisited," *J. Law & Econ.* 23 (1980):289.

For more moderate views, see, in n. 37, Lovett, "Robinson-Patman Act," and Rowe, *Price Discrimination,* together with a recent spectrum of controversy, Areeda & Turner, "Predatory Pricing and Related Practices Under Section 2 of the Sherman Act," *Harv. L. Rev.* 88 (1975):697; Joel Dirlam, "Marginal Cost Pricing Tests for Predation: Naive Welfare Economics and Public Policy," *Antitrust Bull.* 26 (1981):769; F. M. Scherer, "Predatory Pricing and the Sherman Act: A Comment," *Harv. L. Rev.* 89 (1976):869; Oliver Williamson, "Predatory Pricing: A Strategic and Welfare Analysis," *Yale L.J.* 87 (1977):284; Joskow & Klevorick, "A Framework for Analyzing Predatory Pricing Policy," *Yale L.J.* 89 (1979):213; and Brodley & Hay, "Predatory Pricing: Competing Economic Theories and the Evolution of Legal Standards," *Cornell L. Rev.* 66 (1981):738. Recent cases are summarized in ABA Antitrust Section, *Antitrust Law Developments* (Second) (see n. 12), 232–34, 125–30.

82. In this author's twenty-six years of experience in government, private practice, and consulting, a significant amount of predatory and/or competitively injurious pricing discrimination has occurred in high-concentration markets, especially during periods of excess capacity or retrenchment. See also references cited in n. 67, and a perceptive new article by Harry S. Gerla, "The Psychology of Predatory Pricing: Why Predatory Pricing Pays," *Southwestern Law J.* 39 (1985):755.
83. Statute of Monopolies (see n. 7). "IV [I]f any person . . . shall be hindered, grieved, disturbed or disquieted, or their goods or chattels seized, attached, destroyed, taken, carried away or detained by occasion or pretext of any monopoly . . . in every such case [they] shall and may have their remedy at common law, and . . . shall recover three times . . . the damages . . . sustained and double costs." *Statutes of the Realm* (see n. 7), 1212.
84. Sherman Act, original Section 7, 26 Stat. 209 (1890), and Clayton Act, Section 4, 38 Stat. 730 (1914), 15 U.S.C. 15 (as amended).
85. See references in n. 84. "Little" FTC acts in many states, however, make "unfair or deceptive acts or practice in commerce" privately actionable to some degree. See William A. Lovett, "State Deceptive Trade Practice Legislation," *Tulane L. Rev.* 46 (1972):724, 743–49. For more recent developments, see *Unfair and Deceptive Acts and Practices* (Boston: National Consumer Law Center), with 1985 Supplement, chap. 5.
86. See references cited in n. 45.
87. For articles illustrating the growing interest in private antitrust actions, see *Journal of Reprints for Antitrust Law* 2 (Winter 1970); and 2, no. 4 (Spring 1971) (Federal Legal Publications). For a widely employed guide to practioners, see Carla Hills, ed., *Antitrust Adviser* (Colo. Springs: Shepherds), with new editions or supplements in 1971, 1974, 1980, and 1985.
88. For more extended discussion, see William A. Lovett, "Where Antitrust Is Going Wrong: The Case for Strong Judges and Bigger Defendants," *Antitrust Law and Economics Review* 15 (1983):87; *Antitrust Law and Economics Review* 16 (1984):77. The best way (in this author's experience) to manage large antitrust cases responsibly is for trial judges to appoint their own independent economist as adviser to the court and assess costs to the parties. This economic adviser should help define issues, supervise discovery, and interpret evidence and expert testimony.
89. For a convenient summary, see John M. Dobson, *Two Centuries of Tariffs: The Background and Emergence of the US International Trade Commission* (Washington, D.C., ITC, 1976). See also C. Fred Bergsten and William R. Cline, *Trade Policy in the 1980's* (Washington, D.C.: Inst. for Int'l Economics, November 1982); Robert E. Baldwin and Anne Krueger, eds., *The Structure and Evolution of Recent U.S. Trade Policy,* NBER (Chicago: University of Chicago, 1984).
90. *Global Competition: The New Reality,* Report of the President's National Commission on Industrial Competitiveness, vol. 1, 1 January 1985, 9.
91. Ibid, generally. See also, *U.S. Trade: Performance in 1984 and Outlook,* International Trade Administration, U.S. Dept. of Commerce, June 1985; Barry Bluestone and Bennett Harrison, *The Deindustrialization of America* (New York; Basic, 1982).
92. See U.S. Congress, House Committee on the Budget, *International Trade and the Federal Deficit,* Hearing from the Task Force on Economic Policy, 99th Cong., 1st sess., 19 October 1985; Stephen Maris, *Deficits and the Dollar: The World Econ-*

omy at Risk (Washington, D.C.: Inst. Int'l Econ., 1985); and Norman Fieleke, "The Foreign Trade Deficit and American Industry," *N.E. Econ. Rev.* (Boston: Fed. Res. Bank of Boston, July/August 1985). But note, *Global Competition: The New Reality* (see n. 90), 14–15, that an overvalued dollar explains only part of the recent decline in U.S. industrial competitiveness.

93. *Global Competition: The New Reality* (see n. 90). See also, for the "multilateralist" outlook, Robert E. Baldwin and J. David Richardson, *International Trade and Finance, Readings*, 3d ed. (Boston: Little Brown, 1986). In addition, see Mark Andersen, "America's Foreign Trade Crisis," reprinted from the *AFL-CIO American Federationist*, 14 Oct. 1984; *The National Economy and Trade*, AFL-CIO Policy Recommendations for 1986, March 1986; John Culbertson, *International Trade and the Future of the West* (Madison, WI: 21st Century Press, 1984); and John Culbertson, *The Dangers of Free Trade* (Madison, WI: 21st Century Press, 1985). For a comprehensive industrial policy proposal, see Lester C. Thurow, *The Zero-Sum Solution: Building a World-Class American Economy* (New York: Simon and Schuster, 1985). See also William A. Lovett, *Competitive Industrial Policies and the World Bazaar*, Report prepared for the Subcommittee on Economic Stabilization of the House Committee on Banking, Finance and Urban Affairs, 98th Cong., 2d sess., November 1984 (with an extensive bibliography). See also references cited in n. 110.

94. For a history of industrial organization economics, see Almarin Phillips and Rodney E. Stevenson, "The Historical Development of Industrial Organization," *History of Political Economy* 6 (Fall 1974); 324; and most of the sources cited in n. 48, together with W. F. Mueller, "The New Attack on Antitrust," this volume. But compare George Stigler, "Perfect Competition, Historically Contemplated," *Journal of Political Economy* 65 (February 1957):1. See also Melvin Reder, "Chicago Economics: Permanence and Change," *Jrl. Econ. Lit.* 20 (March 1982):1, 29–30.

95. For good discussions of workable competition, see Scherer *Industrial Market Structure* (see n. 48), chap. 2; Jesse Markham, "An Alternative Approach to the Concept of Workable Competition," *Amer. Econ. Rev.* 40 (March 1950):349; and Joe S. Bain, "Workable Competition in Oligopoly," *Amer. Econ. Rev.* 40 (May 1950):35.

96. Among these "hard-liners" were staff members of the antitrust agencies (Antitrust Division and FTC) and the Senate Subcommittee on Antitrust and Monopoly (under Senators Estes Kefauver, Phil Hart, and Ted Kennedy). See, for example, Estes Kefauver (completed by Irene Till), *In a Few Hands: Monopoly Power in America* (Baltimore: Penguin, 1965). But some "liberal" critics of antitrust insisted that its "weakness" was inherent. John Kenneth Galbraith, *The New Industrial State* (Boston: Houghton Mifflin, 1967), 194–207.

97. See Stigler, *Organization of Industry* (see n. 48), together with Robert Bork, *The Antitrust Paradox* (New York: Basic, 1978); and Richard A. Posner, *Antitrust Law: An Economic Perspective* (Chicago: University of Chicago, 1976). See also Roger Leroy Miller, "Where Joe Bain, Mike Scherer, and Fritz Mueller Went Wrong: A Libertarian View," *Antitrust Law & Economics Rev.* 14 (1982):15; George Stigler, "The Economic Effects of the Antitrust Laws," *Jrl. of Law & Econ.* 9 (1966):225; and Reder, "Chicago Economics" (see n. 94).

98. See Bork, *Antitrust Paradox* (see n. 97). See also "Antitrust and Economic Efficiency," a conference sponsored by the Hoover Institution, *Journal of Law and*

50   William A. Lovett

Economics 28 (May 1985): 245; and Frank Easterbrook, "The Limits of Antitrust," *Texas L. Rev.* 63 (1984): 1. But see text and sources cited in references 67–82.
99. A good example is Goldschmid, Mann, and Weston, *Industrial Concentration* (see n. 48); and a subsequent example (with somewhat less balance that reflects a drift toward less vigorous antitrust policy), Eleanor Fox and James Halverson, eds. *Industrial Concentration and the Market System* (see n. 1). A more "structuralist" conference at Middlebury College, Vermont, yielded papers edited by John Craven, *Industrial Organization, Antitrust, and Public Policy* (Boston: Kluwer-Nijhoff, 1983).
100. For analysis of the 1982 Merger Guidelines, see "Symposium: 1982 Merger Guidelines," *Calif. L. Rev.* 71 (March 1983): 281. Limited further revisions were made in the 1984 *Merger Guidelines,* 14 June 1984. For contrasting policies in other countries, see *Merger Policies and Recent Trends in Mergers* (Paris: OECD, 1984), esp. table 1, pp. 12–13.

Recently Congress also liberalized opportunities for joint R&D efforts in the National Cooperative Research Act of 1984, P.L. No. 98-462, 98 Stat. 1815 (1984) (codified at 15 U.S.C. 4301-4305). For an analysis see Marc S. Firestone, "The National Cooperative Research Act: Antitrust Policy in an Era of Declining U.S. Competitiveness," Tulane Law School, 1985, Photocopy. For critical commentary on the dangers of U.S.-foreign joint ventures, see Robert Reich and Eric Mankin, "Joint Ventures with Japan Give Away Our Future," *Harv. Bus. Rev.* (March/April, 1986): 78. But U.S. government policies could enforce a balanced sharing of technology with more aggressive supervision from the U.S. antitrust agencies, U.S. Department of Commerce, and U.S. Trade Representative's Office.
101. Special Supplement, U.S. Dept. of Justice *Vertical Restraint Guidelines,* 23 January 1985, *Antitrust and Trade Regulation Rept.* 48, no. 1199, 24 January 1985.
102. For analysis of the *Vertical Restraint Guidelines,* see *Antitrust and Trade Regulation Rept.* 48 (24 January 1985): 193; and critical reactions, *Antitrust and Trade Regulations Rept.* 48 (31 January 1985): 237. See also William Baxter, "Vertical Restraints and Resale Price Maintenance: A Rule of Reason Approach," *Antitrust Law & Economics Rev.* 14 (1982): 13.
103. Statement by Attorney General Edwin Meese, III, 19 February 1986. For critical reactions in the House of Representatives, see "Evisceration of Antitrust Enforcement Scored During House Oversight Hearing," *Antitrust and Trade Regulation Rept.* 50 (27 February 1986): 351. See also Willard F. Mueller, "The New Attack on Antitrust," this volume (with extensive citations and bibliography).
104. For reports on the recent surge of merger activity, see "Merger Tango," *Time,* 23 December 1985; "Let's Make a Deal: A Wave of Raids and Acquisitions Is Changing the Face of U.S. Industry," *Time,* 23 December 1985, 42–51; and "High Times for T. Boone Pickens: A Wiley Raider Shakes Up Corporate America," *Time,* 4 March 1985, 52–67. For critical appraisal of a further enlargement of merger and consolidation activity, see *Antitrust and Trade Regulation Rept.* 50 (27 February 1986): 351. See also, Mueller, "New Attack on Antitrust" (see n. 103).
105. Reagan-era income and corporate tax cuts have improved savings and profits for upper-middle income and wealthier Americans, while increased unemployment,

greater foreign competition, and weakened unions have led to relative wage reductions (and even wage cuts) in some sectors. See, for example, Bennett Harrison, Chris Tilly, and Barry Bluestone, "Wage Inequality Takes a Great U-Turn," *Challenge* (March/April 1986); Frank Levy and Richard Michel, "An Economic Bust for the Baby Boom," *Challenge* (March/April 1986).

106. For recent inflation data, see Economic Report of the President, February 1986, 315–26. Key price indices were as follows:

	Consumer Price Index	Producer Price Index (finished goods)
1982	3.9	3.7
1983	3.8	.6
1984	4.0	1.7
1985	3.8	1.8

Sources: Table B-58, p. 319; table B-63, p. 326.

107. See references cited in nn. 90, 91, and 92.
108. See, for example, *Antitrust and Trade Regulation Rept.* 50 (27 February 1986):351.
109. Ibid.
110. The intensity of antitrust enforcement has varied considerably. From the early Sherman Act, the Rule of Reason, Wilson's New Freedom, the Good Trust era, NRA, Thurman Arnold, World War II, Post-War resumption, the Warren Court structuralists, moderate easing, to the Reagan relaxation, different interpretations of antitrust law express the "felt necessities of the time." While the great majority of citizens solidly supports antitrust in America, precise definition is left largely to the executive branch, the Antitrust Division (Department of Justice), and the Federal Trade Commmission, subject to congressional oversight and appropriations discipline.
111. See William A. Lovett, *World Trade Rivalry: Trade Equity and Competing Industrial Policies* (Lexington, MA: Lexington–D. C. Heath, 1987). Three major positions have emerged in the recent U.S. trade policy controversy: *(a) free trade*—(illustrated by Baldwin and Krueger, *Recent U.S. Trade Policy* [see n. 89]; Baldwin and Richardson, *International Trade and Finance* [see n. 93]) to encourage more open U.S. and foreign markets; *(b) more balanced and equal restrictions*—(illustrated by Culbertson, *International Trade* [see n. 93]; Bluestone and Harrison, *Deindustrialization of America* [see n. 91]; and the AFL-CIO Policy Recommendations [see n. 93]) to offset foreign protection, industrial development, targeting, and export subsidy policies; and *(c) stronger new industrial development policies* (emulating Japan)—to rejuvenate U.S. industry and manufacturing with productivity-oriented industrial policies and some offsets to foreign restrictions and subsidies (illustrated by the President's Commission on Industrial Competitiveness, *Global Competition: The New Reality* [see n. 90]; Otto Eckstein, et al, *The DRI Report on U.S. Manufacturing Industries* [New York: McGraw-Hill, 1984]; Kevin P. Phillips, *Staying On Top* [New York: Random House, 1984]; and Thurow, *The Zero-Sum Solution* [see n. 93]).

In Lovett's view, each alternative makes considerable sense, but the best, and most likely, policy evolution is a gradual synthesis towards *(a)* substantial, and more equal trade openness; *(b)* more balanced and reciprocal use of industrial support, mutual encouragement, and technology exchange; and *(c)* a stronger policy of fostering U.S. industrial rejuvenation, with more profit sharing, widespread ESOPs, extensive R&D support, and enforced technology sharing with major trading partners (including Japan, Europe, and the USSR). See Lovett, *World Trade Rivalry* (see this note above); and Lovett, *Competing Industrial Policies* (see n. 93).

Note: An early, abbreviated version of this paper appeared as William A. Lovett, "Theory and Practice of Antitrust," in *Issues after a Century of Federal Antitrust Policy,* ed. Robert L. Wills et al. (Lexington, MA: Lexington–D. C. Heath, 1987).

3. The New Attack on Antitrust

Willard F. Mueller

ANTITRUST is under unprecedented attack. Although support for antitrust has waxed and waned since passage of the Sherman Act in 1890, the current attack is unique in its breadth and success. Not only have the new attackers urged drastic "reforms" but they already have accomplished much of their agenda. They have staffed the antitrust agencies and, to an increasing degree, the federal courts with their adherents. And unlike previous attackers, their agenda is based on a body of economic ideas that allegedly represents a new orthodoxy as to how a capitalistic market economy works.

Just how did this all come about? How much have things really changed? How sound are the economic foundations upon which the attackers built their case? What does the future hold? Before turning to these questions, let us review briefly the status of antitrust before the recent attack was launched. (Although antitrust is currently being attacked from both the left and right of the political and economic spectrums, these remarks are addressed to the attack from the right. I have addressed elsewhere [Mueller 1983] the assault by some on the left, who sometimes have been unwitting handmaidens of the attackers from the right.)

Until the 1980s, students of antitrust generally accepted Richard Hofstadter's (1966, 116) observation that "antitrust as legal-administrative enterprise has been solidly institutionalized in the past quarter of a century." This explained why, whereas "once the United States had an antitrust movement without prosecutions, in our time there have been antitrust prosecutions without an antitrust movement."

Although antitrust has never accomplished as much as its staunchest advocates had hoped for, it clearly has performed better than its most ardent detractors have claimed. Nowhere is this more clear than in the experience with enforcement of the Celler-Kefauver Act of 1950, which amended the Clayton Act's prohibition of certain mergers. During the twenty-seven years following 1950, the Department of Justice (DOJ) and the Federal Trade Commission (FTC) challenged 1,021 mergers and acquisitions in 289 complaints (Mueller 1979). In the 1950s, the agencies challenged virtually every sizable horizontal merger. For example, in 1956, the record year in challenging such mergers, the agencies challenged 48 percent (measured in assets) of all large (assets exceeding $10 million) acquisitions of manufacturing and mining corporations. These cases culminated in lower court and Supreme Court decisions establishing tough legal standards for horizontal mergers that had the effect of stopping virtually all such anticompetitive mergers for a time. Students of public policy generally agree that this enforcement effort served as a powerful deterrent of horizontal mergers (Mueller 1965; Stigler 1966; Audretsch 1986). There is little doubt that without this effort highly concentrated industries would be the rule today, not the exception.

During the 1960s, the Supreme Court also handed down several decisions finding conglomerate mergers illegal. In 1969, Nixon's first antitrust chief, Richard W. McLaren, initiated a vigorous enforcement effort to discover the reach of the law toward conglomerate mergers (Mueller 1973). From 1969 to 1970, the antitrust agencies challenged nearly 30 percent (measured by assets) of all large mergers in manufacturing and mining (Mueller 1979). But McLaren's heroic effort foundered, as Henry C. Simons might have said, on the orderly process of democratic corruption. The three ITT cases, the centerpiece of McLaren's assault on conglomerate mergers, were prevented from reaching the Supreme Court when President Nixon ordered that they be settled with a consent decree favorable to ITT (Mueller 1983).

The ITT cases aside, the agencies' merger effort represented an enormous enforcement push as judged by past antitrust efforts. Although enforcement efforts toward conglomerates flagged during the 1970s because of what Justice White (1974) characterized as the "new antitrust majority" of the Burger Court, other antitrust enforcement proceeded pretty much as usual. Indeed, the 1970s saw a number of innovative efforts, e.g., the FTC's shared monopoly case in the cereal industry, as well as vigorous antitrust enforcement by private parties. But all of this changed rapidly, drastically, and largely unexpectedly beginning in 1981.

Unlike previous presidents, Democrats and Republicans alike, President Reagan entered office with an agenda aimed at eliminating or greatly reducing government interference in all areas of business affairs. Antitrust "reform" was near the top of his agenda.

Regulatory policy can be changed in three ways: (1) changing enforcement personnel and policies of the antitrust agencies; (2) appointing judges with a known antiregulatory bias; and (3) repealing or amending the law through the legislative process. To date the Reagan administration has not succeeded in changing the legislative foundations of antitrust, although it recently laid out its agenda in this area as well. However, it has been successful in changing antitrust policy beyond the fondest hopes of the enemies of antitrust and the greatest fears of its friends.

Changes in the Agencies

Reagan's first step in "deregulating" antitrust was to appoint agency heads with known records of hostility to antitrust as enforced before 1981. William F. Baxter, a brilliant, laissez-faire lawyer-economist, was appointed head of the Antitrust Division, and an equally zealous laissez-faire economist, Dr. James Miller III, was appointed chairman of the FTC.[1] Prior to his appointment, Miller had worked for Office of Management and Budget head David Stockman, who had led the administration's effort to wipe out the FTC's antitrust enforcement arm, the Bureau of Competition (Warner 1981).

Both agency heads were doctrinaire disciples of the Chicago School of economics, which holds that the guiding and sole principle of antitrust is, or should be, the pursuit of economic efficiency. In this view, all business conduct should and can be evaluated in terms of its contribution to economic efficiency as predicted by static microeconomic models. This approach tends to resolve all disputes concerning the intent and consequences of particular practices in favor of the businessman making them, since the theory assumes rational decision makers are always motivated by a quest for greater economic efficiency. These latter-day devotees of Adam Smith (Miller always wore an Adam Smith tie while head of the FTC) have even greater faith in the businessman's proclivity for competition than did Smith. Indeed, in the area of vertical price fixing, Baxter and Miller might have rewritten Smith's often-quoted admonition concerning businessmen's propensity to conspire so that it reads: "Manufacturers and retailers seldom meet together, even for merriment or diversion, but the conversation ends in a conspiracy to fix retail prices in order to enhance consumers' welfare."

The remarkable thing about Baxter and Miller is not their view of the world; Chicago School economists have expressed these views for decades. But never before had they received such a felicitous reception by public policymakers. For example, whereas in 1969 the Stigler White House Task Force on Productivity and Competition made several rather drastic proposals to change antitrust, they were largely ignored during the Nixon-Ford years. Nixon's antitrust chief, Richard W. McLaren, considered Stigler's arguments as theoretical nonsense not relevant to the real world. But Baxter and Miller did more than advocate theories before academic audiences. Commanding large legal and economic staffs, many of whose members has passed the Chicago School litmus test, Baxter and Miller set about changing enforcement standards and court-made law. Considerations of space permits only a brief review of the Baxter-Miller accomplishments.

Since Baxter and Miller view businessmen's decisions as generally reflecting the pursuit of greater efficiency, they presume mergers seldom pose a public policy problem. This view is consistent with President Reagan's campaign statements in which he said efforts to slow the conglomerate merger tide were "arbitrary, unnecessary and economically unsound."[2] Both antitrust agencies have adopted new *Merger Guidelines* that essentially give a green light to all mergers except horizontal mergers that result in very high levels of concentration. Under these guidelines, most mergers found illegal by the Supreme Court during the 1960s would not even be challenged today—all this without any change in the laws enforced by the agencies. The result has been to unleash a new "merger mania" among large corporations. Since the Chicagoans have great faith in the "market for corporate control," they are pleased, not bothered by the likes of Boone Pickens, Irv Jacobs, and other merger makers who are restructuring American business for their own private gain and personal aggrandizement. Most large conglomerate mergers have absolutely nothing to do with increasing economic efficiency (Greer 1986; D. C. Mueller 1985), while carrying a potential for anticompetitive effects (Mueller 1982). Nonetheless, FTC Chairman Miller (1984) proudly proclaimed that from 1981 to 1984 the FTC did not open an investigation into a single conglomerate merger. Neither did the agencies challenge any vertical mergers. Although they challenged a number of horizontal mergers, these were largely paper victories ending with consent decrees permitting the mergers after requiring modest partial divestiture. The agencies have even failed to challenge horizontal mergers that violated the Justice Department's *Merger Guidelines*. The FTC was tardy in challenging Pepsi-Cola's proposed acquisition of Seven-Up and Coca-Cola's acquisition of Dr. Pepper, although each of these mergers clearly violated Section 7 of the Clayton Act.[3] Indeed, the FTC did not challenge these actions until RC Cola brought a private suit that succeeded in getting a temporary restraining order blocking the proposed mergers. The experience illustrates anew the critical role of private antitrust actions.

Baxter and Miller also changed enforcement policy in the area of vertical restraints, including vertical price fixing, or so-called resale price maintenance (RPM). Both antitrust agencies have sought to repeal the existing law of vertical restraints through administrative actions. Not only have the agencies failed to bring any RPM cases but they have urged the courts to change their interpretation of the law in this area. To accomplish this, the U.S. Department of Justice (1985) promulgated *Vertical Restraint Guidelines* that would permit much conduct that is illegal under existing law. The Justice Department also has filed amicus briefs in behalf of defendants in private antitrust suits involving RPM and other vertical restraints, a practice it also has followed in other areas of antitrust.

Baxter's views have met with varying success before the federal courts. One federal judge observed: "While there may be some merit to the opinions of [Mr. Baxter], his opinions are not law. The same is true of analyses performed by academics."[4] (The reference to "academics" is to Chicago School economists.) In 1984, Baxter was unsuccessful when he intervened on behalf of the Monsanto Company in an RPM case before the Supreme Court.[5] Although Monsanto had not even raised a free-rider defense, Baxter urged the Court to declare that it would consider such defenses in future RPM cases. The Court said that in the circumstances it was unnecessary to reach the issue. Despite this, given the changing composition of the lower courts and prospective changes in the Supreme Court, if present trends continue the Chicago School may yet carry the day on RPM.

There are many other examples that reflect the Reagan administration's attitude toward antitrust. Under Miller, the Federal Trade Commission brought no vertical price-fixing, price discrimination, or monopolization cases. Moreover, it has dismissed important monopoly and merger cases brought by prior Republican and Democratic administrations. Among the most important of these was a case challenging three companies with having a "shared monopoly" in the prepared breakfast cereal industry. This was a pioneer case designed to determine whether three firms dominating an industry could be found guilty of "monopolizing" under the law. Although this admittedly was a novel interpretation of the monopoly law that hitherto had been applied only to single firm dominance, a majority of the Miller Commission took the unprecedented step of dismissing the case without reviewing the record.

In an important monopolization case, *Borden, Inc.—ReaLemon*,[6] the commission requested the Supreme Court *not* to hear the case despite the fact that in 1978 the prior commission had found the company guilty of monopolizing, a decision that was subsequently approved by an appellate court.[7] The commission then settled the case on grounds satisfactory to the defendant.[8] Commissioner Pertschuk, in dissenting from the predation standard spelled out in the consent decree, said that while the rule "may appeal to some as embodying the height of economic rationality, as a practical matter, the standard in this order would take the Commission out of the business of policing predation."[9]

Likewise, in 1984 the commission dismissed an attempt to monopolize a case involving *ITT-Continental* after an administrative law judge had found ITT guilty.[10] In dissenting from the decision, Commissioner Patricia P. Bailey stated that the FTC majority had sent a signal to the business community that, in the immortal words of Cole Porter, "Anything goes." She added, "It would be simpler, and surely a great saving of everybody's time if the commission today had simply announced that it does not believe predatory pricing exists."[11]

There is only one notable exception to the Reagan administration's soft antitrust policy—horizontal price-fixing agreements. Mr. Baxter has aggressively pursued price fixers. Although the prior administration had begun a probe of highway contractors, Baxter devoted substantial resources to this effort, resulting in fines of $47 million and the jailing of 127 businessman for a cumulative total of forty-seven years.[12] In Baxter's view, "this is garden-variety criminal activity and incarceration of the offending executives is absolutely essential."[13] In view of his great aversion to price fixing, it is incongruous that Mr. Baxter is unconcerned with mergers and other conduct that cause highly concentrated markets where overt price fixing may be unnecessary because competitors recognize their common interests and is virtually impossible to detect when practiced. Apparently Baxter could find little price fixing outside the construction industry, since he brought few price-fixing cases in other industries.

The New Learning Becomes the New Orthodoxy

The intellectual foundations of the policies pursued by Baxter, Miller, and their successors are found in the so-called Chicago School of industrial organization economics. While the ideas are not new, they did not achieve much credibility in antitrust policy until the 1980s. Reagan's first FTC chairman, James C. Miller III, credits their current prominence to superior theory and empirical analysis. As a result, he says, "the ascendancy of the Chicago School now seems all but inevitable" (Miller 1984, 8). In his view, a "new learning" about how markets work has made Chicago School ideas the new orthodoxy.

Just what is this "new learning" we hear so much about these days? How does the Chicago School of industrial organization differ from the majority of economists in this field? Harold Demsetz, himself a leader in the Chicago School, identified the distinction neatly in his paper "Two Systems of Belief about Monopoly." As he expressed it (Demsetz 1974, 164) at the 1974 Airlie House, Virginia, Conference on "Industrial Concentration: The New Learning,"[14] there existed two competing theories about monopoly, and they were "heading for a showdown." The then orthodox theory of the day, which Demsetz called the "self-sufficiency theory," held that monopoly power could develop and survive "without any substantial aid from the government." (This is not to say the theory rejected the notion that government may be a significant source of market power.) The other theory, which Demsetz labeled the "interventionism theory," saw monopoly power as "derivative of government interventions" (164–65). The Chicago School interventionism theory holds that the only thing we have to fear, with minor exceptions, is government policy that purposely or unwittingly confers monopoly power on firms. This is in contrast to the "self-sufficiency theory" that holds that public policy should be concerned with anticompetitive industrial structures and competitive tactics.

Some critics of the Chicago School assert its beliefs rest more on hope than on sound theory and empirical research. But despite such casual criticism, the simple truth is that currently these theories are used to direct or rationalize the public policy actions of the antitrust agencies and increasingly are finding their way into court decisions. Miller proclaimed in 1985, a decade after Demsetz's paper, that the new learning of the Chicago School had triumphed. It had become the new orthodoxy; the old industrial organization theory was dead (Miller 1984, 8–10).

I suggest that is is premature to make funeral arrangements for what had been the mainstream of industrial organization for at least three decades. Let us first examine the new evidence. Do developments in economic thought and research over the past decade support Miller's victory pronouncement?

What I propose doing here is to review the theoretical and empirical work in the two areas where Chicago School "beliefs" about economic affairs have had their greatest impact: market structure-performance relationships and the treatment of vertical restraints. Simply put, the Chicago School believes that (1) oligopolistic market structures are unlikely to adversely affect market performance, and (2) vertical restraints, with few exceptions, improve economic welfare.

I caution readers that what follows is not intended to imply that Chicago School economists have made no significant contributions to industrial organization research. They have. But not surprisingly, since Chicago School economists believe government is the predominant source of monopoly, much of their research focuses on testing hypotheses of the effects of state and federal regulations on competition. These studies generally command high respect among mainstream industrial organization economists. A prominent example of such work is a study of the effects of regulation in the airline industry by former FTC chairman Miller and his colleague Commissioner Douglas (Douglas and Miller 1974).

The New Learning: Oligopoly Does Not Confer Market Power

Since Augustine Cournot explored the subject about 150 years ago, economists have spun a variety of theories to explain the conduct and performance of oligopolists. The problem has not been an absence of theories but the paucity of reliable data to test the theories. Not surprisingly, Bain's (1951) early empirical tests, relying on crude data and statistical techniques, were quickly challenged. But despite data problems, by the 1960s a consensus seemd to have emerged that market power, especially as measured by market concentration and barriers to entry, adversely affected industry performance (Weiss 1971). In his exhaustive review of the literature in 1974, Weiss (1974, 231) concluded: "By and large the relationship holds up for Britain, Canada and Japan, as well as in the United States. In general the data have confirmed the relationship predicted by theory, even though the data are very imperfect and almost certainly biased toward a zero relationship."

But in Demsetz's view, all these studies suffered a fatal flaw. Virtually all of the studies had measured the relationship between market structure and profits. And whereas those conducting the studies believed they had verified a positive relationship between market structure and profits, Demsetz asserted they had unwittingly discovered a positive relationship between concentration and efficiency: the largest firms in an industry had higher profits because they were more efficient, not because they elevated prices.

Demsetz's conclusions, if true, overturned several decades of empirical work and inflicted a deadly blow to what had become the orthodox view of the relationship between industrial structure and performance. The immediate influence of Demsetz's assertions was surprising in view of their fragile empirical foundations. Very briefly, Demsetz had correlated the weighted average concentration ratios of various Internal Revenue Service (IRS) industries with the profit rates of various size groupings of firms within the industries. Anyone familiar with IRS data realizes that they are fraught with problems. The problems inherent in Demsetz's use of these data clearly biased his analysis toward finding a zero relationship between concentration and profits (Appendix A.)[15]

In view of the deficiencies in Demsetz's data, his results are not surprising. He found that the strongest positive correlations tend to be found in the largest class size and negative correlations in the smallest class size. These findings, Demsetz believed, supported the hypothesis that "larger firms in concentrated industries have lower cost because there are scale economies in these industries or because of some inherent superiority of the larger firms in these industries" (Demsetz 1974, 178).[16]

Though not recognized as such at the time, Demsetz's 1974 piece marked the official birthdate of the new learning that concentration promoted efficiency, not market power.[17] Interestingly, leading non–Chicago School scholars attending the Airlie House Conference generally did not take Demsetz's study seriously.[18]

In 1977, Peltzman undertook an ambitious test of the Demsetz hypothesis using a more comprehensive data set and more sophisticated analysis. Peltzman (1977, 251) concluded that "long period changes in market structures are accompanied by increased efficiency. This efficiency gain is most pronounced where concentration is high and rising and where demand is growing." This is perhaps the most cited empirical work supporting the concentration-efficiency hypothesis. But as Scherer (1980, 289) has observed, Peltzman's "interpretation of the results suffers from serious flaws, mostly related to his failure to look behind the numbers and ascertain how things were derived and what was actually happening in the industries analyzed." Scherer predicted that had Peltzman examined the industries experiencing rapid concentration increases, he would have found them to be primarily consumer goods industries.

Scherer's expectations that Peltzman's model was driven by the consumer goods industries in his sample may be tested by redoing the analysis separately for consumer and producer goods. Vita (1984) recently did just that. The analysis used superior data and a slightly improved Peltzman model. Vita's initial analysis, based on a large sample of consumer and producer goods industries, seemed to confirm the Demsetz-Peltzman thesis. But when Vita reran his model separately for consumer goods and producer goods, the confirmation evaporated. The analysis based on producer goods did not support Peltzman's findings, despite the fact that, a priori, producer goods provide the most unequivocal test of the hypothesis.[19] On the other hand, the analysis involving consumer goods industries yielded results similar to Peltzman's. Thus Vita confirmed Scherer's expectation that Peltzman's results depended on his consumer goods observations.

These findings are consistent with other empirical work. As Mueller and Rogers (1980, 1984) have demonstrated, since World War II consumer goods industries have experienced persistent increases in concentration (whereas producer goods industries have experienced no upward trend), with the main cause for the increase related to advantages of large scale in television advertising. And as Wills (1983) has shown, the leading firms in consumer goods industries have substantially higher prices than do smaller sellers in these industries. Moveover, Kelton (1980) found that consumer industries with the greatest advertising experienced the greatest increases in prices. Nor did Kelton (1983) find a significant relationship between concentration and change in productivity.

The above evidence refutes the Demsetz hypothesis. High profits of concentrated industries are due in large part to higher prices, not lower costs. And if, as I believe to be true, the price differences between concentrated industries and less concentrated industries often are greater than the differences in their respective profit rates, many concentrated industries have higher costs as well as higher prices.

Sometimes the various structure-profit studies based on FTC Line-of-Business (LOB) data are cited as support for the new learning. These studies have contributed much to our learning, and the profession is indebted to the FTC for collecting these data for several years. It is a mistake, however, to infer that these studies support the Chicago School thesis merely because the findings differ in some respects from earlier studies. One of the unique findings of these studies is the important role played by individual firm market shares, a phenomenom identified as being significant in an earlier study (Kelly 1969) and by others (Imel and Helmberger 1971; Shepherd 1972; Marion et al. 1979). Some make much of the finding that when market share is included in the model using FTC LOB data the relationship between market concentration and profits sometimes is not statistically significant and the relationship is sometimes negative (Ravenscraft 1983). But these findings are by no means at odds with earlier work. As Weiss (1971) pointed out some years ago, the concentration-profit relationship tends to break down during periods of inflation. Seldom mentioned is the fact that all of the LOB data were collected for years of substantial inflation, 1974–77. Significantly, an analysis (Ravenscraft 1983) using LOB data for the food manufacturing industries found a significant positive relationship between profits and concentration as well as between profits and market shares, which is consistent with other structure-profit studies in these industries (Connor et al. 1985; Rogers 1979, 1985). This is as one would expect: these industries are less susceptible to inflation since the demand for food shifts much less over a business cycle than does demand in most other manufacturing industries. Thus, the jury is still out as to what LOB data would show during noninflationary years. Additionally, these analyses suffer because of the high correlation between market share and concentration ratios, which presents a special problem in the LOB data set because it consists only of large firms, which typically hold the leading positions in their industries (Connor et al. 1985).

Although the preceding demonstrates that the Demsetz concentration-efficiency hypothesis has scant empirical support, there is a growing body of reliable evidence disproving the hypothesis entirely. I am alluding to studies that make a direct test of the hypothesis that market concentration, after adjusting for barriers to entry and other variables, elevates prices above costs. Concentration-price studies are especially relevant because, as Weiss (1985) emphasizes, "for the most part oligopoly theory makes predictions about prices rather than profits. [Therefore] the proper test of oligopoly theory is one where price is the dependent variable." Almost without exception, these studies have found that concentration is positively associated with price levels. Not only do these studies refute Chicago School "beliefs" about the relevance of concentration, but they fly in the face of another revisionist "be-

The New Attack on Antitrust 63

lief," the theory of "contestable markets." Proponents of this theory argue that market concentration does not confer market power as long as a market is "contestable," i.e., that there are no significant barriers to entry or exit (Baumol 1982). If real-world markets were as readily contestable as Baumol believes, the level of concentration would not be positively related to prices in a market. The price studies, therefore, confirm Shepherd's (1984, 585) observation regarding contestable market theory: "The 'new' analysis gives no persuasive reason to shift attention away from competition within the market."

Because the concentration-price studies usually examine the relationship between concentration and prices across geographic markets for a particular product or service, they are not plagued with problems common to *all* cross-industry studies.[20] Indeed, the price studies use data that are superior to even the most reliable data, such as FTC LOB data, which are used in cross-industry studies.

Because of the availability of data and the interest of Federal Reserve economists such as Stephen A. Rhoades, many of the concentration-price studies have examined financial markets. A partial list includes Slater (1956), Edwards (1964), Bell and Murphy (1969), Aspinwall (1970), Jacobs (1971), Kessel (1971), Greer and Shay (1973), Heggestad and Mingo (1976), Rhoades (1977), Graddy and Kyle (1979), Hester (1979), and Marlow (1982). All of the studies cited above found a positive net relationship between concentration and various measures of price, e.g., checking service charges, mortgage interest rates, and bond underwriters' spreads.

There have been at least six studies of air fares since airline deregulation in 1978 (Graham, Kaplan and Sibley 1983; Milliman and Weiss 1983; Bailey, Graham and Kaplan 1984; Call and Keller 1985; Moore 1985; Strassman 1986). The airlines are particularly relevant to the contestability hypothesis. Since entry into another market would seem to be quite easy, many consider airlines one of the closest approximations to contestable markets in the real world. Yet, as Alfred E. Kahn, former chairman of the Civil Aeronautics Board, says of the concentration-price studies: "Every one of them concludes that how many carriers you have in a market makes a difference. If entry were a sufficient discipline, you wouldn't see different fares whether there is one carrier in the market or five" (Vise and Behr 1986).

In food retailing, four studies using different methods, data, and time periods found a positive relationshp between concentration and price levels (Marion et al. 1979; Lamm 1981; Meyer 1983; Cotterill 1986). Except for Lamm's, these studies examined firm prices and found prices positively associated with both market share and concentration. Moreover, Marion et al., who examined both the level of profits and prices, found that in highly concentrated markets price overcharges as a percent of sales were greater than profits as a percent of sales, suggesting that concentration increased costs as well as prices and profits. The results of this study are cited by Leibenstein (1979) as an example of X-inefficiency due to market power.

Virtually all auction market theory points to higher buying prices and lower selling prices as the number of bidders grow. The theory is supported by empirical studies in municipal bond underwriting, bidding for offshore oil, and bidding for national forest timber (Brannman, Klein, and Weiss 1986).

Other concentration-price studies have been made in such diverse industries as life insurance (Cummins, Denenberg, and Scheel 1972); newspaper and television advertising (Landon 1971; Owen 1973; Thompson 1984); gasoline retailing (Marvel 1980); prescription drugs (FTC 1975); cement (Koller and Weiss 1985); and microfilm (Barton and Sherman 1984). All of these studies found a positive relationship between market concentration and prices. Finally, a study by Wills (1983) using exceptionally high quality data examined the relationship between prices and both advertising and market share of the brands of 145 food products. The results demonstrated that prices of the leading brands were substantially higher than even the second- to fourth-largest brands and greater still than prices of minor brands and retailers' private brands. This evidence likely explains why studies such as Peltzman's that combine consumer goods industries and producer goods industries result in false conclusions. Their empirical results are driven by the consumer goods industries in their samples. The market-share–profit relationship in those consumer industries is generated by the impact of advertising on price, not by the efficiencies that Demsetz and company supposed.

The consistency of the price studies cited above is quite amazing. They clearly are at odds with the Demsetz hypothesis and the findings of Peltzman, as well as the beliefs of proponents of the theory of contestable markets. Moreover, it cannot be overemphasized in evaluating these findings that the data used in most of the price studies are far superior to Demsetz's study and virtually all profit studies, including those based on FTC Line-of-Business data. The superior scientific quality of the price studies is often neglected by literature reviewers who are enamored with econometric technique to the neglect of data quality.

The New Learning: Vertical Restraints Promote Consumer Welfare

Chicago School models have reached their fullest flower in the area of vertical restraints, including vertical price fixing, i.e., resale price maintenance (RPM). Since 1911, the Supreme Court has held it per se illegal for a manufacturer to enter into price-fixing agreements with the distributors of its products. For some years, RPM was made an exception to the antitrust laws by a federal law permitting states to authorize RPM. But in 1975, during the Ford administration, these so-called "fair trade" laws were prohibited in favor of the historic antitrust treatment of RPM.

Despite this legislative mandate, the Reagan antitrust agencies have sought more permissive treatment of all types of vertical restraints. FTC Chairman Miller (1983) said his "aim is to persuade you that RPM deserves to be judged by a rule of reason." But let there be no mistake about the ultimate objective of Chicago School policymakers. Very simply, they hope to eliminate the per se prohibitions against RPM as well as the current rule of reason standards applied to nonprice vertical restraints. Richard Posner (1981), formerly of the University of Chicago Law School and currently a federal judge, states it most plainly. He asserts that the appropriate legal rule for all vertical restraints in distribution is one which declares them per se legal. Robert Bork earlier had made a similar argument.

The advocates of the "new learning" about vertical restraints base their case on the Chicago School theory that a manufacturer generally would not set the retail price of his products unless he were motivated by efficiency considerations.[21] This theory has its origins in the writings of Bowman (1957), Telser (1960), and Bork (1966). These scholars argue that a manufacturer can only induce its distributors to furnish the ideal mix of services to customers if the manufacturer guarantees distributors an above competitive price using RPM or other vertical restraints prohibiting intrabrand competition. Without such incentives, some distributors would get a free ride by not providing the needed services, thereby discouraging others from doing so as well.

The Chicago School economists acknowledge that vertical restraints generally result in higher prices, but they argue the increased services shift the demand curve to the right sufficiently to increase the manufacturer's total sales. The test of whether vertical restraints improve economic efficiency is not the price paid by consumers, says the Chicago School, but whether the restraint restricts or increases output, with the former being anticompetitive and latter procompetitive (Bork 1966, 375–76).

But the problem is more complex than this. One relevant question is whether the increased prices paid by consumers are worth the increased services received. F. M. Scherer (1983) and William Comanor (1985) have recently demonstrated that merely because increased services shift retail demand to the right does not prove that economic efficiency has improved. As Comanor (1985, 991–92) puts it: "Societal gains or losses from changes in the product depend on the preference of *all* consumers, not merely those at the margin. . . . If marginal consumers value dealer-provided service less than inframarginal consumers do, the level of such services will be too low. By contrast, if marginal consumers value those services more highly, the level of distribution services will be excessive, and the imposition of vertical restraints to promote such services would be inefficient."

Considerations of space prevent a full treatment of the theoretical argument. But what these authors have done is demonstrate theoretically what many observers long had felt intuitively was wrong with the Chicago School arguments: with restricted distribution, many consumers are forced to pay for services they do not want. Thus, it is wrong to assume that merely because vertical restraints benefit a manufacturer they also must benefit society as whole.

Scherer also has demonstrated that when oligopolists engage in RPM, they may merely push up prices all around without shifting anyone's demand curve to the right.

Not only does the Chicago School's new learning concerning vertical restraints rest on a flawed economic theory but it lacks empirical support. Its argument rests heavily on the illusive concept of free riding. Yet there is scant evidence that a serious free-rider problem exists where RPM and other vertical restraints are practiced. Although free riding may occur in some cases, most claims of free riding are exaggerated or false. As someone has said, free riding is like the Loch Ness monster, much talked about but never seen.

Although it is not discussed at length here, a rich body of empirical evidence exists that demonstrates that consumers are injured by RPM and other vertical restraints. Students of distribution have long been impressed with the broad spectrum of product-service mixes provided by different distributors in the absence of vertical restraints. Food retailing provides an obvious example: store formats range from high-margin, high-service convenience stores to low-margin, low-service warehouse stores. Similar diversity emerges whenever retailers are free to adopt their formats to unique market segments reflecting the price-service preferences of different consumers. I find it ironic in the extreme that Chicago School economists, who yield to no one in their faith that markets provide the best test of what consumers want, believe that vertical price fixing is acceptable because a manufacturer knows better than its distributors what consumers want. It is questionable whether the great diversity that is the hallmark of the American distribution system would have emerged had restricted distribution been per se legal, as advocated by Posner and other Chicago School economists.

In sum, not only was FTC Chairman Miller premature in claiming that "The New Learning" had carried the day but he was flat-out wrong. Both the theory and empirical work of Chicago School economists is seriously flawed. It has displaced neither the mainstream of industrial organization nor what Demsetz labeled the "self-sufficiency theory." This "mainstream" of industrial organization originated in the ideas of Chamberlin, Mason, and Bain and was widened and deepened by the work of such current leaders in this tradition as Leonard Weiss, F. M. Scherer, William Shepherd, Alfred Kahn, Douglas Greer, and William Comanor, to name a few. The new learning gained many true believers, some economists and many laypersons. Its main effect, however, has been to muddy the waters of knowledge. But as the waters clear we see that the mainstream has not been altered significantly. The Chicago School has merely dredged a channel of its own, leading nowhere and filling rapidly with stagnant promises.

Revising Antitrust through Court Appointments

American presidents appoint, with confirmation by the Senate, all members to the federal judiciary. President Reagan's appointments have generally reflected his conservative views. As with his antitrust agency appointments, the president has appointed several Chicago School judges to the appellate courts.

The most controversial such appointee is Richard A. Posner, a former University of Chicago Law School professor appointed to the 7th Circuit Court of Appeals. Judge Posner applies economic analysis in all areas of law: antitrust, torts, contracts, family law, and constitutional law. For example, in his view a free market in private suits will solve the unlawful search and seizure problem (Warren 1983, 76). Improper policy conduct will be deterred if enough private suits result in large jury awards. This faith in "free-market" solutions to problems ignores the reality that victims of improper police conduct often do not have adequate legal counsel, that jury awards generally are small, and that some city governments would pay much to protect a modern-day Bull Connor.

Judge Posner's remoteness from reality was further illustrated in an antitrust decision in which he reasoned that a plaintiff should not be granted discovery until an antitrust violation had been proved. He did not explain just how a plaintiff was to prove his case without prior discovery. In dissenting from this decision, Justice Potter Stewart, a recently retired conservative member of the Supreme Court, criticized Posner for forging "new ground, despite the absence of a factual record . . . and despite the existence of contrary precedent." [22]

No area of law is beyond the reach of Posnerian economics. In one decision he made a cost-benefit analysis of a high school rule prohibiting a student from playing basketball wearing a yarmulke (a cap worn by some Jews) pinned on with a bobby pin (Wermiel 1984). Posner concluded the safety costs outweighed the value of the religious beliefs of the student.

Professor Ponsoldt (1983) of the University of Georgia Law School has accused Posner of "not remembering that he is no longer speaking as a law professor from the University of Chicago." Despite such criticisms, Posner is among the leading contenders for the next vacancy on the Supreme Court.

Ironically, President Reagan pledged to appoint judges who practiced "judicial restraint." Yet the Chicago School antitrust appointees are actually radical activists, prepared to upset any precedent that diverges from their view of the economic world. Judge Posner, whose activism extends to all areas of law, has redefined judicial restraint to mean judicial activism. While he acknowledges it would be "pretty wild" to overrule *Marbury v. Madison,* the leading precedent in American law, in his view this would represent judicial restraint because "it would reduce the power of the federal courts vis-à-vis the other organs of government" (Posner 1985, 210). Such doublespeak is too much for Posner's former colleague, Professor Philip Kurland of the University of Chicago Law School, "a pillar of old-fashioned restraint." As he sees it: "Judges are being appointed in the expectation that they will rewrite laws and the Constitution to the administration's liking. Reagan's judges are activists in support of conservative dogma" (Caplan 1986, 62).

By the end of his term, President Reagan will have appointed over one-half of the sitting federal judges. To date the president has appointed only one member to the Supreme Court. But with five of its nine members now over age seventy, the composition of the Court could well change dramatically by November 1988. Some have suggested that in confirming federal judges the Senate should scrutinize more closely those having "extralegal" views of the judicial process. Speaking specifically of Judge Posner, Professor Ponsoldt (1983) has said:

> Judge Posner's writing and consulting had long been known for its revisionist, anti-populist critique of the existing body of antitrust legislation and Supreme Court case law. . . .
>
> Perhaps, therefore, it should come as no surprise that Judge Posner's opinion in *Marrese* relied on his own views and ignored at least six relevant Supreme Court decisions, constituting the 50-year development of the law to the present day. . . .
>
> The Posner opinion in *Marrese* represents the imperial judiciary in its extreme. The possibility of similar nullification, based upon ideology, should be addressed specifically by the Senate in its confirmation hearings, at least where the nominee is so publicly associated with an extralegal view of public policy.

Ultimately, if the U.S. Senate fails to stem the tide of activist appointees to the federal courts, judges of the Chicago School persuasion will turn antitrust law upside down.

Revising Antitrust by Legislative Action

The changes in antitrust policy discussed above were accomplished without any legislative changes in the antitrust laws. Indeed, to date the Congress has shown considerable hostility to the agencies' failure to enforce existing laws and their practice of intervening in behalf of defendants in private cases.

On 19 February 1986, the Department of Justice sent to the Congress five legislative proposals for "improvements in American antitrust laws." The proposals had been fashioned by the late Commerce Secretary Malcolm Baldrige and Attorney General Edwin Meese III.

The proposals deal with mergers, industries affected by import competition, antitrust remedies, interlocking directorates, and the extraterritoriality of the antitrust laws. Considerations of space permit brief discussion of only the first two of these. Suffice it to say of the third, antitrust remedies, that it also could have disastrous effects on one of the bulwarks of effective antitrust enforcement, private plaintiffs acting as private attorneys general. Having effectively squelched federal antitrust enforcement through administrative actions, the proposed act would spike the guns of private enforcement, long the major source of enforcement in certain areas.

Attorney General Edwin Meese (1986) made plain that the proposed new laws rest on the new learning of Chicago School economists. As he put it: "During the past 20 years advances in economic theory have shown that the antitrust laws should protect consumer welfare and promote economic efficiency. Unfortunately, current antitrust laws have instead been applied at times in a way that inhibits business activities that would benefit consumers." With this as a foundation, the nature and purposes of the proposed "reforms" will come as no surprise to those familiar with "the new learning," which teaches that economic concentration promotes efficiency, not market power.

Mergers

The proposed Merger Modernization Act of 1986 would make fundamental changes in the language of Section 7 of the Clayton Act. Whereas the existing law prohibits mergers whose effects "may" substantially lessen competition, the proposed act would require proof that the merger "will substantially increase the ability to exercise market power." The proposed act also incorporates the Justice Department's *Merger Guidelines* provisions that raise the threshold for illegal mergers. These changes would go far toward permitting all mergers except those that result in substantial market power. This would effectively repeal the Celler-Kefauver Act of 1950, which was designed to strike at accumulations of power by merger well before they reached monopoly proportions. The legislative history of the act made it unmistakably clear that it was directed at *incipient* monopoly and that Sherman Act (i.e. monopoly) standards were not to be used. The Merger Modernization Act of 1986 would repeal this rule.

The Department of Justice "analysis" (Meese 1986) of the proposed act declares that it is "necessary to fine-tune the antitrust laws" because "the body of economic learning upon which antitrust enforcement policy and judicial doctrine regarding mergers is based has changed substantially." From whence came this new economic learning?

Simply put, the new body of learning underlying the new merger proposal is the Chicago School "belief" that private market power is seldom a problem unless it is abetted by government. This is why the *Merger Guidelines* are little concerned unless a merger results in highly concentrated markets. Since the market power concepts in the proposed merger law rest squarely on the Chicago School's new learning, the case for the law is no stronger than the empirical foundations of this learning. As discussed above, the best available empirical evidence regarding the relationship between concentration and performance demonstrates that the Chicago School "beliefs" have no basis in empirical evidence. And insofar as the proposal rests on the belief that mergers are necessary to increase efficiency, here too a growing body of evidence demonstrates that more often than not mergers promote inefficiency, not efficiency (D. C. Mueller 1985; Ravenscraft and Scherer 1986).

Industries Affected by Imports

The proposed Promoting Competition in Distressed Industries Act of 1986 is designed "to provide a new form of relief for domestic industries injured by increased imports." The new "relief" contemplated by the proposal is to give the president authority to grant an antitrust exemption to mergers and acquisitions among members of the injured industry. The Department of Justice "analysis" (Meese 1986) gives the following rationale for the proposal: "Economists now recognize that mergers and acquisitions can create economies of scale and efficiencies. Business may, in turn, translate resulting cost savings into lower prices or better quality products or services in order to repair market share or profitability lost to imports."

This proposal assumes foreign firms outcompete American firms because the latter are not large enough to enjoy economies of scale enjoyed by foreign businesses. This is largely nonsense. American firms claiming they are unable to compete often far surpass in size their foreign rivals and are large enough to enjoy all economies of scale. Consider two of the industries hardest hit by imports, automobiles and steel.

American automobile companies dwarf their foreign competitors. For example, the combined sales of General Motors and Ford are as great as the combined sales of twelve foreign automobile companies (the three largest in Japan, Germany, France, and Britain). Most Japanese automobile companies are midgets compared to their American competitors. General Motors alone has sales about as great as nine Japanese automakers, and Chrysler is larger than all but two of the Japanese companies. Even Japan's fourth largest automobile company, Honda Motor, is little more than 10 percent as large as General Motors and is smaller than Chrysler.

Similarly, leading American steel companies generally dwarf their foreign competitors. And a recent study by the staff of the Federal Trade Commission (Frankena and Paulter 1985) found that all eight of the largest American integrated steel companies are large enough to enjoy full economies of scale.

True, American companies have failed to meet the competitive challenge in many industries. But this has been due to a variety of complex factors unrelated to their size, including the overvalued dollar and lower foreign labor costs. These are not matters that can be changed by concentrating American business into the hands of a few huge firms. Greater size does not necessarily increase efficiency. As Robert Townsend (1970, 17B) has said, those who confuse bigness with efficiency are "like the poor lady who thought all she had to do to become an opera singer was to drink lots of heavy cream." Particular big business organizations are efficient; but often their current size largely reflects their innovativeness when they were smaller. Large size, as Leibenstein observes, often leads to laxity and managerial problems. Such inefficiencies escape public attention when firms possess market power that confers high profits despite inflated cost structures.

The late Secretary of Commerce Malcolm Baldrige, the chief administration champion of this proposal, should haved learned a lesson from the experience of Japanese government officials who at one time held views identical to his. The Japanese Ministry of International Trade and Industry (MITI) in the 1960s attempted to consolidate Japan's nine automobile companies into two large companies to better compete with U.S. firms. The Japanese automakers refused to give up their independence and have thrived since then, despite their having remained small by American standards.

The Future of Antitrust

How, then, can we explain the great impact of Chicago School economics on antitrust policy? To hear former FTC Chairman Miller tell it, the success reflects the triumph of superior theory and empirical work of Chicago School scholars. This, of course, is nonsense. On close examination, "the new learning" is written on tablets of sand. We must look elsewhere for reasons of its recent ascendancy. As observed by one of Chicago's own, Professor Melvin W.

Reder (1982, 36), in speaking of the school's two current intellectual leaders, "the Friedman-Stigler policy position was too attractive ideologically, and too successful as propaganda, for hesitant conservatives to refuse support."[23] Their ideas have triumphed, for now, because they map a course many vested interests wish to travel. Will Chicago School "beliefs" survive even though effectively challenged in the marketplace of ideas? The answer would be less ambiguous were economics a "hard" science. But the appealing simplicity of Chicago School beliefs, abetted by their ideological attractiveness and fervor, gives them a unique ability to survive. This alone makes their future impact on antitrust policy a disturbing specter.

Appendix A. Data Used in Demsetz's Analysis

The Demsetz analysis discussed in the text at notes 14–18 used data reported in the IRS *Source Book for Corporate Income Tax Returns*. In this report, IRS typically places firms in three-digit minor industry groupings that embrace more than a single relevant economic market. This results in placing firms operating in different industries (properly defined) in the same group. For example, in 1979, IRS minor industry group 371, motor vehicles and equipment, had 1,677 firms. They included automobile companies, other motor vehicle companies and makers of all types of motor vehicle equipment. Demsetz computed a weighted average concentration ratio for IRS minor industry group 371, using Census of Manufacturers concentration ratios and value of shipments of Census industry group SIC 371. The resulting concentration ratio largely reflects concentration of the automobile industry. Demsetz assumed that this concentration ratio provided an accurate measure of concentration in each size category in IRS minor group 371. Below are the number of firms and their assets in group IRS 371 distributed in the size classes used by Demsetz:

Asset size ($000)	*No. of firms*	*Assets ($ millions)*
0–500	1,089	188
500–5,000	479	660
5,000–50,000	83	1,069
50,000–100,000	8	520
100,000 and up	18	39,829
	1,677	42,266

It requires little knowledge of the motor vehicle and parts industries to appreciate the problems inherent in these data. As a starter, an observer may properly wonder, who are the eighteen firms in the $100 million and over class? They obviously include much more than the four automobile companies. But more important, what about firms in the other size classes? It is absurd to assume that the 1,089 firms in the smallest class, as well as in the other smaller classes, sell the same products as those in the largest size class.

This problem is not unique to the motor vehicle industry group. To varying degrees it afflicts every group used by Demsetz. For example, the soft drink bottling industry group has 1,796 firms. Only two of these are in the $100 million and over group. These two presumably are Coca-Cola and Pepsi-Cola, which make and sell mainly soft drink syrups and other products that clearly are in different relevant product and geographic markets than are the hundreds of smaller companies, which consist primarily of soft drink bottlers.

Additionally, there also is a problem in the weighted-average concentration ratio that Demsetz derived using Census Bureau industry shipments data. A problem arises because Demsetz's procedures assume that firms in a particular IRS 3-digit minor industry group sell the same mix of products as those that comprise a Census Bureau three-digit SIC industry group. In fact, there often is little correspondence between the two. IRS places a firm in an IRS industry group based on the firm's most important product. All large diversified corporations operate in more than one three-digit industry group because the major product of a company like ITT may be baking, although its Continental Baking operations constitututed less than 10 percent of its income. In that event all of ITT's sales and profits would be included in the IRS industry group including baking. As a result, there need be little correspondence between the concentration ratio derived for a three-digit Census industry group and the average concentration ratios of the firms operating in an IRS industry group.

Notes

1. Baxter resigned as head of the Antitrust Division in December 1983; his two successors have continued his policies. Miller remained head of the FTC until September 1985, when he became head of the Office of Management and Budget. There have been no discernible changes in enforcement philosophy under their successors.
2. "Government May Abandon Fight to Stem Conglomerate Takeovers," *Wall Street Journal*, 14 November 1980, 23.
3. The *Merger Guidelines* declare that "the Department is likely to challenge any merger in [markets with Herfindahl indexes over 1,800] that produce an increase . . . of more than 50 points." The soft drink industry has a premerger Herfindahl index exceeding 2,500. Pepsi-Cola's acquisition of Seven-Up would increase the Herfindahl index by about 300 points, and Coca-Cola's acquisition of Dr. Pepper would increase the Herfindhal index by some 550 points.

4. *Shafer v. Bulk Petroleum Corp., Antitrust & Trade Regulation Report* (BNA) 45 (29 August 1983), 313–314.
5. *Monsanto Co. v. Spray-Rite Service Corp.*, 104 U.S. 1464 (1984).
6. *Borden, Inc. v. Federal Trade Commission*, 674 F. 2d. 498 (1982).
7. Borden, Inc., 92 F.T.C. 669 (1978).
8. "FTC's Proposed Settlement of Borden Case," *Antitrust & Trade Regulation Report* 44 (3 March 1983), 525.
9. Ibid., 528.
10. ITT Continental Baking Co., FTC Docket No. 9009, BNA, *Antitrust & Trade Regulation Report* 47, no. 1177 (9 August 1984), 283.
11. ITT Continental Baking Co. (see n. 10), 311.
12. *Business Week*, 29 August 1983, 50.
13. Ibid.
14. The proceedings of the conference, which was held 1 and 2 May 1974, were published in Goldschmid, Mann, and Weston 1974. According to one of the conference organizers, Professor Harvey J. Goldschmid, Columbia University Law School, the conference was attended by "most of the nation's leading thinkers on industrial concentration" (Goldschmid, Mann, and Weston 1974, viii).
15. Chicago School economists seem especially fond of using these crude IRS data. Telser (1964), in an earlier, much quoted study, used IRS data to examine the relationship between advertising and concentration and reported an "unimpressive" correlation, which contradicted the findings of virtually all other researchers. Mann (1974) attributed Telser's results to his use of IRS data poorly suited for such analyses.
16. As observed in Appendix A, the data Demsetz used were biased toward finding a zero relationship. The flaws in his data were somewhat less serious for the largest firms because their weighted concentration ratios were more likely to reflect the actual concentration of industries in which they operated than those in which the firms in smaller size classes operated. It seems most plausible that Demsetz's observed negative correlations in small class sizes reflect that small firms in IRS minor industry groups operate in more competitive market segments than do the largest firms in these groups. See the motor vehicle example in Appendix A.
17. Demsetz had published a piece setting forth his ideas and some of his data in 1973, but his presentation at the Airlie House Conference on The New Learning in 1974 was more complete, presented before an influential audience, and subsequently published in a widely read book (Goldschmid, Mann, and Weston 1974).
18. Leonard Weiss, who commented on the study in his presentation at the conference, pointed out some of the serious flaws in the study (Weiss 1974, 225–27).
19. There is less variation in price among sellers of producer goods than among sellers of consumer goods because the latter are differentiated.
20. Although most cross-industry studies use data superior to those employed by Demsetz, nonetheless all have serious problems in defining meaningful product and geographic markets. For example, the geographic dispersion index often used to correct for market size is crude at best. Similarly, even adjusted Census product or industry definitions leave much to be desired (Weiss 1972). Finally, economic theory teaches that the price elasticity of demand is crucial in determining the size of monopoly overcharges. Yet cross-industry studies must implicitly assume all industries have the same elasticity of demand. Price studies that are based on a single industry suffer from each of these defects to a far smaller degree than do

cross-industry studies. The recent work of Scott and Pascol (1986) indicates that profit differences among industries are influenced significantly by the capital intensity of sellers. This influence is minimized in structure-price studies based on data for a single industry.
21. The only exception, in their view, is where RPM facilitates collusion among manufacturers or their distributors. But not only is such collusion rare, they believe, if it occurs it should be challenged as a horizontal restraint rather than a vertical restraint.
22. *Marrese v. American Academy of Orthopaedic Surgeons* 692 D. 2d 1083 (1982).
23. In a footnote, Reder added: "In 'support' I include grants for research, conferences, and so forth. But also, and more important, I include access to conservative politicians and business leaders, and to the media" (Reder 1982, 36).

References

Aspinwall, R. C. 1970. Market structure and commercial bank mortgage interest rates. *Southern Economic Journal* 36:376–84.
Audretsch, S. 1986. The Cellar-Kefauver Act and the deterrent effect. *Review of Industrial Organization* 2:322.
Bailey, E. E., D. Graham, and D. Kaplan. 1984. *Deregulating the airlines.* MIT Press.
Bain, J. S. 1951. Relation of profit-rate to industry concentration: American manufacturing, 1936–1940. *Quarterly Journal of Economics* 65:293.
Barton, D., and R. Sherman. 1984. The price and profit effects of horizontal merger. *Journal of Industrial Economics.* 38:165–78.
Baumol, W. J. 1982. Contestable markets: An uprising in the theory of industry structure. *American Economic Review* 72:1.
Bell, F., and N. Murphy. 1969. Impact of market structure on the price of a commercial banking service. *Review of Economics and Statistics* 51:210–13.
Bork, R. 1966. The rule of reason and per se concept: Price fixing and market division. *Yale Law Journal* 75:373.
Bowman, W. 1957. Tying arrangements and the leverage problem. *Yale Law Journal* 67 (November):19–36.
Brannman, L., J. Klein, and L. Weiss. 1986. The price effects of increased competition in auction markets. University of Wisconsin–Madison. Photocopy.
Call, G., and T. Keller. 1985. Airline deregulation, fares, and market behavior: Some empirical evidence. In *Analytical studies in transport economics*, edited by Andrew F. Daughety.
Caplan, L. 1986. Judicial restraint means activism on the right. *Washington Post*, 19 January, G2–G3.
Comanor, W. S. 1985. Vertical price fixing, vertical market restrictions, and the new antitrust policy. *Harvard Law Review* 98:983.
Connor, J. M., R. T. Rogers, B. W. Marion, and W. F. Mueller. 1985. *The food manufacturing industries: Structure, strategies, performance and profits.* Lexington, MA: Lexington Books.
Consumer credit in the United States. 1972. Report of the National Commission on Consumer Finance (December): 118–19.
Cotterill, R. 1986. Market power in the retail food industry: Evidence from Vermont. *Review of Economics and Statistics* 68:379–86.

Cummins, J. D., H. S. Denenberg, and W. C. Scheel. 1972. Concentration in the U.S. life insurance industry. *Journal of Risk and Insurance* (June): 177–99.

de Jong, H. W. 1975. Industrial structure and the price problem: Experience in the European Economic Community. In *The roots of inflation*, edited by G. C. Means et al., 199–209. New York: Burt Franklin & Co.

Demsetz, H. 1973. Industry structure, market rivalry, and public policy. *Journal of Law and Economics* 16:1–10.

———. 1974. Two systems of belief about monopoly. In Goldschmid, Mann, and Weston (1974, 164–83).

Douglas, W., and J. C. Miller III. 1974. Quality competition, industry equilibrium and efficiency in the price constrained airline market. *American Economic Review* 657 (September).

Edwards, F. R. 1964. Concentration in banking and its effect on business loan rates. *Review of Economics and Statistics* (August): 294–300.

———. 1965. The banking competition controversy. *National Banking Review* (September): 1–34.

Federal Trade Commission. 1975. *Prescription drug price disclosures*, Staff Report to the Federal Trade Commission, pt. 3, 41–44.

———. 1985. *Vertical restraint guidelines*. FTC.

Frankena, M. W., and P. A. Paulter, 1985. *Antitrust policy for declining industries*. Bureau of Economics, Federal Trade Commission, October.

Goldschmid, H. J., H. M. Mann, and J. F. Weston, eds. 1974. *Industrial concentration: The new learning*. Boston: Little Brown & Co.

Graddy, D. B., and R. Kyle III. 1979. The simultaneity of bank decision-making market structure, and bank performance. *Journal of Finance* (March): 1–18.

Graham, D., D. Kaplan, and D. Sibley. 1983. Efficiency and competition in the airline industry. *Bell Journal of Economics* 14:118–38.

Greer, D. F. 1986. Acquiring in order to avoid acquisition. *Antitrust Bulletin* 31: 155–86.

Greer, Douglas F., and R. P. Shay. 1973. *An economic analysis of consumer credit markets in the United States*. Technical Study vol. 4, National Commission on Consumer Finance, chaps. 2, 4. Washington, D.C.

Hall, L., A. Schmitz, and J. Cothern. 1979. Beef wholesale-retail marketing margins and concentration. *Economica* F46:295–300.

Heggestad, A., and J. Mingo. 1976. Prices, nonprices, and concentration in banking. *Journal of Money, Credit & Banking* 8:107–17.

Hester, Donald. 1979. Customer relationships and terms of loans—Evidence from a pilot survey: A note. *Journal of Money, Credit and Banking* 11:349–57.

Hofstader, R. 1966. What happened to the American antitrust movement. In *The business establishment*, edited by E. F. Chiet. New York: John Wiley & Sons.

Imel, B., and P. Helmberger. 1971. Estimation of structure-profit relationships with application to the food processing sector. *American Economic Review* 61, no. 4: 614–27.

Jacobs, D. 1971. *Business loan costs and bank market structure*. New York: Columbia University Press.

Kaufman, George. 1966. Bank structure and performance: The evidence from Iowa. *Southern Economic Journal* (April): 429–39.

Kelly, W. H. 1969. *The influence of market structure on the profit performance of food manufacturing companies*. Economic Report to the Federal Trade Commission. Washington, D.C.: GPO.

Kelton, C. 1980. The administered-pricing thesis. Food Systems Research Group, University of Wisconsin. Working Paper No. 43.
———. 1983. Operational efficiency in food and tobacco manufacturing. Food Systems Research Group, University of Wisconsin. Working Paper No. 72.
Kessel, Rueben. 1971. A study of the effects of competition in the tax-exempt bond market. *Journal of Political Economy* 79:706–38.
Koller, R., and L. W. Weiss, 1985. Price levels and seller concentration—The case of Portland Cement. University of Wisconsin-Madison. Processed.
Lamm, R. M. 1981. Prices and concentration in the food retailing industry. *Journal of Industrial Economics* 30:67–78.
Landon, J. 1971. The relation of market concentration and advertising rates: The newspaper industry. *Antitrust Bulletin* 16:53–100.
Leibenstein, H. 1979. X-efficiency; From concept to theory. *Challenge* (September–October):12–22.
Lurie, A. R. 1978. Mergers under the Burger Court: An anti-antitrust bias and its implications. *Villanova Law Review* 23 (January):214.
Mann, H. M. 1974. Advertising, concentration, and profitability: The state of the knowledge and direction of public policy. In Goldschmid, Mann, and Weston (1974, 143–44).
Marion, Bruce W., Willard F. Mueller, Ronald W. Cotterill, Frederick E. Geithman, and John R. Schmelzer. 1979. *The food retailing industry: Market structure, profits and prices.* New York: Praeger.
Marlow, M. L. 1982. Bank structure and mortgage rates. *Journal of Economics and Business,* no. 2:135–42.
Marvel, H. 1978. Competition and price levels in the retail gasoline market. *Rev. Econ. Stat.* 60:252–58.
———. 1980. Collusion and the pattern of rates of return. *Southern Economic Journal* 47:375–87.
Meese, Edwin III. 1986. Statement by Attorney General, Accompanying Proposed Antitrust Laws, and Analysis, Department of Justice (February 19).
Meyer, P. 1983. Concentration and performance in local markets. In *Industrial Organization, Antitrust, and Public Policy,* edited by J. V. Craven, 145–64. Boston: Nijhoff Publishing.
Meyer, P. A. 1967. Price Discrimination, regional loan rates, and the structure of the banking industry. *Journal of Finance* (March):37–48.
Miller, J. 1983. Speech before the International Franchise Association, 18 January.
Miller, J. C. III. 1984. Interview with James C. Miller III, Chairman, Federal Trade Commission. *Antitrust Law Journal* 53:11.
Milliman, S., and L. Weiss, 1983. Competition in regulated air fares. University of Wisconsin-Madison. Processed.
Moore, T. G. 1985. U.S. airline deregulation. Paper delivered at the Southern Economic Association Meetings, November.
Mueller, D. C. 1985. Mergers and market share. *Review of Economics and Statistics* 67 (May):259–67.
Mueller, W. F. 1965. The scope of the current merger movement. *Hearing on Economic Concentration.* Subcommittee on Antitrust and Monopoly of the Senate Committee on the Judiciary. 16 March, pp. 501–536.
———. 1973. The ITT settlement: A deal with justice? *Industrial Organization Review* 1, no. 1:67–86.
———. 1979. *The Celler-Kefauver Act: The First 27 Years.* Study prepared for the

Subcommittee on Monopolies and Commercial Law of the House Committee of the Judiciary. 96th Cong., 1st sess.
———. 1982. Conglomerates: A nonindustry. In *The Structure of American Industry*, edited by W. Adams, 427–74. New York: Macmillan Publishing Co.
———. 1983. The anti-antitrust movement. In *Industrial Organization, Antitrust, and Public Policy*, edited by J. V. Craven. New York: Bluwer-Nijhoff Publishing.
Mueller, W. F. and R. T. Rogers. 1980. The role of advertising in changing concentration of manufacturing industries. *Review of Economics and Statistics* 52:89–95.
———. 1984. Changes in market concentration of manufacturing industries. *Review of Industrial Organization* 1 (Spring):1.
Owen, B. M. 1973. Newspaper and television station joint ownership. *Antitrust Bulletin* (Winter): 787–807.
Peltzman, S. 1977. The gains and losses from industrial concentration. *Journal of Law and Economics* 20:229–64.
Phillips, Almarin. 1967. Evidence on concentrations in banking markets and interest rates. *Federal Reserve Bulletin* (June):916–26.
Ponsoldt, J. F. 1983. Letter to the editor, *National Law Journal*, 7 Feburary.
Posner R. A. 1981. The next step in the antitrust treatment of restricted distribution: Per se legality. *The University of Chicago Law Review* 48:6.
———. 1985. *The federal courts: Crisis and reform.* Cambridge: Harvard University Press.
Ravenscraft, David. 1983. Structure-profit relationships at the line of business and industry level. *Review of Economics and Statistics* 60:22–31.
Ravenscraft, D. J., and F. M. Scherer. 1986. Mergers and managerial performance. Bureau of Economics, Federal Trade Commission. Working Paper No. 137.
Reder, M. 1982. Chicago economics: Performance and change. *Journal of Economic Literature* 20 (March):35–36.
Rhoades, S. A., 1977. Does the market matter in banking? In *Research Papers in Banking and Financial Economics*. Washington, D.C.: Federal Reserve Board.
Rhoades, S. A., and R. D. Rutz. 1982. The impact of bank holding companies. *Journal of Economics and Business*, no. 4:355–65.
Rogers, R. T. 1979. Structure-profit relationship in food manufacturing firms. In Mueller 1979, Appendix D.
———. 1985. A structure-price-cost margin model estimated over time for food and tobacco product classes, 1954 to 1977. Food Systems Research Group, University of Wisconsin-Madison. Working Paper No. 75.
Scherer, F. M. 1979. The causes and consequences of rising industrial concentration. *Journal of Law and Economics* 22:191–208.
———. 1980. *Industrial market structure and economic performance.* 2d ed. Chicago: Rand McNally.
———. 1983. The economics of vertical restraints. *Antitrust Law Journal* 3:687.
Scott, J. T., and G. Pascol. 1986. Beyond firm and industry effects on profitability in imperfect markets. *Review of Economics and Statistics* 68 (May):284–92.
Shepherd, William G. 1972. The elements of market structure. *Review of Economics and Statistics* 59:25–37.
———. 1984. Contestability vs. competition. *American Economic Review* 74:1572.
———. 1986. *Mainstreams in industrial organization.* Martinus Nijhoff Press.
Slater, C. C. 1956. *Banking in America: Market organization and competition.* Evanston: Northwestern University Press.

Stigler, G. 1966. An economic effect of the antitrust laws. *Journal of Law and Economics:* 225–28.

Strassman, D. L. 1986. Contestable markets and dynamic limit pricing in the deregulated airline industry: An empirical test. Economics Department, Rice University. Photocopy.

Telser, L. G. 1960. Why manufacturers want fair trade. *Journal of Law & Economics* 3:86.

———. 1964. Advertising and Competition. *Journal of Political Economy* 72.

Thompson, R. S. 1984. Structure and conduct in local advertising markets. *Journal of Industrial Economics* 38:241–50.

Townsend, Robert. 1970. *Up the organization.* New York: Alfred A. Knopf.

Vise, D. A., and P. Behr. 1986. Airline consolidation takes off. *Washington Post,* 2 March, F1.

Vita, M. G. 1984. Profits, concentration, and the collusion-efficiency debate: A simultaneous equation model. Ph.D. diss. University of Wisconsin.

Warner, M. G. 1981. Reagan pick to head FTC, James Miller, plans major changes but no dismantling. *Wall Street Journal,* 29 June, 12.

Warren, J. 1983. Richard Posner shakes up the bench. *The American Lawyer* (September).

Weiss, Leonard. 1971. Quantitative studies of industrial organization. In *Frontiers of Quantitative Economics,* edited by M.D. Intriligator. New York: North-Holland.

———. 1972. The geographic size of markets in manufacturing. *Review of Economics and Statistics.* 54:245–57.

———. 1974. The concentration-profits relationship and antitrust. In Goldschmid, Mann, and Weston (1974).

———. 1985. Concentration and price—Not concentration and profits. University of Wisconsin-Madison. Processed.

Wermiel, S. 1984. Scholars blend law, economics. *Wall Street Journal,* 18 December, 64.

White, Justice Bryon. 1974. Dissent in *United States v. Marine Bancorporation, Inc.* 418 U.S. 602, 643.

Wills, R. L. 1983. The impact of market structure and advertising on brand pricing in processed food products. Ph.D. diss. University of Wisconsin-Madison.

Part II. Antitrust Economics

4. Vertical Integration of a Monopolist: *Paschall* v. *Kansas City Star*

Roger D. Blair and James M. Fesmire

FOR SOME REASON, monopoly appears to be the rule rather than the exception in daily newspaper publication. In fact, there are only seventeen cities in the United States that have more than one daily newspaper.[1] This is cause for some concern for two reasons. First, there is the familiar social welfare loss that results from the monopolistic restriction of output. Second, we are uncomfortable with monopoly control of news and views in the community.[2] Our focus in this paper, however, is not on the publishing monopolist.[3] Instead, we direct our attention to an analysis of how the monopoly publisher distributes its newspapers. Usually, newspapers are distributed according to exclusive territories, which creates successive monopoly problems. The recent decision in *Paschall v. Kansas City Star*[4] provides a convenient vehicle for examining some of the economic and legal problems associated with successive monopoly.[5]

First, we present the economist's conventional wisdom regarding the theory of successive monopoly and the corresponding benefits of vertical integration. Following this, we move on to an examination of the *Paschall* litigation, where we will see that the court adopted the economic analysis presented in the preceding section. It appears, however, that several "disturbing" facts that appear to be inconsistent with the economist's received doctrine were present. We shall attempt to reconcile these discordant facts and conclude that the final decision in *Paschall* was correct after all.

Note: The authors appreciate the financial support of the Public Policy Research Center at the University of Florida and a grant from the University of Tampa.

1. Benefits of Vertical Integration: Received Doctrine[6]

In the presence of successive monopoly, the benefits of vertical integration are easy to establish in principle. Suppose that the market demand for a home-delivered newspaper is given by

(1) $$P_H = a - bQ_H \quad a,b > 0,$$

where P_H and Q_H represent the price and quantity, respectively, of home-delivered newspapers. We assume that the marginal (and average) costs of delivering the newspapers are constant and equal to MC_D. In order to maximize its profits, the distribution monopolist will equate its marginal revenue to its marginal cost, which is composed of the wholesale price of newspapers (P_N) plus the marginal cost of delivering the newspapers (MC_D):

(2) $$a - 2bQ_H = P_N + MC_D.$$

Algebraic rearrangement yields the newspaper publisher's derived demand for newspapers:

(3) $$P_N = a - 2bQ_N - MC_D,$$

where $Q_N \doteq Q_H$, i.e., the distributor must buy one newspaper at wholesale for each newspaper delivered to a customer.

In an effort to maximize its profits, the newspaper publisher will equate its marginal revenue (MR_N) to its marginal publication costs (MC_P), which are assumed to be constant for expositional convenience:

(4) $$a - 4bQ_N - MC_D = MC_P.$$

Solving (4) for Q_N, we find that the optimal quantity is

(5) $$Q_N^* = \frac{a - MC_P - MC_D}{4b}$$

and substituting (5) into (3), we find the optimal price to be

(6) $$P_N^* = \frac{a + MC_P - MC_D}{2}.$$

The newspaper publisher's maximum profit will be

$$\Pi_N^* = P_N^* Q_N^* - MC_P Q_N^*$$

(7)
$$= \frac{(a - MC_D - MC_P)^2}{8b},$$

given its decision to distribute its newspaper through independent distributors. The distributor will behave as described in first-order condition (2):

(8)
$$a - 2bQ_H = \frac{a + MC_P - MC_D}{2} + MC_D.$$

As we should expect, algebraic rearrangement of (8) reveals that the optimal number of home-delivered newspapers is

(9)
$$Q_H^* = \frac{a - MC_P - MC_D}{4b},$$

which is precisely equal to Q_N^*.

Substituting (9) into (1), we find that the profit-maximizing home-delivered price is

(10)
$$P_H^* = \frac{3a + MC_P + MC_D}{4}.$$

The distributor's maximum profit will be

$$\Pi_H^* = P_H^* Q_H^* - (MC_D + P_N^*) Q_H^*$$

(11)
$$= \frac{(a - MC_D - MC_P)^2}{16b}.$$

These results in the presence of successive monopoly can be contrasted to those of a vertically integrated newspaper monopolist that publishes and distributes its newspapers. Given our assumptions regarding demand and cost, the vertically integrated publisher's profit function will be

$$\Pi_V = P_H Q_H - (MC_P + MC_D) Q_H$$

(12)
$$= (a - bQ_H) Q_H - (MC_P + MC_D) Q_H,$$

with first-order condition

(13)
$$a - 2bQ_H - MC_P - MC_D = 0.$$

Solving (13) for the profit-maximizing quantity yields

(14) $$\hat{Q}_H = \frac{a - MC_P - MC_D}{2b}.$$

Substituting $\hat{Q}_H$ into the demand function (1), we have the optimal price

(15) $$\hat{P}_H = \frac{a + MC_P + MC_D}{2}.$$

Using the results in (14) and (15) along with (12), we find that the maximum profit for the vertically integrated monopolist is

(16) $$\Pi_V^* = \frac{(a - MC_P - MC_D)^2}{4b}.$$

By comparing equations (9) and (14), we see that the vertically integrated monopolist publishes and distributes twice as many newspapers as the successive monopolists. This, of course, means that the home-delivered price must be lower with vertical integration. A comparison of equations (10) and (15) confirms that this is correct.[7] Thus, the quantity consumed expands while the price falls as a result of vertical integration. Finally, we can see that the publisher has a profit incentive for vertically integrating forward because its profits with vertical integration [equation (16)] are twice as large as its profits with successive monopoly. Interestingly, although the publisher gets only one-half of the maximum profit with successive monopoly, the distributor does *not* get the other half. In other words,

$$\Pi_N^* + \Pi_D^* < \Pi_V^*$$

as a comparison of equations (7) and (11) with equation (16) confirms.

These results can be shown graphically as well.[8] In figure 4.1, the straight line labeled D_H represents the demand for newspapers in one of the exclusive territories while the associated marginal revenue is denoted by MR_H. Marginal (and average) distribution costs are shown as MC_D. Now, profit maximization on the part of the distributor will lead him to operate where marginal revenue equals the sum of marginal distribution costs and the wholesale price of the newspaper. Knowing that, the publisher must select the wholesale price that will maximize its profits. In order to display this result, we must find the demand and marginal revenue curves that confront the publisher.

The demand by the distributors for newspapers is derived from the subscribers' demand for the newspaper. As profit maximizers, the distributors will demand newspapers up to the quantity where marginal revenue (MR_H)

Vertical Integration of a Monopolist 87

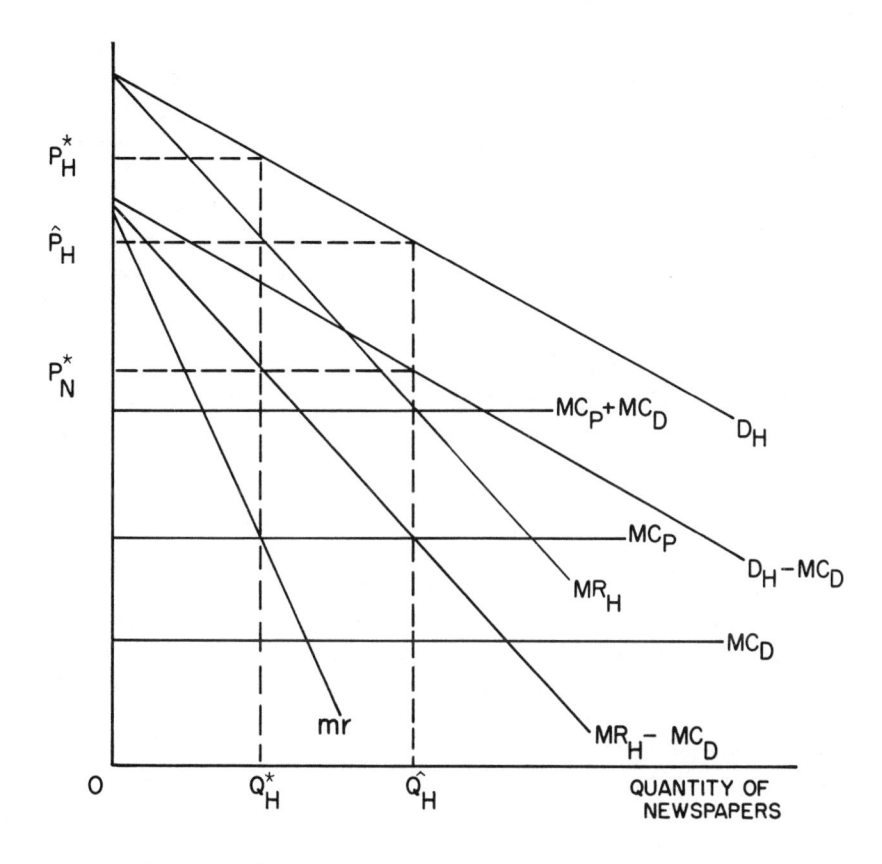

Fig. 4.1. Newspaper demand and cost relationships.

equals marginal distribution cost (MC_D) plus the wholesale price of the paper (P_N). Thus, one could say that the wholesale price equals marginal revenue minus the marginal costs of distribution ($P_N = MR_H - MC_D$). This, in fact, is the derived demand for newspapers, which is shown in figure 4.1 as the line $MR_H - MC_D$. For the publisher, marginal revenue is the line labeled mr. In order to determine the optimal (i.e., profit-maximizing) price and output, the publisher will equate its marginal cost of publishing (MC_P) to the marginal revenue associated with the derived demand curve (mr). In figure 4.1, this occurs at an output equal to Q_H^* newspapers, which will carry a wholesale price of P_N^* each. The publisher earns a profit equal to the per unit markup ($P_N^* - MC_P$) times the quantity sold (Q_H^*).

The distributor purchases newspapers at the wholesale price P_N^*. In order to select the optimal home-delivered price, marginal distribution costs (MC_D) are added to the wholesale price and equated to the marginal revenue associated with subscriber demand. In figure 4.1, one can see that $MC_D + P_N^*$ equals MR_H at an output of Q_H^* newspapers and a home-delivered price of P_H^*. The distributor's profits will be equal to its per unit markup ($P_H^* - MC_D - P_N^*$) times the quantity sold (Q_H^*).

Once again, we can compare the results when the monopolist publishes and distributes its own newspapers with those when it only publishes the newspapers and an independent, exclusive distributor acts as a successive monopolist. If the monopolist publishes and distributes its newspapers, profit maximization will lead it to publish and distribute that number of papers where marginal revenue (MR) equals the sum of the marginal cost of publication and distribution ($MC_P + MC_D$). We see that this occurs at an output of $\hat{Q}_H$ newspapers. The profit-maximizing home-delivered price is $\hat{P}_H$. For the monopolist, profit equals the difference between price and cost ($\hat{P}_H - MC_P - MC_D$) times the quantity sold ($\hat{Q}_H$). This is the maximum profit that can be extracted from this market for newspapers; no alternative organization will yield a larger profit.

For public policy purposes, it is irrelevant which firm obtains how much profit; what is important for consumer welfare is price and output. We can see that successive monopoly results in a reduction in the number of newspapers sold from $\hat{Q}_H$ to Q_H^*. At the same time, the home-delivered price rises from $\hat{P}_H$ to P_H^*. Thus, consumer welfare is reduced by the compound restriction of output that is caused by having two monopolies linked in the vertical chain of distribution.

The publisher will not be indifferent to the organization of publication and distribution of its newspaper. When it publishes and distributes its newspapers, the publisher's profits equal $(\hat{P}_H - MC_P - MC_D)\hat{Q}_H$. In contrast, its profits are only $(P_N^* - MC_P)Q_H^*$ when an exclusive distributor delivers the newspapers to the subscribers. A close look at figure 4.1 reveals that Q_H^* is one-half of $\hat{Q}_H$. Since $\hat{P}_H$ is precisely equal to $P_N^* + MC_D$, the publisher's profits are twice as high when it delivers its own newspapers. This outcome is not simply due to sharing the profit with the distributor because the distributor's profits are only $(P_H^* - P_N^* - MC_D)Q_H^*$, which is less than one-half of $(\hat{P}_H - MC_P - MC_D)\hat{Q}_H$. In other words, there is a dead weight loss due to the second monopolist's restriction of output.

2. Contractual Alternatives to Vertical Integration[9]

The distributor's monopoly power flows from the publisher's grant of an exclusive territory. Thus, it would appear that the newspaper could eliminate the need for vertical integration simply by eliminating territorial exclusivity.

This, however, is an illusion, because the home distribution of newspapers is a *natural* monopoly.[10] In other words, the cost of performing the distribution function is lowest when it is performed by a single firm. As a result, competitive pricing is inconsistent with natural monopoly because of the losses incurred by the rival distributors. Ultimately, only one firm will survive the competitive struggle. The newspaper publisher introduced a system of exclusive territories in recognition of the fact that monopoly in distribution will emerge in any event. By assigning exclusive territories, the newspaper hopes to retain sufficient control over the distributors to prevent their charging more than a competitive price for the distribution services. This can be accomplished by several contractual alternatives, each of which is economically equivalent to ownership integration.

Maximum Resale Prices

First, the publisher could set a maximum home-delivered price to prevent the distributor from charging an excessive price. In the current example, the publisher would sell the newspapers to the distributor at P_N^* and limit the home-delivered subscription rate to $P_N^* + MC_D$, which is equal to the profit-maximizing rate of $\hat{P}_H$. Unfortunately for the publisher, setting maximum resale prices is illegal,[11] as witnessed by the Supreme Court's *Albrecht*[12] decision. The *Globe-Democrat*, a St. Louis newspaper, assigned exclusive territories to its distributors. Because each distributor was given a territorial monopoly, the *Globe-Democrat* retained the power to terminate distributors who charged more than its advertised price. Although Albrecht, a distributor, was aware of the maximum price limitation, he ignored it and charged a higher price. After several customer complaints, the *Globe-Democrat* warned Albrecht that he was jeopardizing his distributorship. Nevertheless, Albrecht continued to overcharge his customers. In response, the *Globe-Democrat* assigned a portion of Albrecht's territory to another distributor. Albrecht then brought suit claiming that the pricing scheme violated Section 1 of the Sherman Act. Consequently, the *Globe-Democrat* terminated his route and forced him to sell his distributorship. The economic rationale for fixing maximum resale prices was explained by the defense and understood by Justice Stewart, but the fact that such an arrangement would protect subscribers from overcharging by distributors apparently was unpersuasive. The Court ruled that "the assertion that illegal price fixing is justified because it blunts the pernicious consequences of another distribution practice is unpersuasive."[13] Concerned about the distributor's ability to compete freely within the marketplace,[14] the Court held that the price-fixing arrangement violated Section 1 of the Sherman Act. There is no apparent judicial inclination to move away from this myopic position.

Performance Standards

A second option is available to the publisher. It could set performance standards for the distributor. If the publisher had sufficient information, it would set the wholesale price equal to P_N^* and permit the distributor to select any home-delivered price that it desired subject to the provision that the distributor sell at least $\hat{Q}_H$ newspapers. This would accomplish the same thing as fixing maximum resale prices, because the only way that $\hat{Q}_H$ newspapers can be sold is to charge a home-delivered subscription rate of $\hat{P}_H$. Any higher price will lead to fewer newspapers being sold and therefore to a failure to satisfy the performance standard. One caveat is in order: there may be franchiser-franchisee problems with enforcing this standard.

Dual Distribution

A third option is to engage in dual distribution. In this case, the publisher would offer to serve any customer at a home-delivered rate of $\hat{P}_H$. This would make it impossible for the independent distributor to charge a price in excess of $\hat{P}_H$ because the subscriber can always turn to the publisher and get a lower price. In fact, this is the procedure that the *Kansas City Star* actually employed. Although dual distribution is not without its perils, it is not clearly illegal. But dual distribution is a cumbersome way of dealing with the successive monopoly problem—especially if the *Star* actually had to service many subscribers. Moreover, given the natural monopoly aspect of newspaper distribution, this is an expensive way of dealing with the problem unless its deterrent effect is absolute.

These three contractual arrangements all result in the same price and output combination for the subscribers. If each works perfectly, the same profits result for the publisher and for the distributor. The publisher gets all of the monopoly profit and the distributor gets none of it. As an economic proposition, there is nothing to commend one arrangement over another. Since these three arrangements along with ownership integration are economically equivalent, there is no apparent reason why they should receive divergent legal treatment.

3. The Paschall Litigation

Since 1942, the *Kansas City Star* Company has published the only daily metropolitan newspapers in the Kansas City, Missouri, and Kansas City, Kansas area.[15] Historically, the *Star* sold its newspapers to independent carriers at wholesale prices. Each carrier resold and delivered the newspapers to the subscribers along its exclusive delivery route. Due to this exclusivity, each carrier had a monopoly of home delivery within its assigned territory. According to the terms of its agreement with its distributors, the *Star* reserved the right to sell and deliver its newspapers to any customer. In fact, however, the *Star* rarely exercised this right. Its presence as a potential competitor on the edge of the distribution market apparently had an influence on the behavior of its distributors.

On 24 May 1974, the *Star* informed each of its independent carriers that it might alter its system of distribution. Starting on 1 July 1974 the *Star* required an acknowledgment in writing from anyone signing a new independent carrier contract that he was aware of the fact that the distribution system might be changed. The existing distributors, of course, were dismayed by this turn of events because they were losing valuable assets.[16] As a result, in January of 1975, one of the independent carriers, Gweldon Paschall, challenged the *Star*'s freedom to alter its distribution system. During the autumn of 1977, the *Star* announced that the independent carriers would be replaced by its own agents. No newspapers would be sold at wholesale prices, and therefore the independent carriers would be unable to compete with the agents. To soften the blow a bit, the *Star* offered agency agreements to the existing carriers that would provide approximately the same income as they were earning currently.

Paschall I Decision

Unappeased by this offer, the independent carriers—Paschall and about 250 others—asked for a temporary restraining order and a preliminary injunction, which were granted. Following a nonjury trial, the district court found that the *Star*'s proposal to discontinue wholesaling its papers to the independent carriers constituted an illegal expansion of its publishing monopoly in violation of Section 2 of the Sherman Act. Subsequently, a permanent injunction was issued and the *Star* was precluded from implementing its new distribution policy. The *Star* appealed this decision to the Eighth Circuit Court of Appeals.

Initially, the *Star*'s appeal failed.[17] In spite of an amicus curiae brief filed by the Department of Justice on behalf of the *Star*, the Eighth Circuit affirmed the district court's decision. The court found that the *Star* had a monopoly of metropolitan daily newspapers sold at wholesale in the seven-county metropolitan area of Kansas City. Moreover, the *Star*'s refusal to sell newspapers at wholesale prices to the independent carriers would extend its publishing monopoly into retail distribution. The legal question is whether that extension is an illegal abuse of monopoly power. Although the court recognized that a seller's unilateral refusal to deal is usually legal,[18] it also found that a monopolist may have an obligation to deal in some circumstances. In this case, the court found that a refusal to deal that is designed to accomplish vertical integration violates Section 2 when "such vertical integration will result in substantial anticompetitive effects that are not offset by production economies, savings in market transactions, or other competitive benefit."[19]

The court was unpersuaded by the economist's conventional wisdom as spelled out in section 1 above. Instead, it found that the anticompetitive consequences of the *Star*'s refusal to deal would likely outweigh any competitive benefits. First, the proposed refusal would eliminate the *Star* as a potential competitor in the retail market.[20] Moreover, it would likely result in higher prices and lower quality service to subscribers. We return to this claim in the next section. Finally, the proposed refusal would not be likely to lead to a more efficient delivery system.

Paschall II Decision

The *Star* petitioned for a rehearing *en banc* at the Eighth Circuit. In *Paschall II*, the Eighth Circuit overruled *en banc* its earlier decision and vacated the permanent injunction.

The opinion of the *en banc* majority was not a model of economic analysis in spite of the fact that it reached the correct conclusion. First, the analysis of potential competition was weak. The court recognized the loss of a competitive check on distribution but felt that it was outweighed by the procompetitive effects of vertical integration. For the procompetitive effects, the court looked to the conventional economic wisdom presented in section 2 above. Frankly, the majority's analysis was disappointing, as it finessed several apparently inconsistent facts. We turn to an analysis of these discordant facts in the next section.

4. The Analysis and the Evidence

Vertical integration in the presence of successive monopoly leads to a lower price and a greater quantity for consumers, thereby enhancing consumer welfare. As we have seen, there are contractual alternatives to integration that can lead to economically equivalent results. But these alternatives to vertical integration are not without legal problems and difficulties in implementation, as shown above. In *Paschall II*, the court adopted reasoning that leads to the conclusion that the *Star*'s forward integration was procompetitive on balance. At times, however, its analysis was not compelling. Further, the dissent rejected the theoretical analysis and instead pointed to "hard" evidence that it felt supported a finding of net anticompetitive effects associated with the integration.[21] That is, the dissent argued that the independent carriers operated to hold down prices to consumers and "to protect them from the full exercise of unlawfully achieved economic power."[22] The dissent went on to regret not only the alleged harm to consumers that results from vertical integration but also the destruction of 250 independent businesses, the owners of which have "treated their customers fairly and have given them good service" while delivering their newspapers "economically and efficiently."[23] In addition, the dissent agreed with the majority that the elimination of the *Star* as a potential competitor removed a check on the ability of distributors to raise prices.

In this section we argue that the dissent is apparently confused in its understanding of the "Chicago School" theory and that the "hard" evidence that it used to refute the theory's conclusions is neither "hard" nor evidence of the theory's lack of validity. We shall note that there is "evidence" that the *Star*'s role as potential competitor may have been largely ineffective and that the new management of the *Star* may have been acting to overcome that deficiency and also to overcome the previous mismanagement of the *Star*. Finally, we observe that the destruction of the independent carriers was to some degree compelled by the illegality of maximum price fixing and that the *Star*'s forward integration was an attempt to circumvent the Supreme Court's ill-conceived *Albrecht* rule with a less desirable alternative.

Confusion about Successive Monopoly and Potential Competition

It should be noted here that Judge Heaney, who wrote the Eighth Circuit's majority opinion in *Paschall I*, which affirmed the district court's decision enjoining the *Star* from refusing to sell its newspapers to independents at wholesale rates, also wrote the later dissent from the *en banc* decision overruling that opinion. For purposes of exposition, we will treat Judge Heaney's comments in both instances as the dissenting opinion. This allows us to draw heavily from the earlier opinion's more detailed analysis of the facts while discussing the *en banc* dissent. Moreover, it will eliminate the confusion that would accompany frequent referrals to his two written opinions. Judge Heaney's summary of the *Star* and "amicus" theory included:

> Under any given cost and demand conditions, there is a single price which will maximize a monopolist's profit. If the monopolist charges more than the profit-maximizing price, its profit will be less than optimal because the decrease in revenue from decreased sales, due to the higher price, will exceed the increase in revenue from the higher price. Moreover, a monopolist can extract its maximum profit only once from the sale of any given end product. If a monopolist attempts to increase that profit by integrating forward and charging a higher retail price, again, the decline in revenue from the decreased demand will exceed the increase from the higher price.[24]

All of this is generally true and did no violence to the case at hand. Unfortunately, Judge Heaney elected to continue: "Consequently, a monopolist cannot increase its profits by integrating forward unless it can directly distribute its product at a lower cost than the independent distributors."[25] This is true only if the monopoly producer faces a system of competitive distributors, which was not the case in *Paschall*. The *Star* faced a system of independent monopolists. As a result, the *Star* could integrate forward, lower the retail price, increase the quantity sold, and still increase its profits even if it could not distribute at any lower cost than the independent carriers. This is the essence of the successive monopoly theory presented in section 1 above. Judge Heaney's confusion of the results of integration by a monopolist with competitive distributors with those when a monopolist integrates with monopoly distributors led him to his incorrect conclusion.

This same confusion led to more mischief later when Judge Heaney explained: "Moreover, even though vertical integration by a monopolist might theoretically lead to pro-competitive results, some commentators have suggested it nonetheless may be beneficial to preserve competition at the retail level because competitors are often more efficient or innovative than monopolists."[26] Once again, it might be true that competitors are more efficient and innovative than monopolists, but the judge again failed to recognize that the distributors are monopolists in their respective territories. In fact, these exclusive territories are granted because newspaper distribution is a "natural" monopoly.

The *Star* as Potential Competition

Against this background of misunderstanding, Judge Heaney stated that the record does not support the *Star*'s claims that integration will lead to lower retail prices and better customer service. Instead, he said that the elimination of the *Star* as a "potential competitor in the retail market will likely result in higher prices and poorer services to readers, and will not lead to a more efficient delivery system."[27] The potential competition doctrine holds that the potential entry of a firm acts as a restraining influence on the price and other behavior of firms already in the industry. Thus, poised and ready to enter the market if a greedy distributor raised its price or reduced the quality of its service, the *Star* provided a competitive check on the distributors through the threat of entry.

It is true that the *Star*'s contracts with its distributors permitted it to compete directly with them. In fact, the *Star* had exercised this right once in 1970 at the request of a subscriber group in an apartment complex. Moreover, the *Star* did try to provide this competitive check by engaging in actions that could only be construed as communicating to the independents the *Star*'s willingness and ability to enter the market.[28] But this was to be expected because of the *Star*'s interest in low retail prices.

Why was the *Star* interested in low prices? The analysis in section 1 makes this clear. A monopolistic producer who faces a monopolistic distributor has a clear interest in preventing the distributor from charging a price above his cost. This not only permits the monopoly producer to extract all of the monopoly profit for itself but it also limits the distributor to a competitive rate of return by preventing him from extracting monopoly profits by raising the resale price. As shown in section 1, this is beneficial to the consumer because it lowers price below what an unfettered monopolistic distributor would charge and increases newspaper sales beyond those that the distributor would make. The newspaper, as a successive monopolist, has a clear interest in holding down the retail price and increasing distribution. The newspaper clearly is a potential competitor and has a clear interest in being a successful one.

But the *Star* had another reason for wanting the price of newspapers to remain low. The *Star* does not just sell newspapers. It also sells advertising in those newspapers. "Newspaper publishers suffer from reduced circulation not because of the effect on revenues derived from newspapers but because of its effect on advertising rates. Monopolistic pricing by a newspaper carrier is likely to have a trivial impact on net revenues that the newspaper obtains from newspaper sales. Most newspapers sell copies to independent carriers for less than the cost of the newsprint and ink to print them."[29] But advertising rates vary directly with circulation. If circulation is down, advertising revenue is down, and advertising accounts for approximately 80 percent of a newspaper's revenues. The *Star* then had a very strong incentive to provide a competitive check by providing potential competition for the distributors. If distributors raise their prices above the level that yields a competitive return on distribution, the publisher loses profits in his role as a successive monopolist and, in addition, loses advertising revenues as well.

The *Star* maximizes its profits when distributors charge a price that just yields a competitive return on distribution. The *Star*'s role as a potential competitor was to hold retail prices down to that level if possible. Unfortunately, the *Star* did not play that role very well.

The monopoly power that each exclusive distributor possessed was a creation of the *Star*. In spite of the *Star*'s policy of not recognizing a carrier's proprietary right in its assigned route, routes were sold to third parties for up to $300,000. This sum represents the capitalized value of the monopoly profits. In section 1, we saw that the distributor will earn monopoly profits equal to $(P_H^* - MC_D - P_N^*)Q_H^*$ per period. The market value of this asset is the discounted present value of the stream of monopoly profits over time. In this case, the present value went as high as $300,000.

Since it is unlikely that a distributor can fully capitalize the profit stream due to business risks and the risks of termination,[30] the market prices of the routes understate the divergence between competitive and actual performance. If the *Star* had been doing a good job as a potential competitor, then the high values placed on these distributorships would not have existed. Thus, we are driven to the conclusion that the *Star* was doing a poor job as a potential competitor. Since the *Star* was doing a poor job as a potential competitor, its elimination from that role can hardly be viewed as seriously anticompetitive. Moreover, even if the *Star* had been doing an excellent job in curtailing the home-delivered price, its behavior would not change following vertical integration. It would retain the very same interest in holding down the home-delivered price.

The Price Evidence

Under the old system, the independent carriers set their own prices and terms. Following vertical integration, the *Star* intended to replace the existing hodgepodge of rates with a single, uniform price for all subscribers. The dissent made much of the fact that this meant that 149,728 of its full-subscription subscribers would experience price increases and only 5,990 would have their rates decreased.[31] At first blush, this seems inconsistent with the successive monopoly theory, which says that the publisher should desire lower rates than would the carriers. Why then would the *Star* not reduce rates upon forward integration?

First, it is possible that the new owners felt that the revenues from newspaper sales had been too low. Paschall's expert witness, Dr. Frederick Kirby, "testified that the $125 million purchase price paid by Capital Cities for the *Star* could not be justified by the newspaper's existing assets, its past profits, or the previous return on equity enjoyed by Capital Cities shareholders. He concluded, therefore, that the *Star* would have to increase its profit level to justify the purchase price" and "that the *Star* likely could only improve its profit by increasing revenue rather than reducing costs."[32] If the *Star*'s purchase price is not justified by its profits and if the only way to increase profits is to raise revenues, then rate increases designed to raise revenues are understandable. One reason why Capital Cities would pay more for the *Star* than its profits would justify is that Capital Cities felt that the *Star* was being mismanaged and that the profit picture could be improved. Otherwise, the purchase would be irrational. Therefore, following Capital Cities' acquisition of the *Star*, it took actions to raise revenues and improve profits. The important question, though, is whether the *Star*'s actions to increase revenues in order to improve profits constitute evidence that successive monopoly theory is contradicted by these price increases. Either implicitly or explicitly, the economic theory of successive monopoly is based in part upon an assumption of profit maximization. If, in fact, one or the other party behaves nonoptimally, the theory will not necessarily provide accurate predictions. To the extent that the

Star failed to maximize its profits prior to the acquisition, we would expect prices to adjust following the acquisition irrespective of vertical integration.

Second, it is possible that cost increases called for price increases regardless of whether *Star* integrated forward or retained the system of independent carriers. Surely, price increases for newspapers were not rare during the 1970s. There is no evidence in the opinions for or against cost justifications for price increases.

Finally, it is possible that the increased subscription rates were just a big mistake. Capital Cities just moved into the Kansas City market and could not be expected to know precisely what prices were optimal. Nonetheless, Capital Cities has a powerful profit motive to discover the correct prices. Thus, incorrect prices are not stable and we would expect them to be corrected over time. Moreover, it is inappropriate to employ the antitrust laws to correct or prevent managerial mistakes.

In summary, the situation appears to be this: Capital Cities purchased the *Kansas City Star* for which profits failed to justify the price that Capital Cities paid. Consequently, Capital Cities most certainly believed that it must improve profits. Economic theory dictates that the *Star* should integrate forward, lower the retail price, increase circulation, and experience greater profits. Instead, the *Star* replaced a mixed bag of prices in different territories with a uniform price that constituted a price increase for the majority of its subscribers. We do not feel that this action by the *Star* constitutes conclusive evidence that the successive monopoly theory is bankrupt and therefore that the anticompetitive effects of the *Star*'s integration outweigh any procompetitive effects. There are several explanations for the *Star*'s behavior: (1) the original prices may have been nonoptimal, (2) cost increases may have called for higher prices, or (3) the new management may have made a mistake. These explanations do *not* call for antitrust remedies.

The Service Evidence

The dissent also alleges anticompetitive effect in the form of reduced service resulting from the *Star*'s forward integration into distribution. It argues that because of the *Star*'s integration efforts the number of subscription options is reduced from ten to three.[33] Of course, these ten different subscription options include the total number of options available to all of the subscribers in the *Star*'s circulation area. It is unlikely that any one subscriber in any one territory ever had access to all ten options. Each carrier is a monopolist, and therefore each subscriber has access to only the options offered by its (monopoly) carrier. It is quite possible that the "average" subscriber will find the options expanded when offered a choice of three. The evidence is not clear on this point.

It is also pointed out that the independent carriers generally provided newspapers to "country" routes twice a day, while the *Star*'s agents would deliver papers on "country" routes only once a day. While it is not clear why this happened from the evidence in the record, it seems clear that the cost of delivering papers on sparsely populated country routes is greater than it would be on more densely populated city routes. It also seems likely that country routes with their higher costs had higher rates under the independent carrier system. It is also likely then that these customers had their rates reduced under the uniform pricing scheme imposed by the *Star*. It seems then that it is quite likely that the delivery of a second, less popular paper would become unprofitable under a uniform pricing system.

Finally, "the district court found, and the majority does not disagree, that the *Star* had legitimate business reasons for its decision which included such efficiency considerations as the assurance of more rapid 'starts' for new subscribers, and the establishment of uniform policies regarding collection, payments, and customer complaints, all of which were recognized by the district court as problems under the independent dealer system."[34] On balance it does not seem clear that customer service was reduced under *Star*'s new system.

5. Concluding Remarks

Economic theory does not address one issue that Judge Bright raised in his dissent: the fate of the distributors. He descried the majority's decision, which permitted "a monopolist to destroy hundreds of independent businesses."[35] Judge Bright pointed to some language in *Brown Shoe* indicating that Congress passed the antitrust laws "to promote competition through the protection of viable, small, locally owned businesses."[36] But this concern is misplaced. First, it is likely that the *Albrecht* rule is responsible for the demise of these independent businesses. Historically, newspaper publishers generally organized the distribution of their newspapers as the *Star* had. When the *Albrecht* decision made it extremely hazardous to impose maximum resale prices, the independent distributor began to disappear. Since the newspapers seem to have preferred independent distributors, the antitrust rule of *Albrecht* seems to have introduced some inefficiency along with the demise of the independent carrier.

This is not to say that the independent distributors would not be hurt by their termination. When routes were assigned initially, the *Star* gave something of great value to each distributor. Subsequently, some of these distributors sold their routes and the monopoly profit was partially capitalized in the sales price. The new owner of the route must continue to set price at the (successive) monopoly level in order to earn a competitive return on its investment in the route. If it is terminated as a distributor, it will lose the amount that it paid for the route. This does not necessarily mean that the distributors should be compensated. First, anyone who buys a flow of monopoly profit surely recognizes that there are risks associated with the acquisition. One of the obvious risks is that the newspaper will terminate the distributor. Second, it is not clear that the displaced distributors suffered any antitrust injury.[37] Finally, the distributors were offered an opportunity to enter agency agreements with the *Star* that guaranteed them the same income that they earned as independent carriers.

The agency offer is not inconsistent with economic theory. As we saw in section 1, total profits for the *Star* were $(P_N^* - MC_P)Q_N^*$ and were $(P_H^* - P_N^* - MC_D)Q_H^*$ for the distributor with successive monopoly. Under an agency agreement, total profits for the *Star* would be $(\hat{P}_H - MC_P - MC_D)\hat{Q}_H$. It could pay the distributor an amount equal to the distributor's former profit and still increase its own profit by a like amount. The *Star*'s willingness to share the profit may be explained by a desire to retain as many of the existing carriers as possible at least through some transition period. It may have thought—mistakenly as it turns out—that such an offer would prevent legal action by the carriers. Moreover, it may have adopted this strategy as a short-run approach. As the agents quit, retired, or died, the *Star* could replace them with employees.

The *en banc* decision of the Eighth Circuit in *Paschall v. Kansas City Star* provided an excellent opportunity to evaluate the economic analysis of the judiciary. In our opinion, the majority got the right answer for the wrong reason. It accepted the so-called Chicago School analysis of vertical integration by ignoring several jarring facts. We believe that we have reconciled the theory with these discordant facts.

Notes

1. The reasons for monopoly in newspaper publication are not obvious. For purposes of this paper, however, we shall not investigate this interesting issue.
2. Our concern may be overstated because there are competitive sources of news: radio, television, and magazines.
3. If our concern were with monopoly at the publishing stage, we would advocate Section 2, Sherman Act prosecution with a meaningful remedy. We shall return to this later.
4. Actually, there were two decisions that provide some interesting contrasts. The original decision was *Paschall v. Kansas City Star Company*, 695 F.2d 322 (8th Cir. 1982). A rehearing *en banc* was granted and the subsequent opinion was reported at 727 F.2d 692 (8th Cir. 1984).
5. This effort was begun in Blair and Maurer (1983). The main focus of the present paper is somewhat different.

6. The received doctrine has been developed over an extended period. For some of the seminal contributions, see Spengler (1950) and Machlup and Taber (1960). For an extensive survey of motives for vertical integration, see Kaserman (1978), Blair and Kaserman (1983), and Blair and Kaserman (1985).
7. From equations (10) and (15), we want to show that

$$\frac{3a + MC_P + MC_D}{4} - \frac{a + MC_P + MC_D}{2} > 0.$$

Algebra reveals that this will be true provided that $a > MC_P + MC_D$. But this must be true if output is positive since a is the intercept of the demand curve.
8. A thorough graphical analysis is contained in Blair and Kaserman (1985) and Blair and Fesmire (1986).
9. Contractual means of acquiring vertical control and their equivalence to vertical integration are explored in some detail in Blair and Kaserman (1983).
10. See Hovenkamp (1984) for a discussion of this point.
11. The illogic of making maximum resale price fixing illegal is explored in Blair and Kaserman (1981) and Easterbrook (1981).
12. *Albrecht v. Herald Co.*, 390 U.S. 145 (1968).
13. 390 U.S. 145, 154 (1968).
14. 390 U.S. 145, 152–153 (1968).
15. The *Star* was convicted of attempted and actual monopolization of newspaper publication in violation of Section 2 of the Sherman Act due to its use of predatory practices in driving its competitors out of business and preventing others from entering the market. *Kansas City Star Co. v. United States*, 240 F.2d 643 (8th Cir. 1957). Nonetheless, its monopoly control persists, which does not say much for the remedies employed in 1957.
16. Although the *Star* did not recognize any property rights of the carriers in their assigned territories, the routes typically were sold at prices ranging up to $300,000.
17. See *Paschall v. Kansas City Star Company*, 695 F.2d 322 (8th Cir. 1982).
18. This was first considered by the Supreme Court in *United States v. Colgate & Co.*, 250 U.S. 300 (1919), in a resale price maintenance case.
19. 695 F.2d 322, 325 (8th Cir. 1982) citing *Auburn News Co. v. Providence Journal Co.*, 659 F.2d 273, 278 (1st Cir. 1981), and *Byars v. Bluff City News Co.*, 609 F.2d 843, 859–863 (6th Cir. 1979).
20. Usually, the potential competition doctrine is used in merger cases to express a social preference for internal expansion. Here it was used to block internal expansion. The use of potential competition in *Paschall* was ridiculous. For a further analysis, see Areeda (1982) at par. 729.4b5 and 729.7f. This misapplication of potential competition was rejected in *Paschall II*, 727 F.2d 692 (8th Cir. 1984).
21. 727 F.2d 692, 706 (1984).
22. 727 F.2d 692, 706 (1984).
23. 727 F.2d 692, 706 (1984).
24. 695 F.2d 322, 328 (1982).
25. 695 F.2d 322, 328 (1982).
26. 695 F.2d 322, 328 (1982).
27. 695 F.2d 322, 328–29 (1982).
28. 695 F.2d 322, 328–30 (1982).
29. See Hovenkamp (1984, 455).
30. See Bierman and Tollison (1970) for a brief discussion.

31. 695 F.2d 322, 330 (1982).
32. 695 F.2d 322, 332 (1982).
33. 695 F.2d 322, 330–331 (1982).
34. 695 F.2d 322, 341 (1982).
35. 727 F.2d 692, 706 (1984).
36. *Brown Shoe Co. v. United States*, 370 U.S. 294, 344 (1962).
37. The antitrust injury doctrine is concerned with whether the injury suffered flows from the anticompetitive aspect of an antitrust violation. *Brunswick Corp. v. Pueblo Bowl-O-Mat, Inc.*, 429 U.S. 477 (1977). For an economic analysis, see Page (1980).

References

Areeda, Phillip E. 1982. *Antitrust law—1982 Supplement*. Boston: Little, Brown and Company.
Bierman, Harold, and Robert Tollison. 1970. Monopoly rent capitalization and antitrust policy. *Western Economic Journal* 8 (December):385–89.
Blair, Roger D., and James M. Fesmire. 1986. Maximum price fixing and the goals of antitrust. *Syracuse Law Review* 37 (June):43–77.
Blair, Roger D., and David L. Kaserman. 1981. The *Albrecht* rule and consumer welfare: An economic analysis. *University of Florida Law Review* 33 (Summer):461–84.
———. 1983. *Law and economics of vertical integration and control*. New York: Academic Press, Inc.
———. 1985. *Antitrust economics*. Homewood, IL.: Richard D. Irwin.
Blair, Roger D., and Virginia G. Maurer. 1983. Forward integration and successive monopolies: Is there room for reason in the rule of reason. Typescript.
Easterbrook, Frank H. 1981. Maximum price fixing. *University of Chicago Law Review* 48 (Fall):886–910.
Hovenkamp, Herbert. 1984. Vertical integration by the newspaper monopolist. *Iowa Law Review* 69 (January):451–67.
Page, William H. 1980. Antitrust damages and economic efficiency: An approach to antitrust injury. *University of Chicago Law Review* 47 (Spring):467–504.
Machlup, Fritz, and Martha Taber. 1960. Bilateral monopoly, successive monopoly, and vertical integration. *Economica* 27 (May):101–19.
Spengler, Joseph J. 1950. Vertical integration and antitrust policy. *Journal of Political Economy* 58 (August):347–52.

5. A Note on Delivered Pricing Systems

Yoram C. Peles

Abstract

THE PAPER offers justification for delivered pricing systems based on two sources of savings they offer. First, savings result from economies of scale in arranging transportation services. These savings can occur in a perfectly competitive setting. Second, producers save by having monopsony power. I show when the savings can be brought to delivered pricing and when to FOB pricing. The theory is supported by actual pricing cases of both systems.

A widely used pricing practice that has won considerable attention in the economic literature is the delivered pricing system. Machlup (1949) described and analyzed this phenomenon at length. One well-known rationale for the delivered pricing system was suggested by Stigler (1949), and two recent contributions to the literature offer additional analyses. David Haddock (1982) explains this pricing system by the existence of economies of long haul, while Dennis Carlton (1983) points to the system's superior ability to detect price reductions by firms participating in cartels. This paper focuses on efficiency as an explanation of the delivered pricing system, which can prevail both in a competitive market and when a cartel exists. That is, this pricing system can be explained either by the above-mentioned cartel theories or by the economic benefits of the system that are described below.

The difference between the delivered price and the FOB price stems from transportation costs (including insurance, etc.). Given the customers' demand function, the lower the transportation costs, the higher the derived demand producers face at their factories' gates (FOB). Hence, it is in the producers' interest to lower the transportation costs. Therefore, the question is, Under what market conditions can producers endeavor to lower the costs of transportation?

There are industries in which there are fewer producers than buyers, such that each producer sells greater quantities of a specific product than the quantities bought by each customer (from all sources). For example, in the steel industry the total quantity produced and sold by any mill is usually larger than the quantity purchased by any individual customer. The cement industry also seems to be characterized by this structure. Under these circumstances, producers might be able to save on the transportation cost in either or both of two ways:

(1) *Savings resulting from economies of scale in arranging the transportation services.* The producer may know the appropriate administrative channels to transportation firms and so be more efficient in organizing the shipment than individual buyers. These economies of scale should be distinguished from the economies of long haul suggested by Haddock. Savings can also occur if the transportation industry is perfectly competitive. Thus, the producers are just serving as agents of the buyers for the purpose of shipping the product.

(2) *Benefits to the producers resulting from having a monopsony power.* The market structure of the transportation industry can be characterized by very few firms operating in certain locations and/or certain modes of transportation. There is specific equipment used for transportation of some specific kinds of products, and the market may be quite localized, either because of administrative or cartel arrangements or for technological reasons. Hit-and-run phenomena can be very rare or not significant in this industry.

Hence, the demand the producers are facing is not just the total demand of the buyers reduced by the marginal costs of transportation. The freighters who have some monopoly power over selling their services can take advantage of this power and reap a larger share of the total revenue obtained from the buyers. They can do this either by splitting the monopoly profits of the producers (if the producers have this power) or by lowering the quantity produced and shipped (and raising prices).

However, as suggested above, each producer sells larger quantities of the product than the quantities purchased by each buyer. Each producer (and, of course, a cartel of producers) has more market power than any individual buyer; that is, the producer can exercise a monopsony power over the companies operating the transportation facilities. In other words, whereas the interrelation between the transportation companies and the buyers is basically oligopoly of the transportation companies, the position of the transportation companies versus the producers is more of the bilateral oligopoly type (or even oligopoly-monopoly type, if the producers are organized in a cartel). Hence, if the transaction is arranged by the producers, they will pay prices for transportation services equal to or lower than those the buyers would have to pay if the transaction were between the transportation companies and the buyers. The savings here can accrue to the producers.

Notice that the above argument is valid whether the producers are operating independently or (and with possible higher benefits) are organized in a cartel.

An alternative to the structure described above is one in which, instead of using independent freighters, the producers operate transportation facilities, effecting a vertical integration between producers and freighters. However, that is not always more efficient than the system in which production and transportation are organized and managed independently.

A similar argument can be made when independent buyers or a cartel of buyers buy larger quantities than each producer can sell independently. Again, the two sources of savings exist, but with the buyers making all the transportation arrangements and having the monopsony (oligopsony) power in the transportation industry. Here there is an advantage to the FOB pricing system over the delivered pricing system.

Moreover, the existence of economies of scale in freight may bring enforcement of delivery pricing in a competitive market. Thus, a declining long-run average cost of transportation means having a marginal cost lower than the average cost. If the usual transportation cost imposed on customers is the (declining) average cost, then it is possible to find producers "absorbing" freight costs for some marginal customers, while actually the cost charged for transportation is not lower than the marginal cost.

Also, in cases where the producers have some monopoly power even without any cartel agreement with other producers, they may enforce a delivery pricing system such that by increasing the quantity shipped the average cost of transportation declines. Thus, a producer can negotiate a declining price per unit of transportation (e.g., with a train company). Where a buyer has his own transportation arrangement at a cost lower than the (average) price arranged by the producer, the buyer's specific cost of transportation can be higher than the marginal cost implied by the arrangement made by the producer. It may be in the interest of the producer (and the buyers as a group) to force the customer to use the transportation arrangement organized by the producers, either by absorbing freight costs or by charging a delivery price. The group of buyers paying an average cost price for transportation enjoys a positive "externality" by having a larger group of buyers.

Therefore, it is not uncommon to find all buyers using the same carrier (such as trains) without any collusive agreement, although some buyers could have arranged for transportation at a cost lower than the (average cost) price charged by this common carrier.

Also, under these conditions the introduction of a new technology with a high degree of divisibility (i.e., no economies of scale) may bring about the abolishment of the delivery pricing system. Scherer (1980, 332) claims that "when the steel industry shifted from basing point to FOB mill pricing the share of trucks increased from almost nothing in 1953 to 44 percent of total shipment tonnage in 1963 and 54 percent in 1972." The above-mentioned existence of an association between the shift from the delivered pricing system to FOB mill pricing and the increase in the share of trucks in total shipment is consistent with a causation opposite of that suggested by Scherer. That is, the progress made in the trucking system caused the switch in the pricing system. This line of reasoning is supported by the fact that the share of trucks in total shipment tonnage has increased over the last decades, not only in the steel industry but also in most industries.

It is interesting to note that even in an industry notorious for using delivery prices there are several exceptions that can be explained by the above savings. These exceptions are big business buyers who organize transportation by themselves. Machlup (1949, 64–65) claims that "steel rails for railroads were exempted from the basing point practice after the railroad companies reached an understanding with the steel producers in 1908" and "exceptions of particular destinations seems to have been permitted. . . . one of the destinations was Detroit, the location of the Ford Company and other automobile producers." Notice that the exception was not limited to the Ford Company (which was a steel producer itself) but also included all buyers in that area.

The following example can illustrate the savings that producers can enjoy by exercising their monopoly power in the transportation industry. Suppose an industry (cartel) is facing a linear inverse demand curve

$$P = a - bQ,$$

where P = price at delivery point and Q = quantity.

The producers' marginal cost is given by $P = a/10$ and the freighters' marginal cost is $P = a/20$. The producers' net FOB inverse demand (after subtracting the payments for transportation) is given by $P_p = a - P_t - bQ$, where P_p = FOB price of producers, and P_t = prices for transportation charged by the freighters. The producers then will maximize their profits by producing the (cartel) quantity given by

$$Q = \frac{0.9a - P_t}{2b}.$$

If the freighters behave competitively and charge marginal cost pricing, then $P_t = a/20$. In this market structure, the optimal solution for a cartel of the producers is to sell a quantity of $Q = (17/40)(a/b)$ at FOB price of $P_p = (21/40)a$, having a net income of $(17)^2/(40)^2 \cdot a^2/b$ or approximately $0.18\ a^2/b$. (Notice that the profit [and Q] is also the optimal joint profit [and Q] of the producers and freighters together.)

Now, suppose the producers leave the transportation arrangement to the buyers and that freighters behave monopolistically. That is, the freighters charge the price that will maximize their own net income under the assumption that they know the behavior pattern of the producers. They know the producers will maximize their own net income given their net FOB demand curve (after the freighters charge their own price). The producers then face $P_t > a/20$, which is determined as follows: The transportation industry faces a demand curve given by $P_t = a - P_p - bQ$, where both P_p and Q are determined in the producers/buyers market, as assumed above. With the usual optimal solution for the transportation industry of marginal revenue equals marginal costs, we obtain the solution that $MR_t = a - P_p - 2bQ = a/20$. Incorporating P_p and Q as determined by the producers/buyers and solving for P_t, we determine the transporters' (cartel) optimal price to be $P_t = (1/3)a$. Hence the producers' quantity and price are determined to be $Q = 17/60 \cdot a/b$ and $P_p = 23/60a$, giving the producers a net income of $(17/60)^2 \cdot a^2/b$ or about $0.08\ a^2/b$. In other words, in this example,[1] producers organizing and acting in a cartel who also organize the transportation and sell using the delivered pricing system can obtain a net income of $0.18\ a^2/b$. If they sell at FOB prices and leave the buyers to negotiate and organize their transportation, the producers can earn a net income as low as $0.08\ a^2/b$.

One example where the transportation services are supplied by sellers for reasons of efficiency is found in liquefied gas or minerals and other chemical industries. The producers are usually large relative to buyers, and transportation is executed with specialized equipment.

Examples in which prices are set FOB and the buyers are usually those who organize the transportation for reasons of efficiency can be found in international trade. Suppliers of raw materials and other unsophisticated products are often small and lack organizational skills, so that the buyers must assume the organization of the transportation. Thus, big American firms not only buy apparel at FOB prices in the Far East but in many cases also design the clothes. Another example is the Israeli cartel (official) of producers of plywood, which buys the wood in Africa at FOB prices and organizes the transportation. The major reasons are economies of scale in using ships and the poor organizational skills of the suppliers of wood.

Probably the best known cartel is OPEC, which until recently set its prices

FOB. In addition, the cartel allocated the total quantity agreed upon between members in order to prevent intracompetition. Stigler (1949) predicted that a cartel that faces a fluctuation demand would use delivered pricing systems. OPEC, which adheres to FOB pricing, certainly does not bear out this prediction. The main reason for this seems to be the inability of OPEC members to organize, operate, and control the means of transportation. Moreover, the oil companies that buy the oil supplied by OPEC in many cases both operate the oil fields and perform the exploration and the development of new oil fields. Transportation is an obvious extension of their involvement.[2]

Notes

1. Note that the analysis here is based on the assumption that both the producers and the freighters independently determine their own price assuming the other price is given. In a way, both parties are followers in the duopoly terminology. An alternative analysis is to let the producers be the followers and to determine a reaction line—their optimal quantity given the freighters' price. This line serves as the derived demand curve ($Q = (0.9a - P_t)/2b$) the freighters are facing. The freighters then maximize their profits. They are in a way "leaders." They will then charge a price of $P_t = (19/40)a$ for $Q = (17/40)(a/2b)$ having a profit of 0.09 a^2/b, which exceeds their profits as "followers." The producers' profits are higher when the freighters behave as "followers" rather than "leaders," hence the producers' incentive to exercise delivered pricing is even higher under the threat of the freighters being leaders.
2. It is interesting to note that the above pricing system was not always prevalent. On 17 September 1928 the three major oil companies that dominated the oil industry outside the United States—Standard Oil of New Jersey, Shell, and Anglo Persian BP—established a delivery pricing system known as "ACHNACARRY Agreement" or "As Is" Agreement. The system established the Gulf of Mexico as the basing point. Thus oil sold in India that originated in the Persian Gulf was sold at the above basing point plus cost of transportation from the Gulf of Mexico. This pricing system ("though never entirely successful") prevailed until 1944–45 when another basing point was added: the Persian Gulf (see Seymour [1980, 6–8]).

References

Carlton, Dennis W. 1983. A reexamination of delivered pricing systems. *Journal of Law and Economics* 26 (April):51–70.
Haddock, David D. 1982. Basing-point pricing: Competitive vs. collusive theories. *A.E.R.* 72, no. 3 (June):289–306.
Machlup, F. 1949. *The basing-point system*. Blakiston.
Scherer, Frederick M. 1980. *Industrial market structure and economic performance*. 2d ed. Rand McNally.
Seymour, Ian. 1980. *OPEC: instrument of change*. Macmillan.
Stigler, George J. 1949. A theory of uniform delivered prices. *A.E.R.* 39, no. 6 (December):1143–59.

6. Quality of Service, Contestable Markets, and the Effectiveness of Motor Carrier Rate Bureaus as Cartels

Arthur DeVany and Thomas R. Saving

THE PASSAGE of the Motor Carrier Act of 1980 signaled the end of three decades of collective rate making in the trucking industry. The act set 1984 as the expiration of the broad antitrust exemption originally granted to motor carrier rate bureaus by the Reed-Bullwinkle Act. Some parts of the general exemption remain intact: rate bureau members may still agree on general rate increases and broad rate structures as they relate to costs of the average firm, but the industry must adjust to increased scrutiny by the Justice Department.

The effect on the trucking industry of the removal of antitrust immunity will depend on how effective the industry had been in making use of the exemption from prosecution. Immunity from antitrust prosecution certainly contributed to the ability of rate bureaus to engage in price-fixing activities. Competitive pressure, however, could have made antitrust immunity an unimportant component in the determination of the equilibrium rate structure.

Rate bureaus were allowed to organize the carriers in their region and hold rate conferences for the purpose of the joint determination of tariffs. The legality of these organizations, however, did not imply effectiveness. The industry was only partially regulated by the Interstate Commerce Commission. Three important classes of competition were unregulated: intrastate carriers, agricultural carriers, and firms who did their own shipping. Rate bureaus, however, were allowed to organize both regulated and unregulated carriers, but no carrier was required to join a rate bureau.

The overall impact of the antitrust exemption on rates during the period before 1984 is open to question. Analysis of the antitrust exemption period is complicated by the fact that some liberalization of trucking regulation occurred in the early 1970s, and the Motor Carrier Act of 1980 provided some immediate further deregulation.

By viewing rate bureaus across regions as having differing degrees of success in maximizing industry profits, we have been able to utilize a combination of cross-section and time-series data to test the hypothesis that rate bureaus have had anticompetitive effects. This test requires that those characteristics of rate bureaus that imply a stronger organization be identified. Using the data supplied to the ICC by those rate bureaus that requested antitrust exemptions, we have identified four characteristics that can be associated with organization strength. Then, using a marginal revenue approach based on the proposition that the greater the effectiveness of a rate bureau, the greater the marginal revenue of shipments, we are able to directly test the proposition that rate bureaus were effective in using the antitrust exemption to achieve noncompetitive results.

Motor Carrier Rate Bureaus

While rate bureaus differed in many important respects, all rate bureaus published the rates of member trucking firms. A significant subset also provided procedures for the joint approval of individual member firms' rate changes. The joint publishing of rates has not been a subject of serious controversy. The joint approval of rates by rate bureaus, however, has many of the attributes of price fixing by cartels and has been the subject of heated controversy since the 1940s.

With the encouragement of the ICC, motor carrier rate bureaus developed soon after federal regulation of trucking rates began in 1935 (Davis and Sherwood, 1975, chap. 2). Using the Sherman Act, the Department of Justice launched a campaign against motor carrier and railroad rate bureaus in the 1940s. The department alleged that the joint approval required for rate changes by member firms was price fixing, despite the required ICC review of any rates approved by the bureaus. In 1948 Congress settled the legal question by passing the Reed-Bullwinkle Act. It added section 5a to the Interstate Commerce Act and provided that, under certain conditions, the ICC could grant rate bureaus exemption from the antitrust laws.[1]

A principal argument against rate bureaus has been that they were cartels that facilitated the setting of prices above the levels that would have existed without them. The operation of the rate bureaus enabled trucking firms to obtain accurate information about other firms' rate changes before the prices were changed, much like the open-price trade associations that were convicted of Sherman Act violations. In addition to providing a forum for obtaining accurate information about other firms' proposed rate changes, rate bureaus also explicitly provided for review of rate changes by one or more committees made up of representatives of competing trucking firms.[2]

The power of rate bureaus, however, was limited by several important factors.

1. Not all carriers were regulated: intrastate and agricultural carriers were exempted from regulation.

2. Any shipper dissatisfied with rates could provide its own trucking services.

Both factors (1) and (2) made the trucking industry an excellent candidate for the type of competitive pressure envisioned in the work of Saving (1972) on market power and in the work of Baumol, Panzer, and Willig (1982) on "contestable" markets.

3. Rate bureaus did not have the final say in proposed rate changes by member firms.

Rejection of a proposed rate change by the rate bureau committee evaluating the proposal did not necessarily kill the rate change. A trucking firm had the right to file the rate change through the rate bureau or through publication elsewhere as an independent action, which was subject to review by the ICC but not by the rate bureau. These independent actions provided a possible limitation on the rate bureau's ability to act as a cartel since only the ICC's approval was required and the rate bureau had to accept the ICC's ruling.

4. Motor carrier firms were not required by law or regulation to belong to a rate bureau.

5. Rate bureaus could not expel a carrier for failing to comply with bureau-established rates.[3]

Table 6.1. Ten rate bureaus

CENSO	Central and Southern Motor Freight Tariff Association
CENST	Central States Motor Freight Bureau
EACEN	Eastern Central Motor Carriers Association
MIDAT	Middle Atlantic Conference
MIDWST	Middlewest Freight Bureau
MOCAR	Motor Carriers Traffic Association
NENG	New England Motor Rate Bureau
PACIN	Pacific Inland Tariff Bureau
ROCM	Rocky Mountain Tariff Bureau
SOMO	Southern Motor Carriers Rate Conference

Effectiveness of Motor Carrier Rate Bureaus as Cartels   111

Carriers were required, however, to charge only ICC-approved rates on regulated shipments.
6. Rate bureaus were not allowed explicitly to pool revenues.[4]

Table 6.2. Basic statistics, rate bureaus, 1971–77

Rate bureau	Members' M/(SD)	Members' trend[a]	Indep. actions per reg. prop.	Indep. actions D/A per reg. prop.	Total actions per reg. prop.
CENSO	123	0.019	0.254	0.072	0.326
	(7.2)	(2.21)	(0.093)	(0.032)	(0.200)
CENST	533	−0.009	1.058	0.003	1.062
	(26.3)	(−1.04)	(0.230)	(0.003)	(0.229)
EACEN	303	0.082	0.491	0.145	0.636
	(84.6)	(1.18)	(0.103)	(0.030)	(0.121)
MIDAT	1028	−0.016	0.401	0.109	0.510
	(43.9)	(−2.79)	(0.232)	(0.130)	(0.241)
MIDWST	1068	−0.025	0.351	0.019	0.370
	(59.6)	(−9.29)	(0.495)	(0.006)	(0.494)
MOCAR	412	−0.038	1.831	0.014	1.854
	(39.0)	(−6.38)	(0.584)	(0.006)	(0.587)
NENG	1172	−0.018	0.247	0.014	0.261
	(47.9)	(−6.38)	(0.055)	(0.008)	(0.061)
PACIN	208	0.034	0.018	0.005	0.023
	(25.1)	(1.71)	(0.009)	(0.004)	(0.013)
ROCM	154	−0.107	0.015	0.030	0.045
	(37.6)	(−3.29)	(0.009)	(0.009)	(0.015)
SOMO	451	[b]	0.793	0.096	0.889
	(1.0)		(0.142)	(0.045)	(0.179)
All	545	−0.014	0.546	0.051	0.597
	(21.0)	(2.72)	(0.132)	(0.013)	(0.132)

[a] t-ratios are in parentheses below trend coefficients.
[b] Data for SOMO were available for only three years.

These limitations imply that, in spite of immunity from antitrust prosecution, *rate bureaus were not legally enforced cartels*. The fact that limitations on the ability of rate bureaus to act as cartels existed does not imply that their effect on rates was zero. In order to evaluate the effectiveness of rate bureaus it will be useful to review some descriptive material in the form of numbers of members and independent actions of two forms. We have calculated these statistics for ten rate bureaus that obtained exemptions from the antitrust laws under the Reed-Bullwinkle Act during the period 1971–77. Table 6.1 contains a listing of the ten rate bureaus.

For these rate bureaus, we have calculated some membership statistics for 1971–77. This information, presented in columns 1 and 2 of table 6.2, indicates that the number of members varies widely across regions. The variation is due in part to the nonuniformity in the size of the regions. One possibly significant feature of the data is that membership was declining in this period. The time trend coefficients indicate that for six of the nine bureaus that had sufficient data to estimate a time trend, the trend was negative (five statistically significant).

Unfortunately, no data on the proportion of all firms in a region that belong to rate bureaus are available. The ICC did not maintain an inventory of operating authorities by region. In addition, each region contained a significant number of unregulated carriers who may or may not have belonged to rate bureaus.

Rate bureaus that have received exemptions from the antitrust laws under the Reed-Bullwinkle Act were required to report considerable data on their activity. Of particular interest is the number of independent actions filed since this factor may be important as a measure of the cartel power of the rate bureau. In columns 3, 4, and 5 of table 6.2, we show some summary figures for the rate of independent actions by the bureaus. These figures reveal a significant variation in the number of independent actions per regular proposal across the bureaus. Even more significant is the rate at which independent actions were generated: more than one independent action for every two regular proposals. The second set of independent action figures in the table show the rate of independent actions during and after a regular proposal. These actions take issue with a specific proposal and may indicate dissatisfaction with the decision at the time it is made. This rate is, however, quite small.[5]

A Revenue Function Model of the Trucking Industry

We do not have direct information on prices, and even if such data were available for the period for which we have other data, the number of commodity classes and rate changes would make analysis of the data impractical. Extensive data based on revenues are available. Profit maximization implies that, in general, marginal revenue must equal marginal cost with the specific marginal revenue depending on the form of anticompetitive activity assumed. Using this general approach, we derive below hypotheses that apply to the derivatives of the revenue function with respect to capacity and shipments. By estimating the marginal revenue of capacity and shipments and regressing these estimates on the degree of rate bureau cartelization, we can test the hypothesis that rate bureaus have had anticompetitive effects.

Our data are industry-level data, which implies that the appropriate revenue function is at the industry level. Assume that industry demand for each commodity class i is a function of full price defined as

$$(1) \qquad P_i = p_i - \eta_i W(q,t),$$

where P_i is the full cost of shipping commodities of class i, p_i is the explicit transport cost of shipping commodities of class i, η_i is the value of time for shippers of the ith class of commodity, and W is the common expected total shipping time which is a function of firm total shipments q and firm capacity t.

The regulated carriers were required by common carrier provisions to treat all shipments on a first-come-first-served basis, which implies a common total shipping time. Following our earlier work (DeVany and Saving 1977) we assume further that costs and quality of service (total transport time) depend on output and capacity. Under these conditions the industry total revenue function can be written as

$$(2) \qquad TR = \Sigma(P_i - \eta_i W)Q_i = F(Q, T, R)$$

where TR represents total industry revenue, Q_i is total industry shipments in commodity class i, $Q = \Sigma Q_i$ is total industry shipments, T is industry capacity, and R represents a measure of rate bureau activity related to the rate bureau's ability to act as a cartel in some or all dimensions; price p, capacity, T, or output, Q.

Model One: Perfect Cartel

The perfect cartel model assumes that rate bureau members are able to choose both monopoly prices and levels of capacity so that industry profits are maximized.[6] Consider the monopoly choice of shipments (output) when T is fixed at its optimal level. For any given distribution of shipments over commodity classes, the appropriate marginal condition for industry profit maximization is

$$(3) \qquad \frac{\partial TR}{\partial Q} = \sum_{i=1}^{n}\left[\left(\frac{\partial P_i}{\partial Q_i} - \eta_i \frac{\partial W}{\partial Q}\right)Q_i + p_i\right] = \frac{\partial C}{\partial Q}$$

where $\partial C/\partial Q$ is marginal shipment cost holding trucks constant, $\partial P_i/\partial Q_i$ is the change in full price of commodity class i resulting from an increase in Q_i, which is negative for every i, and $\eta_i(\partial W/\partial Q)$ is the marginal waiting cost of shipments for commodity class i, which is positive for every i.

The monopolist must consider both the reduction in money price caused by the increased waiting cost incurred as shipments are increased, as well as the fact that full prices fall when output is increased. Equation (3) is the usual marginal-revenue-equals-marginal-cost condition for profit maximization for a multiproduct monopolist with the complication that full price is affected by total shipping time (service quality).

At the optimal level of shipments, capacity must be utilized until its effect on industry profits is zero, implying that

$$(4) \qquad -\sum_{i=1}^{n} \eta_i \frac{\partial W}{\partial T} Q_i = \frac{\partial C}{\partial T}$$

where $\partial C/\partial T$ is the marginal cost of trucks.

We have from (3) and (4) that at the full cartel equilibrium, $F(\ )$ must have the following derivatives

$$(5) \qquad F_Q^M = \frac{\partial C}{\partial Q} > 0$$

$$(6) \qquad F_T^M = \frac{\partial C}{\partial T} > 0$$

where F_Q^M and F_T^M are respectively the industry marginal revenue of shipments and capacity. If the cartel is imperfect in achieving monopoly results because of its inability to control capacity, then the level of industry capacity will exceed the cartel level. The increased level of industry capacity reduces industry prices and reduces the profit-maximizing industry marginal revenue for both shipments and capacity. As a result we have the marginal revenue restrictions $F_Q^{CC} < F_Q^M$ and $F_T^{CC} < F_T^M$, where the CC superscript denotes capacity-competing cartel.

Model Two: Competition

Assume that unrestricted competitive equilibrium holds in both the price and capacity dimensions.[7] As before, assume that, in competition, firms are full-price takers. The firm-level equilibrium conditions are

$$(7) \qquad p_i - \eta_i \frac{\partial W_i}{\partial Q_i} = \frac{\partial C_i}{\partial Q_i}$$

$$(8) \qquad -\eta_i \frac{\partial W_i}{\partial T_i} Q_i = \frac{\partial C_i}{\partial T_i}$$

where the subscript i indicates firm i. In addition, we have the zero-profit condition

$$\sum_{i=1}^{n} p_i q_i = C\left(\frac{Q}{m}, \frac{T}{m}\right) \tag{9}$$

where m is the number of firms.

Assume further that entering firms may replicate the cost functions of firms in the industry so that we have constant long-run costs of output. Then in long-run equilibrium we have that

$$p_i = \frac{C(W)}{q} \tag{10}$$

where $C(W)$ is the constant industry cost of supplying the service quality associated with the expected shipping time W. Thus, for competition, under the assumed conditions, equilibrium output occurs where industry average and marginal cost equal industry average revenue. For the cartel, output is restricted to the level where average and marginal costs equal industry marginal revenue. For the price- and capacity-setting cartel, marginal revenue of shipments exceeds the marginal revenue of shipments in competition. The marginal revenue restrictions are

$$MR_Q^m > MR_Q^c \tag{11}$$

$$MR_T^m > MR_T^c \tag{12}$$

Model Three: Cartel Pricing with Competitive Capacity

Assume that prices are set by a cartel at monopoly levels but the level of trucks cannot be controlled. In this imperfect cartel, the members of the rate bureau achieve monopoly prices and prevent price competition. The bureau does not succeed in limiting capacity, however, and its members engage in service rivalry, expanding capacity until profits are driven to zero. If the ICC does not restrict entry, new firms are also drawn into the industry until profits equal zero.

The industry marginal revenue for the capacity-competing cartel exceeds competitive industry marginal revenue but is less than monopoly marginal revenue. The capacity-competing cartel produces more output than a perfect cartel because it invests in more capacity, which reduces full price and raises output. Imperfect cartel output is less than competitive output, and marginal revenue exceeds the competitive level.

In summary, the restrictions implied by the three possible limiting equilibria are

(13) $$MR^m_Q > MR^{cc}_Q > MR^c_Q$$

(14) $$MR^m_T \le MR^c_T; MR^m_T \le MR^{cc}_T \gtreqless MR^c_T$$

where m, c, and cc denote monopoly, competition, and competing cartel respectively.

The Data

Our analysis is based on differences in cartel effectiveness and the marginal revenue of shipments. We require, therefore, cross-section data on shipments and revenue by rate bureau as well as measures of their effectiveness as cartels. Firms that earn at least 75 percent of their revenue from intercity traffic reported data by truckload and less than truckload categories. These firms are a subset of all regulated class I and class II motor freight carriers, so our data

Table 6.3. Variable definitions

Variable[a]	Definitions
Firms	Number of firms in each region
Tot Rev	Total revenue from intercity freight operations per firm in each region (thousands of 1971 dollars)
TL Rev	Revenue from intercity truckload shipments per firm in each region (thousands of 1971 dollars)
LTV Rev	Revenue from intercity less-than-truckload shipments per firm in each region (thousands of 1971 dollars)
Trucks	Number of trucks per firm in each region, measured at year-end
Trailers	Number of truck-trailers (including semi-trailers) per firm in each region, measured at year-end
Power units	Number of power units (owned and used in intercity and local operations plus those rented) per firm in each region, measured at year-end
TLS	Number of intercity truckload shipments per firm in each region (thousands of shipments)
LTLS	Number of intercity less-than-truckload shipments per firm in each region (thousands of shipments)
TS	Sum of TLS and LTLS

[a] All variables are annual figures, with the exception of trucks, tractors, trailers, and power units.

Effectiveness of Motor Carrier Rate Bureaus as Cartels

Table 6.4. Sample data summary statistics all regions, 1971–77

Variable	Mean	Standard deviation
Firms	53	48
Tot Rev	27,576	36,905
TL Rev	9,738	11,218
LTL Rev	17,838	26,313
Trucks	76	89
Tractors	376	490
Trailers	812	1,053
Power units	364	378
TLS	29	31
LTLS	683	818
TS	713	844

do not cover the entire population of firms. Moreover, regulated class I and II carriers are a subset of all the trucking firms operating in a rate bureau's jurisdiction; the latter include intrastate carriers, exempt carriers, and shippers operating their own trucks.

The data are from the annual reports submitted to the ICC by class I and II motor carriers, as compiled in *TRINC'S Blue Book of the Trucking Industry*. These data cover individual intercity general freight carriers, classified by the region of their headquarters. There are fifteen regions. The data span the period 1971–77. The variables are defined in table 6.3. The population summary statistics are presented for the pooled sample in table 6.4 and for each region in table 6.5.

Rate Bureau Characteristics

What are the characteristics that might indicate or measure the effectiveness of a rate bureau operating as a cartel? Ideally, we would like to identify rate bureau characteristics that imply effectiveness or lack of effectiveness in managing price competition and service competition.

Standard cartel analysis suggests that, as the number of members of a cartel rises, the less effective it becomes in policing its members; rate bureaus with a larger number of members should be less effective. On the other hand, a larger membership means there are fewer members outside the cartel, which makes the rate bureau more effective. There are no data on the number of firms in a region, so there is no direct measure of the extent to which the membership includes every firm in the region of the rate bureau. One measure we can use is the ratio of bureau members to the number of ICC-certificated class I and II carriers. This measure is appropriate if the ratio of rate bureau members to class I and II carriers is associated with the ratio of bureau members to all the firms operating in a region.

Rate bureau members need not accept the rate filings of the bureau; they could file rates independently of the bureau. These independent actions were taken when the carrier did not wish to comply with a regular rate proposal. The extent of these independent actions measures the extent of disagreement

Table 6.5. Summary statistics by region, 1971–77: Mean (standard deviation)

Regions	Firms	TL Rev	LTL Rev	Power units	TLS	LTLS
1	46.1	615.	1406.	52.2	4.2	102.3
	(5.0)	(41.)	(275.)	(4.1)	(.5)	(17.1)
2	151.2	1140.	1956.	66.7	6.5	107.1
	(6.8)	(123.)	(262.)	(10.3)	(.6)	(8.8)
3	148.4	2050.	3076.	90.8	13.2	174.5
	(8.1)	(371.)	(344.)	(21.3)	(2.5)	(11.7)
4	92.0	1290.	2728.	83.0	10.6	206.3
	(9.6)	(276.)	(673.)	(11.0)	(4.3)	(275.6)
5	82.4	1658.	4028.	97.3	7.6	245.1
	(2.1)	(173.)	(250.)	(39.9)	(1.2)	(13.1)
6	34.7	1968.	5918.	143.8	16.1	658.4
	(6.0)	(161.)	(333.)	(32.0)	(.9)	(10.8)
7	73.1	1275.	3745.	93.2	6.9	226.0
	(6.0)	(161.)	(333.)	(32.0)	(.9)	(10.8)
8	35.1	2793.	6155.	168.1	12.6	302.6
	(3.7)	(418.)	(362.)	(36.1)	(1.5)	(13.0)
9	29.9	14647.	20008.	530.6	44.6	768.1
	(1.7)	(1571.)	(1771.)	(133.8)	(5.0)	(49.0)
10	28.0	13996.	17732.	552.1	39.8	641.7
	(3.9)	(1410.)	(1047.)	(161.2)	(4.8)	(27.8)
11	10.0	8023.	11591.	384.5	33.2	562.7
	(1.3)	(1720.)	(2493.)	(226.7)	(10.4)	(120.8)
12	13.7	30292.	25776.	1046.5	88.1	865.5
	(.5)	(6645.)	(4894.)	(142.2)	(14.0)	(124.8)
13	3.3	36641.	100055.	979.0	100.9	3289.8
	(.7)	(4427.)	(13041.)	(223.0)	(63.6)	(487.5)
14	10.6	8758.	12560.	317.2	25.1	574.2
	(.7)	(903.)	(875.)	(135.6)	(5.0)	(64.9)
15	16.6	29732.	54236.	1144.3	56.3	1600.0
	(.9)	(9738.)	(17838.)	(363.8)	(29.4)	(683.1)
All	52.8	9738.	17838.	363.8	29.4	683.1
	(47.9)	(11218.)	(26313.)	(377.9)	(31.0)	(818.5)

Table 6.6. Definitions of rate bureau characteristics

Firm	Number of Class I and Class II firms in region
Mem	Number of rate bureau members
Prop	Total rate proposals (excluding independent action)
IA	Independent actions submitted without a related regular proposal
IA(D+A)	Independent actions during or within two months after a regular rate proposal
Mem/Firm	Rate bureau members per firm
IA(D+A)/Prop	Independent action during or after a regular proposal per total proposals
IA/Mem	Independent actions per member
Prop/Mem	Proposals per member
Prop	Proposals per firm

among rate bureau members. A high ratio of independent actions to the total number of proposals should indicate weakness of the bureau in controlling its members.

The number of annual proposals initiated per member should be highly correlated with the complexity of published tariffs in any region. When the tariffs contain many items, there will be many actions to change them. A complex tariff requires many actions each year just to keep abreast of the market. The number of proposals per firm then is a measure of the degree to which rates are differentiated by commodity. Complex tariffs also embody a high degree of differentiation; the narrow commodity classes and service definitions of complex tariff manuals are the classic trademarks of price discrimination. Narrow classes and definitions also restrict entry in commodity and service areas when they are enforced by the ICC. Tariff complexity should be related to monopolistic pricing. To the extent that proposals per member captures the complexity of tariffs, it should be associated with higher total revenue for each level of output.

The Empirical Model

Equations to be Estimated

Our method uses estimates of the marginal revenues of trailer load (TL) shipments, less than trailer load (LTL) shipments, and capacity (the number of trucks). The estimates of marginal revenues are then used as dependent variables in an equation containing rate bureau characteristics. If rate bureaus had anticompetitive effects, then the characteristics indicative of the strength of the rate bureau organization should affect marginal revenue in the manner indicated by the inequalities derived from the model (equations 13 and 14).

The functional form of the revenue function used to estimate the marginal revenue is

(15) $$Rev_{it} = b_1 \text{ Power units} + b_2 TLS_{it} + b_3 LTLS_{it}$$
$$+ \sum_k C_{Rs} Y_k + \sum_j D_{Rj} R_j + e_{it}$$

where Rev_{it} is revenue in region i, in year t. The b's, C_{Rk}'s and D_{Rj}'s are to be estimated, and the e's are zero-mean, constant-variance errors. Power units is the total number of units used in intercity operations.[8] The Y_k and R_j variables are, respectively, dummy variables for particular year and region. All variables, other than the regional and time dummy variables, are measured in the logs of the variables.

When TL revenue is used in the regression, LTL shipments should have a negative sign, i.e., b_3 should be negative, because as more competing LTL shipments arrive, the capacity to service TL shipments is reduced. The coefficient of TL shipments should be negative when LTL revenues are used for the same reason that b_3 is negative in the TL regression. The coefficient of capacity (b_1) in the LTL regression should be positive, as should the coefficient of TL or LTL shipments (b_2) when the regression was TL or LTL revenue.

The marginal values of power units and of shipments must be calculated from (15); they are

(16) $$MV_{PU} = b_1 \left(\frac{Rev_{it}}{\text{Power units}_{it}} \right)$$

$$MV_{TL} = b_2 \left(\frac{Rev_{it}}{TL \ Q_{it}} \right)$$

$$MV_{LTL} = b_3 \left(\frac{Rev_{it}}{LTL \ Q_{it}} \right)$$

The estimated TL, LTL, and PU marginal revenues differ by region and year. If the pattern of marginal revenues by region matches the pattern of measures of bureau effectiveness, this fact will support the hypothesis that effective bureaus did raise prices.[9] The hypotheses about the effectiveness of rate bureaus as cartels can be tested by using the estimates of marginal revenues calculated from equation (15) to estimate the following equation:

(17) $$MV_{kit} = c_1 \left(\frac{Mem}{Firm}\right)_{it} + c_2 \left(\frac{IA}{Mem}\right)_{it} + c_3 \left(\frac{IA(D+A)}{Prop}\right)_{it}$$
$$+ c_4 \left(\frac{Prop}{Mem}\right)_{it} + \sum_s C_{vs} Y_s + \sum_j D_{vj} R_j + e_{kit}$$

where $k = PU, TL$, and LTL. All variables are measured in the natural logarithms. From the discussion of the effect of the degree of cartelization on the marginal revenues and the discussion of measures of the effectiveness of rate bureaus, it follows that, for the TLS and $LTLS$ regressions, significant coefficients of the following signs imply that rate bureaus had an effect on the degree of competition: $c_1 > 0, c_2 < 0, c_3 < 0, c_4 > 0$.

It is also possible to test the contestable market hypothesis on equation (17). Any firm with sufficient shipping to keep its own truck busy is a potential competitor to the regulated trucking firm. Shippers can contest the regulated carriers by hiring or leasing their own trucks and drivers. This own-shipping activity is most likely to occur for TL shipments. Thus, the contestable market theory says we expect the effect of rate bureaus will be greatest in the LTL market equation.

Estimation Technique

All of the equations were estimated using ordinary least squares, which provides unbiased and efficient estimates. The region and year dummies control for region-specific and year-specific factors, which are not measurable. If these unmeasured factors are not orthogonal to the right-hand-side variables, the inclusion of dummy variables is the correct way to obtain unbiased estimates of the coefficients (Mundlak, 1978).[10]

Joint estimation of all the equations does not produce more efficient estimates than ordinary least squares when the same right-hand-side variables are included in each regression. Ordinary least squares is equivalent to joint estimation (Zellner, 1962) of the model and is the method of estimation used.

Estimates of the Revenue Function

The estimates of the revenue function (equation 15) are presented in table 6.7. The equations are highly significant, as indicated by their high F values, and the sets of dummy variables are significant relative to an ordinary least squares model as indicated by their joint F value. The signs of the output and capacity coefficients are as predicted by the theory, and their statistical significance is good.

Table 6.7. Estimates of the revenue regressions

Right-hand-side variables	Left-hand-side variables				
	Tot Rev	TL Rev	LTL Rev	TL Rev	LTL Rev
Power	.220	.360	.150	.418	.148
units	(7.14)[a]	(6.74)	(4.93)	(9.70)	(4.87)
TLS	.054	.111	.018	.129	
	(2.72)	(3.21)	(.90)	(3.86)	
LTLS	.547	.165	.731		.744
	(10.37)	(1.80)	(13.99)		(14.90)
R^2	.816	.550	.838	.535	.836
$F_V{}^b$	150.5	41.5	175.5	59.3	263.3
$F_D{}^c$	135.4	63.2	165.2	61.6	169.8

[a] t-values are in parentheses below coefficients.
[b] Partial R^2 and F for the capacity and shipments variables.
[c] F-values for the dummy variables.

The capacity variable, power units, has positive and statistically significant estimated coefficients in all of the regressions. This confirms our hypothesis (DeVany and Saving, 1977) that capacity has a positive marginal value; the elasticity is also less than one, as required for stability. The *TL* shipment revenue elasticities are positive and significant in total and *TL* revenue. *LTL* shipments do not affect *TL* revenue. The *LTL* shipment revenue elasticities are positive and significant in the total and *LTL* revenue equations. The last regression in table 6.7 excludes insignificant variables, the R^2, *F,* and *t*-values indicate that these variables do not affect the values of any coefficients.

The regressions using estimates of marginal revenues derived from the coefficients of the total revenue regression in table 6.7 as dependent variables are presented in table 6.8. All of the regressions are statistically significant by the *F*-values. The rate bureau variables explain a large fraction of the variance in marginal revenue of *TL, LTL* shipments, and power units over regions. Although not as high as the partial R^2's in table 6.7, the R^2's in table 6.8 are quite respectable. All but one of the coefficients in table 6.8 have the hypothesized sign, the single exception being proposals per member in the shipment regression, which has a positive sign rather than the expected negative sign.

The signs of the coefficients in the power units regression are consistent with the restrictions we derived: the coverage variable, members per firm, raises marginal revenue, the two independent action variables lower it, and tariff complexity raises it. The members per firm variable is significant at better than the 1 percent level, and tariff complexity (prop/mem) is significant at the 20 percent level. The different sign of prop/member in the *TL* (negative)

Effectiveness of Motor Carrier Rate Bureaus as Cartels

Table 6.8. Estimates of the marginal revenue regressions based on total revenue

Variables	Marginal revenue		
	Power units	TLS	LTLS
Mem/Firm	.229	.179	.218
	(3.48)[a]	(3.95)	(3.40)
IA(D+A)/Prop	−.021	−.040	−.021
	(−.91)	(−1.76)	(−.90)
IA/Mem	−.019	−.082	−.022
	(−.60)	(−1.04)	(−.66)
Prop/Mem	.102	−.058	.086
	(1.50)	(−1.82)	(1.38)
R^2	0.207	0.218	0.199
$F_V{}^b$	6.1	6.5	5.9
$F_D{}^c$	57.6	73.1	66.7

[a] t-values are in parentheses below coefficients.
[b] Partial R^2 and F for the rate bureau variables.
[c] F-values for dummy variables.

Table 6.9. Estimates of the marginal revenue regressions based on TL revenues

Variables	Marginal revenue[a]	
	Power units	TLS
Mem/Firm	.246	.090
	(3.24)[b]	(1.64)
IA(D+A)/Prop	−.018	−.035
	(−.70)	(−1.27)
IA/Mem	.012	.096
	(.33)	(1.02)
Prop/Mem	.237	−.023
	(3.03)	(−.61)
R^2	0.158	0.090
$F_V{}^c$	4.40	2.32
$F_D{}^d$	21.6	41.1

[a] LTL shipments are not included due to the insignificance of this variable. The results are available upon request.
[b] The t-values of regression coefficients are in parentheses.
[c] Partial R^2 and F for the rate bureaus' variables.
[d] F-values for dummy variables.

Table 6.10. Estimates of the marginal revenue regressions based on LTL revenue

Variables	Marginal revenue[a] Power units	LTLS
Mem/Firm	.213	.224
	(3.14)[b]	(4.96)
IA(D+A)/Prop	−.020	−.041
	(−.85)	(−1.79)
IA/Mem	−.040	−.176
	(−1.21)	(−2.25)
Prop/Mem	.029	−.080
	(.42)	(−2.53)
R^2	0.241	0.305
F_V[c]	7.48	10.31
F_D[d]	98.20	114.28

[a] TL shipments are not included due to the insignificance of this variable. The results are available upon request.
[b] The t-values of regression coefficients are in parentheses.
[c] Partial R^2 and F for the rate bureaus' variables.
[d] F-values for dummy variables.

and *LTL* (positive) equations suggests tariff complexity is driven by the *LTL* market and complexity lowers revenue in the more contestable *TL* market.

The separate regressions using estimated marginal revenue of truckload shipments and less than truckload shipments are presented in tables 6.9 and 6.10. The regression of marginal revenues using truckload revenues had insignificant coefficients on the rate bureau variables; the sole exception is the coverage members per firm, which had a positive effect on the marginal revenue of trailerload shipments.

The estimates of marginal revenues in the less-than-truckload market in table 6.10 tell a different story. The contestable market analysis would suggest that rate bureaus would be most effective in the *LTL* segment of the market in any anticompetitive efforts. All of the rate bureau variable coefficients are significant and of the hypothesized sign in the *LTL* marginal revenue equation. This evidence suggests that those rate bureaus that were well organized were effective in increasing shipping rates in the less-than-truckload segment of the market.

Conclusions

Rate bureaus were exempt from antitrust action for almost thirty-five years beginning with the enactment of the Reed-Bullwinkle Act in 1946 and ending with the passage of the Motor Carrier Act of 1980. The bureaus were collective rate-making organizations, with far-reaching tools for defining commodity classes and service and for setting and disseminating rates. It would be surprising if such a powerful institution were to have no effect on how the industry operated.

Collective rate-making procedures contain a bias against lowering prices, which would guide the most innocent and guileless collection of members toward higher prices. There need be no specific intent or overt collective action to raise prices, the procedures—which mandate sharing of information, joint approval, public dissemination of posted prices, and ICC enforcement—would appear to be strong enough to raise prices by themselves. Our results support this view.

The countervailing powers to the procedural bias toward higher prices are dissension among the ranks and competitive pressure from outside the ranks. We find both were important in limiting the upward price bias inherent in collective rate-making. We found that the extent to which a bureau's membership covered all the trucking firms in a region was correlated with higher shipping rates in that region. Independent actions initiated by members were slightly negatively related to rates, indicating that this venue of action was not very effective in countering the upward rate bias of collective rate making. The bureaus were most active in terms of tariff-making proposals in the *LTL* segment of the market and had their greatest effect there as well. They were less likely to raise rates in the *TL* segment. We offer the hypothesis that the *TL* segment of the market is more contestable than the *LTL* segment because shippers are more able to provide their own services through hire or lease of trucks and drivers.

Notes

1. The Reed-Bullwinkle Act is, more formally, the Carriers' Rate Bureau Act of 1948.
2. In this way, trucking firms could find out other firms' evaluations of the effect and desirability of any proposed rate change. The general review of proposed changes may have provided helpful information to the firm requesting a change on the likely response by other firms.
3. Member carriers could be expelled only for failure to pay amounts due the rate bureau.
4. It may be possible, however, that transfers of operating rights at nonmarket prices could be an imperfect substitute for explicit revenue pooling.
5. Over the seven-year period, there appears to have been no consistent trend in the rate of independent actions. In nine of the ten rate bureaus the trend was positive but the trend coefficients were small and in only two cases statistically significant.
6. The ICC must cooperate and close entry to the industry, or these profits will be dissipated through the entry of new firms.

7. This is a strong assumption since it implies that neither the ICC nor the rate bureaus have any effect on the market outcome.
8. In all regressions, capacity is measured using number of power units. A comparison of initial regressions estimated with trucks, tractors, and trailers (or trucks and tractors) and regressions with power units indicates that power units generally provide at least as good a fit.
9. It may be argued that cost factors across regions might account for the differences in marginal revenues. Examination of data, however, shows that regional differences in cost conditions, while substantial due to diesel or road taxes, for example, have been constant over time. In contrast, the time variation of cost conditions due to diesel fuel price effects, for example, has been relatively constant across regions. Since regional and time dummy variables can pick up such variables, only the rate bureau variables are explicitly included in the final regressions.
10. Initial estimates of these regressions had substantially different coefficients when estimated with a fixed-effects and a random-effects model. If the random-effects specifications were correct, these estimates would be similar (Hausman, 1978); estimation with fixed effects was thus indicated.

References

Baumol, William, John Panzer, and Robert Willig. 1982. *Contestable Markets and the Theory of Industry Structure*. New York: Harcourt Brace Jovanovich.
Beilock, Richard. 1985. "Is Regulation Necessary?" *The Rand Journal of Economics* 16 (Spring): 93–102.
Davis, Grant M., and Charles Sherwood. 1975. *Rate Bureaus and Antitrust Conflicts in Transportation*. New York: Praeger Publishers.
DeVany, A. S., and T. R. Saving. 1977. "Product Quality, Uncertainty and Regulation: The Trucking Industry." *American Economic Review* 67 (September): 583–94.
———. 1983. "The Economics of Quality." *The Journal of Political Economy* 91 (December): 979–1000.
Hausman, J. A. 1978. "Specification Tests in Econometrics." *Econometrica* 46 (November): 1251–72.
Mundlak, Yair. 1978. "On the Pooling of Time Series and Cross Section Data." *Econometrica* 46 (January): 69–86.
Saving, T. R. 1970. "Concentration Ratios and the Degree of Monopoly." *International Economic Review* (February).
TRINC'S Blue Book of the Trucking Industry. 1967–77. Washington, D.C.: TRINC Transportation Consultants.
Zellner, Arnold. 1962. "An Efficient Method of Estimating Seemingly Unrelated Regressions and Tests for Aggregation Bias." *Journal of the American Statistical Association* 57 (June): 348–68.

Part III. Regulation and the Theory of the Firm

7. Deregulation, Competition, and Risk in Commercial Banking

Arnold A. Heggestad and Stephen D. Smith

THE SOUNDNESS of the commercial banking industry and the prevention of bank failures have been matters of major public policy concern since the depression of the 1930s. As a result of widespread failures during this period, numerous programs and regulatory constraints were instituted, most of which are still in effect. However, technological innovations in the delivery of financial services, increased competition, and the current administration's philosophy of deregulation of financial markets have caused many of the longstanding soundness programs to be modified or even be removed.

Proponents of deregulation have based their position primarily on the expected benefits to be obtained for increased competition. However, our analysis suggests that deregulation could also lead to significant increases in the risk exposure of commercial banks. This consequence, which we feel has not been given adequate consideration by lawmakers, should be considered in any further deregulation proposals.

Soundness Regulation

Between 1930 and 1933, 9,096 of the 25,000 U.S. commercial banks were suspended from operation and were liquidated or merged into other banks. On an annual basis, 11.3 percent of the banks failed with 4.1 percent of the deposits (Benston 1983). This was catastrophic to the economy and was widely believed to be the cause of the Great Depression. It was clear that the banking system could not continue to function in this type of environment. In an attempt to stabilize the banking system, programs were instituted to restrict the ability of banks to take on excessive financial risk and to provide greater stability in the financial markets in which the banks operate.

Numerous federal programs were instituted during this period. The Federal Deposit Insurance Corporation (FDIC) was established in 1933 with the purpose of insuring all but the very largest depositors against loss. The Glass-Steagall Act, also passed in 1933, permanently enjoined commercial banking and investment banking from being intertwined. The Banking Act of 1933 prohibited the payment of interest on demand deposits. At the same time, practices were established to limit entry into commercial banking by increasing the difficulty of obtaining a charter.

The general intent of these laws was to promote banking stability. The Glass-Steagall Act restricted the riskiness of investments of commercial banks by keeping them from holding or underwriting securities. It also protected commercial banks from competition for their deposits, since only institutions with bank charters, which were limited in availability, could offer deposits.

The FDIC's role was to protect the banking system from a depositor panic with a corresponding liquidity crisis. Depositors were guaranteed they would not suffer losses as a result of the failure of their bank. This significantly lowered the probability of a failure at one bank leading to runs or panics at other institutions. The FDIC thus effectively reduced the joint probability of failures of the entire system; there have been no panics since its inception.

The prohibition of interest on demand deposits was an attempt to limit competitive forces in deposit markets. Reduction in competition for the primary input of commercial banks, deposits, had two possible effects. First, it would increase the general level of profitability of the industry to the extent the rate ceilings were below market rates and could not be circumvented by nonprice competition. This would provide a potentially greater cushion against any unforeseen losses and reduce failure rates. Second, it would reduce the incentive for managers to invest in risky assets, with corresponding losses, to pay for more expensive deposits.

In this study we focus on two major forces, with potentially complementary effects, that are presently taking place in the commercial banking industry. These two forces may have strong adverse consequences for the overall goal of a sound commercial banking system and are directly related to soundness restrictions that were originally developed in the 1930s.

First, both technological and legal innovations as well as regulatory changes have increased the degree of competition in banking markets. Firms have developed new and sophisticated methods to deliver financial services nationally and internationally, significantly broadening the geographic and product base in which large banks may operate. Financial services are delivered electronically to a wide variety of customers. Local market services are provided by a plethora of banklike institutions, including nonbank banks, loan production offices, specialized bank holding company subsidiaries, investment banking houses, and retailers. The net effect of these changes has been to move commercial banking from an industry characterized by highly concentrated local markets to one with extremely competitive markets, at least in the major metropolitan areas.

Second, the legal restrictions on competition for deposits are being removed. The Depository Deregulation and Monetary Control Act of 1980 required a phasing out of Regulation Q, which sharply restricted rate competition for savings deposits, by 1 April 1986. Similarly, new types of accounts, such as NOW accounts, super NOW accounts, and money market accounts, have effectively removed most barriers on the payment of interest on transaction accounts. Thus a major regulatory limitation on competition that had been in place for some fifty years has now been removed.

We do not take the position that these changes are incorrect and should be reconsidered. The restriction of competition has had undesirable consequences on many dimensions of banking performance, including prices for financial services, innovation, and efficiency in the delivery of services (see Heggestad [1984]). Similarly, deposit rate ceilings have severely restricted income and investment opportunities for small savers (Pyle [1975]). We simply wish to consider the possibly adverse effect of these actions on the soundness of the system. It has been demonstrated in theoretical models that increases in the degree of competition are likely to lead to increases in the systematic risk of firms. (See, for example, Subrahmanyam and Thomodakis [1980]; and Morgan and Smith [1985] for the specific case of intermediaries and deposit markets.) In addition, the failure rate of commercial banks has been at record high levels over the past five years. This may be coincidental, but the increased failure rate comes at a time of increased competition and liability rate deregulation.

Rate Ceilings and Bank Risk

Two major studies have considered the implications of deposit rate ceilings on bank risk. In his important 1964 study, Benston analyzed the implications of rate ceilings on bank risk exposure in the 1920s, when no ceilings existed.

Benston argued that the implicit justification for rate ceilings when they were instituted in the 1930s—and the continuing rationale for the ceilings— is the assumption that banks have a minimum target rate of return objective. They raise funds in deposit markets and in turn lend and invest these funds. Their source of profits is derived from the spread or differential between the deposit rate and the yield on loans and other investments. In this formulation, the required return on loans and investments is determined by the cost of funds.

In a competitive deposit market, it is inevitable that some participants will increase deposit rates. Competing banks will be forced to meet the rate increase or lose market share. This will narrow the differential between asset returns and cost of funds. To make their target profit rates, banks would then be under pressure to increase their gross yield on loans and other investments. This could only be achieved by investing in more risky assets. Consequently, an increase in deposit rates will inevitably lead to riskier assets with corresponding greater losses on loans and investments.

An alternative explanation of bank behavior presented by Benston may be termed the profit maximization hypothesis. In an unregulated environment, the bank may attract deposits by increasing rates or by utilizing nonprice forms of competition, such as advertising, premiums, or convenient branch offices. To maximize profits they will use price and nonprice strategies to attract deposits until the marginal cost of one more dollar of deposits from any strategy to attract deposits is exactly equal to the marginal increase in revenue from investing this dollar. Under this hypothesis, there need be no relationship between deposit costs and risk.

This form of the profit maximization hypothesis is nonstochastic. However, if we allow for uncertainty in interest rates and/or in deposit levels but assume the firm acts in a risk-neutral manner so that it maximizes the expected value of profits, the same result holds.

Benston tested these two distinctive models on a sample of New York state banks for the period 1923–34 and on all national banks for the period 1928–33. He found no evidence to support the target rate of return hypothesis. He could find no correlation between the payment of interest on deposits and loan losses. In fact, he found that the failure rate of banks was lower in states where banks paid interest on deposits.

In a more recent study, Mingo (1981) replicated and extended Benston's analysis by considering the effect of rate ceilings in the current economic environment. His study offered several advantages over the Benston study. First, he had current data, which meant he could evaluate the effect of rate ceilings in a world of Regulation Q and the prohibition of interest on demand deposits. Second, he was able to obtain individual firm data on a wide sample of commercial banks. Finally, he was able to apply a multivariate test that controlled for market risk and competitive factors operating on bank risk.

Mingo found that in every test those firms that had aggressively competed for deposits by offering higher rates of interest experienced less risk during the 1961–72 period. Mingo concluded that "relative use of interest payments to attracts funds, as would be the case to a greater extent if Regulation Q were repealed, is associated with lesser, not greater, bank risk" (1981, 140). This conclusion has become the generally accepted view of economists and regulators involved with the banking industry.

Analytical Model

It is clear there is a major conflict in the financial economics literature on the question of the relationship between the degree of competition and the risk exposure of corporations. However, the conflict is not direct in that different propositions are considered by the studies. They differ in their treatment of risk and in their treatment of competition. Benston and Mingo focus on the effect of limitations on rate competition for deposits. Since their nonstochastic models do not allow the firm to trade off risk for return, changes in costs will have no direct impact on risk exposure. Their empirical results, however, strongly suggest a negative correlation between competition for deposits and risk.

The studies that find a positive relationship between systematic risk and competition differ significantly. First, they consider a change in the degree of competition as compared to the effect of a change in the supply function for an input such as deposits. Second, they are concerned only with systematic risk, i.e., the relationship between the returns on investing in the firm and the return on investing in all assets. Their emphasis is on the effect of a change in competition from the viewpoint of a shareholder holding a widely diversified portfolio. Regulators, however, should be concerned with total risk, or asset-specific risk, as their major concern is the probability of bankruptcy rather than a marginal change in the risk of a diversified portfolio. (For a discussion of the appropriate utility function to model financial institution behavior, see Santomero [1984].)

Therefore, it is in the context of total risk that we develop a model of the commercial banking firm to evaluate the proposition that increased competition for funds and the removal of rate ceilings will lead to a change in bank risk. Our model explicitly allows for changes in the degree of competition in the loan and deposit markets as a result of deregulation of deposits and as a result of new entry into banking markets.

We assume the firm operates in imperfect loan and deposit markets but is a perfect competitor in a risk-free market where it may borrow and lend funds. An example of such a market is the Federal Funds market. Further, we assume the firm operates in a risk-averse manner and has a utility function that exhibits constant absolute risk aversion. This form of utility function assumes that a change in the wealth of the firm will have no influence on the degree of risk aversion. (For a discussion of the implications of this assumption, see Edwards and Heggestad [1973].)

The utility function for the firm is defined as:

(1) $$U(X) = Z - e^{-AX},$$

where Z is a constant, $A = -U''/U'$ is the degree of absolute risk aversion, and X is total profits of the firm (see Pratt [1964]).

We assume the bank operates as a quantity setter in the loan market and as a rate setter in the deposit market. In the loan market, the firm is uncertain of the rate it will earn on loans once quantity is set. In the deposit markets, the firm is uncertain of the quantity of deposits it will attract once the deposit rate is set. Furthermore, we assume that rate and quantity uncertainty are both linear and normally distributed.

The deposit supply function is given by

(2) $$D = \delta + \alpha R_D + \mu$$
$$\delta, \alpha > 0,$$

where D is total deposits and R_D is the predetermined deposit rate. The random error term, μ, is assumed to be normally distributed with an expected value of 0 and a constant variance, σ^2_μ.

In this formulation, δ represents the supply of core deposits, i.e., the level of deposits that would be available to the firm if it paid no interest. Similarly, α may be interpreted as a measure of the sensitivity of the deposit supply to a change in the firm's deposit rate. The greater is α, the more competitive is the market. (Note, in this model, α incorporates the conjectural variation. The firm does not have to be concerned that a change in rates will incur any reaction from its rivals. A less restrictive assumption would complicate the analysis but would yield the same results.

The demand function for loans is given by

(3) $$R_L = a - bL + \varepsilon$$
$$a, b \quad 0,$$

where R_L is the rate on loans, L is the quantity of loans, and ε is normally distributed and has expected value of 0 and variance σ^2_ε. R_L is random because of two factors. First, the general level of interest rates could change, causing a change in the loan rate received by the bank. This is most evident for variable rate loans. Second, R_L is a rate net of loan losses. An increase in loan losses would cause the net loan rate, R_L, to fall for a given volume of loans, L.

Deregulation, Competition, and Risk in Commercial Banking   135

The term a represents a shift parameter. An increase in the demand for loans at every level of interest rates would be represented by an increase in a. The coefficient b represents the sensitivity of loan rates to a change in the quantity of loans. *Ceteris paribus,* a decrease in the amount of competition in the market will increase the size of b.

In this model, the firm determines *ex ante* the rate on deposits and the quantity of loans. These two decisions are interdependent and will depend on relative profit opportunities in the two markets.

We also allow for stochastic interaction in the two markets. The covariance between loan rates and deposit supply, $\sigma_{\varepsilon\mu}$, is expected to be positive. Business cycle theory would suggest that a shock that increases deposits is also likely to increase loan rates, as well as other market determined interest rates. The same shock is likely to reduce loan losses as the condition of the economy improves beyond the general level of expectations. Further, at a more micro level, we would expect that if ε is low due to unexpected loan losses, deposits would flow out of the bank, as has been the case in recent years.

The firm sets its deposit rate on the basis of the supply curve for deposits and its intent to invest in loans. If it receives more deposits than it has committed to loan, it invests the residual in the Federal Funds market and receives interest rate p, which is assumed to be known with certainty. This rate will be less than the loan rate. Similarly, if it does not receive enough deposits to fund its loan portfolio, it must borrow in the Federal Funds market at the same cost. This rate will generally exceed the deposit rate and reduce profits.

We assume that $0 < p < a$. The firm must expect to make a profit from loans when it first enters the market, i.e., at $L = 0$. Our assumption that p is known can be justified on the grounds that the time interval between the time the deposit rate is set and deposits flow into the bank is "small." If we allow p to be stochastic, the results become significantly more complex. However, it would have no result on our basic conclusion.

The firm earns a total profit X, which is uncertain.

(4) $$X = R_L L - R_D D - p(L - D).$$

In this model, we abstract from operating costs. While we recognize this is an important element in the firm, we consider it of secondary interest to the risk issue.

Rearranging terms, the expected profit is defined as

(5) $$\bar{X} = aL - bL^2 - (R_D - p)(\delta + \alpha R_D) - pL.$$

The firm is concerned with the variance of profits as a measure of risk, which is given by

(6) $$\sigma^2_x = \sigma^2_\varepsilon L^2 + (R_D - p)^2 \sigma^2_\mu - 2(R_D - p)\sigma_{\mu\varepsilon}L.$$

In this formulation, the first term, $\sigma^2_\varepsilon L^2$ represents the credit and interest rate risk of the firm. The second term $(R_D - p)^2\sigma^2_\mu$ represents liquidity risk. Liquidity risk increases with the spread between the deposit rate and the Federal Funds rate and increases with the variance in deposits σ^2_μ. The last term represents the interaction between liquidity risk and credit risk. Since $R_D < p$, this term will add to the risk of the firm in normal cases as $\sigma_{\mu\varepsilon} > 0$.

The firm maximizes the expected utility of profits. Assuming normality in the distribution of uncertain deposit levels and loan rates, the expected utility of profits may be defined as

(7) $$E[U] = \bar{X} - 0.5A\sigma^2_x,$$

where A in equation (7) is the degree of absolute risk aversion. Higher values of A imply higher risk aversion. Note that if A is zero, the firm maximizes expected profits—i.e., it is risk-neutral.

We substitute equations (5) and (6) into equation (7) and solve for the optimal levels of L and R_D

(8) $$L^* = \frac{\Theta_1(a - p) - \Theta_3(\delta + \alpha p)}{\Theta_1\Theta_2 - \Theta^2_3},$$

where $\Theta_1 = (2\alpha + A\sigma^2_\mu)$; $\Theta_2 = (2b + A\sigma^2_\varepsilon)$; and

$$\Theta_3 = A\sigma_{\mu\varepsilon} \quad \Theta_1 > 0; \Theta_2 > 0; \Theta_3 > 0 \text{ if } \sigma_{\mu\varepsilon} > 0.$$

Similarly,

(9) $$R_D^* = p + \frac{\Theta_1(a - p) - \Theta_2(\delta + \alpha p)}{\Theta_1\Theta_2 - \Theta^2_3}.$$

We utilize the model to do comparative static analysis of changes in the parameters.

Changes in the Supply of Core Deposits (δ)

Deregulation of deposits will effectively remove the supply of low-cost (free) deposits from financial institutions. In the formulation of our model, δ will fall.

In the solution to the model, $dL^*/d\delta = -\text{sign }\sigma_{\mu\varepsilon} < 0$. If the covariance between the supply of deposits and loan rates is positive, a reduction in the supply of core deposits will cause an increase in the optimal quantity of risky

Deregulation, Competition, and Risk in Commercial Banking   137

loans. We would expect this covariance to be positive; as in a period of rising interest rates, more funds would flow into the commercial banks. This result implies that a reduction in low-cost deposits will cause the firm to substitute for more expensive deposits and to invest in higher return loans. This result is exactly contrary to the Benston or Mingo results.

$dR_D^*/d\delta < 0$. A reduction in the supply of core deposits would imply that the optimal deposit rate would increase. This result is consistent with the generally accepted result that consumers will benefit from a reduction in Regulation Q deposit ceilings by receiving higher rates.

Increases in the Competition for Deposits

We model the increases in the competition for deposits by changes in the α term. As competition increases, a change in deposit rates will have a larger influence on deposit levels (α increases).

We find the sign of $dR_D^*/d\alpha = $ sign of $(p - 2R_D)$. The effect of a change in competition for deposits depends on the relationship between the Federal Funds rate, p, and the deposit rate. If deposit rates are substantially below the risk-free rate, the sign is positive. An increase in competition should result in higher deposit rates and a higher level of risky loans since the

$$\text{sign of } dL^*/d\alpha = \text{sign } (\sigma_{\mu\varepsilon}(p - 2R_D)) > 0 \text{ if } p > 2R_D.$$

If we adopt the convention of risk neutrality, for example, $A = 0$ and $R_D^* = 1/2 \ (p - \delta/\alpha)$, so that the above condition is satisfied.

Thus, we see that increases in both average competition, which could be interpreted as decreases in δ, and in marginal competition, increases in α, have the same effect. They cause the bank to increase its deposit rate and to expand its position in risky loans as long as the deposit rate is low and as long as the covariance between loan rates and deposit supplies is positive.

If the deposit rate is relatively close to the risk-free rate, the result is reversed. Increases in marginal competition will cause the bank to reduce its deposit rate and to reduce its holdings of risky loans.

This result may explain the conclusions of Benston on the 1930s. Interest rates had fallen in general to a level so low that there was virtually no difference between money market rates, p, and deposit rates. For example, the prime rate had fallen to 1/2 percent. In this period, increases in deposit rates did not cause banks to take on greater risk, as evidenced by loan losses or failure rates.

Increases in Competition for Loans

The degree of competition for loans is reflected in the slope term of the loan demand equation. As competition increases, the size of b decreases.

We find the sign of $dL^*/db < 0$ and the sign of $dR_D^*/db = -$ sign $\sigma_{\mu\varepsilon} < 0$. An increase in competition will cause the sensitivity of loan demand to a change in interest rates (b) to decrease. The effect of decreased loan sensitivity will be for banks to increase their optimal deposit rates and to increase their holdings of loans. In this case, an increase in competition will have the effect of increasing interest rates on deposits and increasing the amount of loans. Again, increased competition leads to more risky loans.

Increases in Loan-Rate Risk

We find the sign of $dL^*/d\sigma^2_\varepsilon < 0$ and the sign of $dR_D^*/d\sigma^2_\varepsilon = -$ sign $\sigma_{\varepsilon\mu} < 0$. An increase in the risk of the loan portfolio will cause the bank to reduce the optimal amount of loans and to reduce the rate it is willing to pay on deposits. The risk-averse bank will act to compensate for greater risk exposure by limiting its size so as to reduce the variability of its expected profits.

Increases in Deposit-Level Risk

We obtain the expected result on variation in deposit risk.

$$\text{sign } dL^*/d\sigma^2_\mu = \text{sign } (\sigma_{\mu\varepsilon} (p - R_D)) > 0 \text{ and the sign } dR_D/d\sigma^2_\mu$$
$$= \text{sign } (p - R_D) > 0.$$

If the deposit rate is below the Federal Funds rate, the bank will increase the rate it is willing to pay for deposits and reduce the optimal quantity of loans when faced with greater deposit risk. Greater liquidity risk will cause the bank to expand its deposits and loans.

Changes in Variance of Profits

In this section, we evaluate the effect of changes in competition on the variance of deposits. We see that the results depend on the relative contributions of deposit variability and loan rate variability to profitability of the firm and to the risk of profitability.

We first consider the effect of a change in core deposits on profit variability. $d\sigma^2_X/d\delta > 0$ if $(R_D - p) < 0$. The variance of profits increases as core deposits increase and will therefore fall if core deposits are lost.

Similarly, $d\sigma^2_X/d\alpha < 0$ if $(p > 2R_D)$ and >0 if $2R_D > p > R_D$.

Variance of profits will decline as the general level of competition increases if $p > 2R_D$, but will fall if p lies between $2R_D$ and R_D.

In situations where both the loan and the deposit rate are increasing, the variance of profits will fall. The bank is relying less on purchased funds. Note these are changes in the absolute variance, not, for example, in the coefficient of variation. That is, the risk declines because the direct effects of a change in deposit competition on R_D dominate the secondary effects on L.

The loan rate variance results are similar. $d\sigma^2_x/d\,a > 0$ if $R_D < p$ and $d\sigma^2_x/db < 0$. Increases in average monopoly rents increase variance as do increases in marginal monopoly power in the asset markets.

The variance arguments may be summarized as follows. Changes in liability regulations (δ and α) or asset regulations (a and b) influence variance of profits the most through the direct impact on R_D for deposit parameters and on L for loan rate parameters. The variance terms always dominate the covariance terms which are second order effects.

Consequently, any change in liability regulations that causes the institution to increase its deposit rate will cause a *reduction* in variance, since the bank is relying less on purchased funds. In other words, *their liquidity risk has fallen.* Alternatively, any asset regulations that cause the bank to make more loans, such as increasing b, will cause the risk to increase because the firm will face *more interest rate and credit risk.* Therefore, the net effect of deregulation depends on whether liquidity risk or rate risk is the more important for the institution.

Summary

This paper has raised serious questions about the effect of deposit deregulation in an increasingly competitive environment. We find that on many occasions, the rational reaction of financial institutions to increased competitive and deposit cost pressure is to compensate by increased risk. This could well lead to increased failure rate in the economy.

References

Benston, George. 1964. Interest payments on demand deposits and bank investment behavior. *Journal of Political Economy* (October).
———. 1983. Deposit insurance and risk. *Economic Review* (March). Federal Reserve Bank of Atlanta.
Edwards, Franklin R., and Arnold A. Heggestad. 1973. Uncertainty, market structure and performance: The Galbraith-Caves hypothesis and managerial motives in banking. *Quarterly Journal of Economics* 87 (August).
Heggestad, Arnold A. 1984. Comment on market structure and competition: A survey. *Journal of Money, Credit, and Banking* (November).
Mingo, John J. 1981. The economic impact of deposit rate ceilings. In *Regulation of Consumer Financial Services*, ed. A. A. Heggestad. Cambridge: Abt Books.
Morgan, George, and S. Smith. 1985. A theory and test of the effect of competition on risk: The case of DIDMCA. *Bank Structure and Competition*. Federal Reserve Bank of Chicago.

Pratt, J. W. 1964. Risk aversion in the small and in the large. *Econometrica* (January).
Pyle, D. 1975. The losses of savings deposits from interest rate deregulation. *Bell Journal of Economics and Management Science*.
Santomero, A. M. 1984. Modeling the banking firm: A survey. *Journal of Money, Credit and Banking* (November).
Subrahmanyam, N., and S. Thomodakis. 1980. Systematic risk and the theory of the firm. *Quarterly Journal of Economics* (May).

8. The Economics of Regulation: Theory and Policy in the Postdivestiture Telecommunications Industry

David L. Kaserman and John W. Mayo

IN PERFECTLY competitive markets with no externalities, the free interaction of the forces of market supply and demand lead to an optimal allocation of society's resources. This fundamental attribute together with a political mistrust of agglomeration have led to a national affinity for competitive markets. This affinity, in turn, has resulted in the presence of both our antitrust laws and direct economic regulation.

Few would deny that enforcement of the antitrust laws and imposition of direct economic regulation have profoundly affected resource allocation. Yet for many years economists, lawyers, and public officials were content to ascribe to rather naïve notions about the rationale for and the effects of regulation. Beginning in the 1960s, however, economists began to systematically and rigorously investigate various aspects of economic regulation. This work has continued and accelerated in the 1970s and 1980s.

Despite the growing interest and research in the subject of economic regulation, however, the literature remains surprisingly disjoint. In the material that follows, we provide a synthesis of recent and significant research into various aspects of economic regulation. The purposes of this paper, then, are first to explore the foundations of regulatory economics that have evolved over the past two decades and, second, to examine the implications of these fundamental developments for public policy in the postdivestiture telecommunications industry.

The paper proceeds with a major section on the economics of regulation. In that section we first provide a perspective on economic regulation in the United States. We then turn to a discussion of the fundamental areas of inquiry by regulatory economists in recent years. These areas include the study of natural monopoly, theories of regulation, and the economic costs of regulation. In the next section, we turn to a discussion of regulation in the telecommunications industry. Again, we begin the discussion with a historical perspective of public policy in this industry. We then critically examine the present policy structure in the industry, which we refer to as asymmetric regulation. From that discussion, we turn to a presentation of the case for deregulation in this industry. The fifth section of the paper provides an analysis of the current impediments to deregulation. Finally, there is a section of summary and policy conclusions.

The Economics of Regulation

While federal and state governments have been active in regulation for a number of years, the stated justification for regulation has changed over time, and with it the appropriate boundaries of the regulatory process vis-à-vis the market mechanism.[1] The first significant case of economic regulation of private enterprise in the United States occurred over one hundred years ago in the case of *Munn v. Illinois*.[2] In that case, the Supreme Court upheld a state law that controlled the price charged by grain elevators. The Court upheld the law not because of the grain elevators' natural monopoly position, but because the industry was "affected with the public interest." This justification of market regulation was very broad and loosely defined. One reason for this may have been the lack of understanding of exactly what market conditions cause regulation to be truly in the public interest.

It was during that same era that economists began to more clearly articulate the conditions under which the market mechanism could not be expected to result in the optimal allocation of society's resources. One of these conditions that was posited by nineteenth-century economists was the notion of monopoly. Both Augustin Cournot (1838) and Jules Dupuit (1844) depicted monopolies in terms of a single firm that is able to choose its prices rather than having prices dictated by market conditions. It remained, however, for John Stuart Mill to make a critical distinction between two important types of monopolies. Although he did not explicitly use the term "natural," Mill clearly differentiated between what have since been labeled natural monopolies and contrived monopolies. The natural monopoly was not defined in terms of the actual number of firms in the market at a given time or in terms of its ability to manipulate price, but instead in terms of the relative *efficiency* of serving the market with a single firm.[3] The concept of natural monopoly soon began to be identified with the notion of economies of scale. That is, an industry was referred to as a natural monopoly if unit (average) cost fell monotonically with increased output.

During the first half of this century, the distinction between contrived and natural monopoly became (and remains) critical to the development of appropriate public policy toward industry organization. In markets characterized by high concentration, which approached monopoly but had limited scale economies, antitrust laws arose as the appropriate public policy instrument. In markets where economies of scale were thought to be pervasive, however, direct regulation was perceived to be the appropriate public policy. Antitrust policy, in this latter case, is inappropriate because divestiture of a natural monopoly would result in several smaller firms each producing output at higher unit costs. Furthermore, competition between these firms would eventually lead to the exit of all but one. Several industries were identified in the early 1900s that were thought to produce subject to economies of scale and were therefore labeled as natural monopolies. As a result, these industries, which include telecommunications, electricity, railroads, and airlines, came under direct regulation.

This spread of regulation in the past was based on three implicit assumptions that were seldom seriously questioned: (1) markets are fragile and are often apt to operate inefficiently if left alone; (2) regulators are perfectly (or at least well-) informed, public welfare–maximizing agents; and, (3) government regulation of markets is costless or at least relatively inexpensive. In recent years, however, economic analysis has cast severe doubt on the accuracy of these assumptions. In particular, economic analysis has proceeded along three countervailing lines. First, the theory of natural monopoly and its pricing implications have been reformulated. As a result, economists now recognize that the ability of markets to achieve efficient resource allocation (pricing and output) is more robust than was previously believed. Second, extensive work in the theory of regulation indicates that regulators are often placed in a political and economic tug-of-war with no guarantee or even any reasonable assurance that the scope of regulatory activities will be limited to those markets where regulation is in fact in the public interest. Finally, a growing body of research has indicated that regulation of markets is far from costless. We now turn to a somewhat more detailed review of these recent advances in economic thought and their implications for public policy.

The Theory of Natural Monopoly

Beginning with the work of Bonbright (1961) and continuing through the most recent work of Baumol, Panzar, and Willig (1982), the theory of natural monopoly and its implications for resource allocation have been extensively revised. One of the most important revisions is the finding that economies of scale can no longer be relied upon as the exclusive determinant of whether or not an industry is a natural monopoly. Instead, a given industry's output is said to be an *output-specific natural monopoly* if that output can be produced more cheaply by a single firm than for any partition of that output among two or more firms. More generally, an industry is said to constitute a *natural monopoly* if for *any* industry output level the product(s) can be produced most efficiently by a single firm.[4] Once defined in this way it can easily be shown that economies of scale are neither necessary nor sufficient for the existence of natural monopoly.[5] This suggests that the set of naturally monopolistic industries may be significantly different than was earlier believed. Furthermore, the literature indicates that caution should be exercised in the interpretation of product- or stage-specific economies of scale as being indicative of the presence of natural monopoly in an industry.

In addition to making advances in the conceptual notion of natural monopoly, economists working in this area have reexamined and modified the theoretical implications of market structure for pricing. In particular, economists now more widely recognize the very powerful role that potential entry can play in limiting the behavior of incumbent firms. When (1) potential entrants can serve the same market demand and have access to the same general technology and inputs as incumbent firms, (2) potential entrants do not face entry costs greater than those faced by current incumbent firms, and (3) potential entrants evaluate the profitability of entry at the incumbents' preentry prices, then it can be shown that industry pricing, regardless of market structure, will remain efficient due to the threat of entry.[6]

These recent advances in the theory of natural monopoly have some direct and powerful implications for the economic analysis of and public policy toward regulated and potentially regulated industries. The newly elevated status of "potential entry" has called into question the entire relationship between industry concentration and performance. It is now widely recognized that in markets that approximately satisfy conditions (1) through (3) above, efficiency results on pricing, output, and profit (conduct and performance) are likely to occur regardless of the actual number of extant firms. Furthermore, these developments have recently begun to influence public policy toward industries. Indeed, a driving force behind the deregulation of the airline industry was the recognition that despite the presence of some economies of scale and a limited number of firms along a given route, efficient pricing is still likely to occur in this industry.[7]

In summary, economic analysis of the theory of natural monopoly indicates that many industries originally thought to be natural monopolies may or may not be and that even if an industry's output is concentrated among firms it may still approximate the efficiency results of a competitive market.

Theories of Regulation

A second area of advance by economists in recent years has been in the theory of regulation. Beginning with the work of Stigler (1971), economists have investigated the important role of regulators in the regulatory process. Prior to the 1970s, the most widely accepted view of regulation was that it was conducted by clear-sighted, public welfare–maximizing regulators. However, Stigler's work and a rapidly growing body of subsequent economic analysis have posited a somewhat more complicated view of regulation.[8] Collectively, this body of research indicates that the legally binding powers of regulatory bodies are goods that are subject to the pressures of supply and demand just like any other good or service. Furthermore, under the new approach regulators are demoted to the status of utility-maximizing, nonomniscient humans who must allocate the benefits of regulation among competing and often contradictory demands. Consequently, the competition for favorable regulatory treatment is likely to be intense with the "winner" being chosen not necessarily on the basis of efficiency or equity, but rather on the basis of the political survivability of the regulator. This more general view of the regulatory process recognizes, then, that (1) regulators may be "captured" by those they regulate; (2) industries may use regulation to achieve cartel-like price and output; and (3) regulation is likely to result in extensive cross-subsidization. In summary, this literature suggests that the breadth of regulation may be much wider than is economically justified and that there is little guarantee that the benefits of regulation will flow to the appropriate parties. Moreover, this view of the regulatory process engenders a certain degree of cynicism concerning the likelihood of achieving either efficient or equitable outcomes through the decisions of regulators.

The Costs of Regulation

During the 1960s economists began systematically investigating the efficiency properties of market regulation. Averch and Johnson (AJ) (1962) demonstrated that under fairly general conditions rate-of-return regulation will provide an incentive for regulated firms to employ an inefficient input mix. Discovery of this regulation-induced inefficiency has led to the subsequent investigation and verification of other inefficiencies that are likely to emerge in regulated markets. These inefficiencies break down into four rough categories: input mix distortions, technical inefficiency, distortion of innovation and product quality, and administrative costs. While an exhaustive review of the literature on each of these costs of regulation is inappropriate here, we do offer a brief synopsis of the research findings in this area.

First, the literature on input mix distortions in regulated markets has grown rapidly since the original AJ model. The bulk of this theoretical literature indicates that under any of a wide array of plausible starting assumptions rate-of-return regulation will induce inefficiency in the input combinations employed by regulated firms.[9] Second, beginning with the work of Leibenstein

(1966), economists have become increasingly skeptical about whether regulated firms operate in a technically efficient fashion. For the most part, this literature has focused on the propensity of regulated firms to employ too many resources and for labor to overindulge in the consumption of nonpecuniary benefits (e.g., long coffee breaks, three-martini lunches, plush offices, etc.). At a very fundamental level this sort of technical inefficiency is thought to arise from the regulation-induced lack of competitive rivalry.[10]

Third, economists have investigated the role of regulation on firm-level innovation and product quality. Three widely accepted results emerge from this literature: regulation tends to harm consumers by restricting the range of "quality" offered; where price and entry are regulated, the quality of regulated firms' products is likely to be excessive; and regulation tends to attenuate the returns to technological innovation and thereby harms the dynamic efficiency of the firm.[11]

Finally, administrative costs for the regulatory process can be quite high. While these costs do not necessarily represent an inefficiency in firm behavior, they do constitute a social loss to the extent that resources that are dedicated to the administrative regulatory process represent forgone allocation of resources to the efficient production and distribution of the regulated firm's products. Given these changes in economic theory regarding regulation, we now turn to an examination of the implications of these developments for regulatory policy in the telecommunications industry.

Current Regulatory Policy in the Telecommunications Industry

The telecommunications industry is scarcely one hundred years old, yet it has faced virtually every conceivable type of government policy toward business. The industry that began in the 1880s as an unregulated, rivalrous duopoly has subsequently evolved into a divested industry with component parts ranging from completely regulated to completely deregulated. Along the way, the industry has passed from being a heavily patented monopoly to being openly competitive to being a regulated franchise monopoly. Between the mid-1930s and the late 1960s virtually every aspect of the telecommunications industry was regulated by either the Federal Communications Commission (FCC) or the state public utility commissions. During the 1970s and 1980s, however, the FCC and the courts took several major steps toward relaxing regulation in some telecommunications markets.

Most significant among these was the relaxation of entry standards in the 1969 *MCI Decision* and the 1971 *Specialized Common Carrier Decision*. This was followed in the early 1980s by the removal of tariff support regulation to all interstate carriers except AT&T. (See Federal Communications

Commission, *Competitive Carrier Rulemaking*, Fourth Report and Order.) Also in keeping with a 1982 Consent Decree between the U.S. Department of Justice and AT&T, the Bell Operating Companies (BOCs) were divested in January 1984 from AT&T, their parent corporation. As a result, the BOCs provide local telephone service and long-distance service within LATAs.[12] AT&T retained the rights to provide several other products and services, including telephone equipment sales, computer sales and inter-LATA (long distance) telephone service. The rationale for the 1974 antitrust case that culminated in the consent decree was the belief that if AT&T were divested of the local operating companies, the demand and cost conditions in the long-distance telecommunications industry could support vigorous competition.

In light of rapidly changing market structure and relaxed entry conditions, it appeared to many that the 1984 divestiture would pave the way for rapid deregulation of the long-distance telecommunications market. Despite this sentiment, however, efforts to relax the regulator's grip on the inter-LATA telecommunications market have met with only limited success. In most states and at the federal level, the current public policy is to subject AT&T, the traditional provider of long-distance services, to either full-blown rate-of-return regulation or to maintain regulated prices within some relatively narrow bands. In addition, the traditional common carrier obligation to maintain service to all markets has continued to be imposed on this firm in most jurisdictions. At the same time, however, virtually no regulatory controls on price or output are placed on firms that compete with AT&T.[13] Moreover, these newer firms are allowed to freely enter or exit whatever markets they choose. Finally, while all inter-LATA carriers are currently made to pay for access to the local network, these alternative carriers are assessed a charge some 55 percent lower, on a per minute of access basis, than AT&T. We refer to these current policies collectively as asymmetric regulation.

Costs of Asymmetric Regulation in the Telecommunications Industry

Based on the previously discussed generic research on the costs of regulation, we can readily identify several specific problems with the current policy of asymmetric regulation. First, under the current regulatory structure, AT&T alone is regulated in its prices, services, and investments. As a result of this rate-of-return regulation, which attempts to set price equal to average costs, society unnecessarily suffers a relatively large allocative inefficiency. Kahn (1984) has argued that prices by long-distance services are inflated some 60 percent above average costs, which are in turn likely to be significantly higher than the more economically relevant marginal costs.[14] Thus, while there are demanders of long-distance services who value the service more highly than the marginal cost of providing the service, they are inefficiently being dissuaded from consumption by artificially high and inflexible regulatory prices. Moreover, asymmetric regulation impairs the ability of the regulated provider to respond in a timely fashion to changes in technology, market conditions, or the prices and services of its competitors.

Second, since rate-of-return controls are applied in conjunction with a uniform set of prices, there is a distinct possibility that inefficient entry and investment patterns are being fostered. To the extent that this regulatory system involves cross-subsidization, some markets will be attractive targets for entry by unregulated firms while other markets will not. Since unregulated firms are allowed to selectively enter those markets where profits exist, the pattern of observed entry may be more a by-product of artificial incentives created by the regulatory apparatus than a manifestation of socially efficient entry opportunities.[15]

Under current regulatory policies, it is generally not possible to distinguish with confidence entry that is due entirely to cream-skimming opportunities from entry by firms that are at least as efficient as market incumbents. If what we are observing is the former, then the total social (and private) costs of providing service may be increased as a result of encouraging and then allowing entry by relatively high-cost producers. In this case, the appropriate policy is to prohibit entry altogether; or, better yet, to eliminate the cross-subsidization scheme that is encouraging it. But if what we are observing is the latter, then industry costs may well be lowered by the infusion of competitive rivalry. Here, a policy of deregulation is appropriate. To complicate matters further, it may very well be that some of the observed entry into the interexchange market has been by efficient providers while other entry simply represents cream-skimming. So long as a policy of asymmetric regulation remains in effect, however, it will be impossible to distinguish between these hypotheses regarding the genealogy of observed entry. As a result, the appropriate policy response to this entry will remain in doubt, and the risk that regulation is spawning an inefficient industry structure will persist.[16]

Also, the current process of entry, whether by efficient or inefficient firms, is likely to place an ever-increasing burden on regulators that seek to maintain elements of cross-subsidization within the inter-LATA telecommunications industry. Specifically, attempts to maintain cross-subsidization of high-cost customers through revenue from low-cost customers is likely to lead to the pairing of (potentially inefficient) entrants and low-cost customers who previously subscribed to the regulated carrier. The erosion of revenue caused by this entry must lead to ever-increasing price-cost margins for those customers that the regulated firm maintains. This in turn generates even more profitable entry opportunities and the further erosion of the regulated firm's market. Thus, we see that the maintenance of the current regulatory structure will involve a dynamic process of adjustment that at best appears to be a race between increasing price-cost margins from which to generate regulatory-mandated cross-subsidies and technological advance that has the potential for slowing the unstable regulatory cycle. The outcome of this race will be either the achievement of a long-run equilibrium where the regulatory-induced cross-subsidies are collected from a reduced set of regulated firm customers or the eventual elimination of an adequate revenue base from which to generate the subsidies at all. In summary, cross-subsidization *and* successful competition in telecommunications markets simply cannot be maintained in the long run.

A third significant problem with the policy of asymmetric regulation is that it attenuates the returns to innovative activities. It is widely acknowledged that the telecommunications industry has recently been and has the opportunity to continue to be one of the most dynamically progressive industries in our economy. Technological advances, together with regulatory and antitrust reforms, have catalyzed this progress, yet asymmetric regulation currently jeopardizes this progress. In particular, the regulated carrier is placed on the horns of a dilemma that could seriously jeopardize the industry's innovativeness. This is because on one hand changing technology and increased competition mandate that the industry participants undertake innovative (but risky) activities; and on the other hand rate-of-return regulation and artificially low depreciation rates subject AT&T to a low ceiling on risky projects that turn out to be successful. This low return to innovative activities, then, attenuates the firm's incentives to undertake these projects. By discouraging a major market participant from undertaking innovative projects, the current regulatory structure may lead the industry down a path of technological stagnation that would be costly to both current and future consumers.

Fourth, asymmetric regulation diverts resources away from market competition, imposes direct costs on regulatory participants, and introduces potentially costly elements of strategic behavior into the competitive process. Under the current regulatory structure, all market participants realize that their ultimate success or failure will depend not only on the efficiency with which they operate in the market but also on their litigation skills in the regulatory arena. Consequently, valuable resources are shifted toward regulatory activities and away from the marketplace. Moreover, the procedural and evidentiary requirements that a regulated firm must satisfy in order to implement price changes or introduce new services provide its competitors with a powerful strategic weapon. Where rival firms can prevent or at least retard competitive responses by intervening in regulatory hearings, it is extremely unlikely that the public interest will be served.[17]

Moreover, aside from regulation-induced inefficiencies, the direct costs of regulation are currently exerting upward pressure on inter-LATA telecommunications prices. The FCC recognized this upward pressure on prices when it noted: "It is expensive and time consuming for AT&T to prepare cost-justified rate filings and requests for changes in its authorized rate of return. So too it is expensive and time consuming for the Commission to examine them." Subsequently, the Commission indicates, "In at least some ways our scrutiny of AT&T's rates and earnings may result in telecommunications users paying higher prices than, and receiving services that do not satisfy their demands as well as offerings under less burdensome regulation."[18]

Finally, the current regulatory system provides a distortionary intraindustry transfer from long-distance to local customers. This cross-subsidization occurs as long-distance companies are made to pay access charges on a per minute of use basis to local teleophone companies to reimburse the local firms for part of the fixed costs of maintaining the local system. Since the bulk of these fixed costs are attributable to the provision of local service (in the sense that this service cannot be provided without these fixed assets, while the transfer of long-distance calls from one local exchange to another can), this allocation scheme in effect results in a cross-subsidization of the local rates by the tariff placed on long-distance calls. It has been demonstrated elsewhere that this cross-subsidization scheme is impractical, inefficient, inequitable, and dominated by several policy alternatives.[19]

The Case for Deregulation of Inter-LATA Telecommunications

Given the above problems associated with the current policy of asymmetric regulation, the obvious question is whether the public interest would be served by deregulation of this industry. Equally obvious is the question of why divestiture of the long-distance service from the local network should have been instituted if it were not for the purpose of deregulating this sector of the industry. To answer these questions, it is necessary to examine the fundamental structural characteristics of the inter-LATA market to determine whether competitive market forces are likely to be sufficiently strong to elicit desirable industry performance in the absence of regulatory oversight. We turn now to these structrural conditions.

Entry and Exit Conditions

When an industry's output is supplied under natural monopoly conditions, firms are subject to differential access to markets and technology, and entry is blockaded, then prices in excess of marginal costs will appear and market regulation may provide a desirable public policy. Where entry is relatively easy, firms quickly achieve low average production costs, and potential entrants have access to similar technology and markets as incumbents, then market competition, supported by an antitrust backstop, offers a superior policy to market regulation. Thus, in general, the technological conditions under which an industry's outputs are supplied are quite important to the design of appropriate public policy.

The most powerful technological changes to affect telecommunications markets in general and the interexchange services market in particular have been the development of the microprocessor, the dramatic advances in transmission technologies, and the subsequent broadening of both the supply and demand sides of market. In the past, technology dictated that networks specialize in one of three distinct types of information: video, data, or voice. With the rapid growth of digital technology, however, flexible "transmission pipes" are being developed that can provide any or all of these types of service. This suggests, on the demand side, that telecommunications firms of today and tomorrow will compete across a much wider spectrum of consumer demand than was previously envisioned. As we shall see in the next section, this broadening of the demand side of the market has positive implications for the ability of the market to successfully support competition. On the supply side, rapid technological change is quickly blurring the boundary between interexchange services firms and enhanced services firms. Firms that offered only one of these technologies in the past will now have the capacity to compete in data and video transmission, as well as voice transmission. Thus, the number of firms supplying or potentially supplying this broadened market is much larger than would have been the case had the rapid technological change not occurred.

Furthermore, the combination of technological change, marketing innovations, and regulatory reform has drastically reduced both the cost and the risk associated with entry. Technological advances, including fiber optics and the development of terrestrial and satellite microwave, have drastically reduced costs and expanded capacity of developing an interexchange network. The cost of these new technologies is falling rapidly, and as a result the development of a "backbone" interexchange network using these state-of-the-art technologies is much less expensive than the development of such a system would have been during the "copper-wire" era.[20]

Aside from these cost reductions, there are several factors that have reduced the degree of sunk costs in the long distance telecommunications industry.[21] First, the 1984 divestiture of the BOCs from AT&T resulted in the transfer of the bulk of the industry's sunk costs to the local exchange companies. The remaining network costs (only some of which are sunk) appear to constitute less than 15 percent of total operating costs for a typical industry participant.[22] The remaining 85 percent is comprised of access costs paid to local exchange companies, operator services, general administrative costs, and marketing—all of which are very low sunk-cost items.

Second, the nature of telecommunications investments has become more geographically fungible over time.[23] During the "copper-wire" era, when long-distance networks consisted primarily of thousands of miles of buried wire-pairs, investments in the development of a long-distance network were economically, as well as literally, sunk. The sunk-cost nature of these investments created an impediment to free entry. Today, however, long-distance networks are typically constructed with some combination of microwave relay stations, satellites, and fiber optic cables. These investments are significantly less sunk than earlier copper wire investments.[24] In the case of satellite investments, both an active rental market and the ability to easily redirect satellite capacity to alternative geographic markets significantly increase the mobility of telecommunications firms' investments. In addition, satellite capacity is rather easily diverted from voice to nonvoice communications. Similarly, the earth stations and auxiliary ground equipment necessary to support a satellite network are geographically mobile and versatile in their alternative uses. Microwave stations and fiber optic portions of long-distance networks are somewhat more geographically sunk than satellites, though even for these technologies their usefulness as part of an overall network increases the alternative value of these investments and reduces the degree to which they are sunk.

A third factor that has reduced the sunk-cost impediment to free entry conditions in long-distance telecommunications has been the rapid growth of firms that lease transmission capacity in bulk and then resell that long-distance capacity to telecommunications areas. These resellers can enter (and exit) the industry with little or no sunk costs. Initial investment for entry into the resale business has been estimated to be in the $150,000–$500,000 range. (This compares to somewhere around $5 million to enter the personal computer industry.)[25]

Finally, as pointed out by Katz and Willig (1983), an extremely low sunk-cost option is afforded potential entrants who choose to solicit long-term contracts from customers prior to the initial investment by the supplying firm. Technically, this does not alter the degree of sunk costs in the production process but instead reduces the probability that the sunk costs will not be recouped. The implications of the ability of potential entrants to engage in preentry contracting, however, are clear. Namely, such action reduces the deterrent properties of any extant sunk costs.

Beyond the technical conditions of entry and exit for market participants, regulatory policies, reinforced by the courts, have substantially eliminated any regulatory barriers to entry into the long-distance industry. This erosion of regulatory barriers began in 1960 with the Above 890 Decision[26] and has continued until the present. Today, at the federal level (for interstate calling) and in the vast majority of states (for intrastate calling) regulatory agencies erect virtually no barriers to entry. Even in those states that have not officially authorized a competitive presence of the OCCs (an apparent barrier to entry), competitive long-distance carriers have still been able to enter and provide long-distance services under the guise of providing only interstate calling (which is not under the purview of state level regulatory commissions).

Demand characteristics

The demand for interexchange services has several characteristics that have important implications for this market to successfully support active competition. First, the demand for interexchange services is highly skewed. For instance, only 4 percent of all business customers account for 62 percent of all business interstate revenues. In the residential market, 4 percent of residential customers account for nearly 30 percent of interexchange calling.[27] These customers, who account for such a large part of market demand, spend very large amounts of money on their long-distance calling. The three thousand largest business customers in 1975 spent an average of $666,700 per customer on interstate telephone services. It is well known that consumers tend to be more price-conscious the larger the expenditure on a good or service. As a result of this price consciousness and the importance of a relatively few customers to telecommunication firms' revenues, price and quality competition for these customers, if permitted, will be intense.

A second important feature of demand is the rapid rate at which the market is growing. Despite artificially high prices on AT&T's long-distance services, market growth in the interexchange market has been in excess of 10 percent annually in recent years. Moreover, telecommunications markets appear destined for rapid growth in the future.[28] This healthy prognosis on consumer demand in the interexchange services market is based on two basic market attributes. First, advances in microprocessor and transmission technologies and the subsequent decline in the cost of transmitting information, together with the rising cost (both implicit and explicit) of transporting people, suggest that more and more demand will shift to information transmission markets. Second, advances in competition and technology within the industry have resulted in the development of many attractive services that are complementary to long-distance calling. These services include teleconferencing, videoconferencing, facsimile transmission telemarketing, reverse charge (800) services, and so on. The provision of these services offers expanded flexibility in the transmission and uses of long-distance services that will undoubtedly strengthen consumer demand for interexchange services over time. A third factor likely to stimulate the growth of demand for long distance is the decline in price of those related products and services that are complementary to long-distance telecommunications. For instance, the price of customer premises equipment (i.e., telephones, inside wiring, etc.) has fallen sharply with the deregulation of the telecommunications equipment market. This combination of underlying factors that are catalyzing long-distance demand growth will certainly facilitate firm entry and exert competitive pressure on incumbent firms. Since industry growth reduces the likelihood of firm failures, the vulnerability of potential entrants to the presence of sunk costs is mitigated. Moreover, there is growing empirical support that documents a strong and positive relationship between industry growth and firm entry.[29]

In addition to the competitive contributions of demand growth, the demand of individual inter-LATA carriers is becoming increasingly elastic.[30] As already noted, both business and residential demand is highly skewed so customers with heavy telecommunications demands will naturally be sensitive to price-quality differentials among supplier firms. Also, in an era of stable technology the "AT&T" brand name offered a consistent signal to customers regarding product and service quality. Today, however, customers are increasingly aware that rapid technological change has removed any one company's monopoly on price and quality offerings. Thus, whatever brand-name loyalty AT&T might have had as a regulated franchise monopolist appears to be depreciating rapidly in the face of competition. In a truly deregulated market, it appears that service quality and price exclusively will determine market share.

An additional factor that has increased inter-LATA carriers' price elasticity has been the ever-increasing number of competitors for the interexchange services markets. This is particularly true given that these new entrants include both resellers and "least-cost routing" firms. Resellers lease transmission capacity at low cost (in bulk) and make this capacity available to smaller customers who otherwise would not have access to high-volume discount rates. The presence of these resellers increases the incumbent firms' price elasticity in two powerful ways. First, since resellers are leasing capacity in bulk it is in their best interest to shop around among firms with transmission capacity. Second, since the resellers tend to offer rates that are quite attractive to end-users, many customers are likely to avail themselves of these attractive rates by subscribing to resellers' services. Least-cost routing companies have also recently emerged as both customers and competitors of incumbent firms. These firms provide end-user customers with a routing service whereby a subscribing customer's call is routed to its destination via the least-cost provider of the transmission at that time. As subscription to these firms grows, a larger and larger block of interexchange transmissions will become extremely price-sensitive.

Yet another catalyst to the increased price elasticity of demand facing inter-LATA carriers has been the growing awareness by customers that when the price-quality combination offered by incumbent firms is unsatisfactory, self-supply may provide an attractive alternative. That self-supply represents a viable (credible) option has already been demonstrated by the construction of private communications networks by such major businesses as Federal Express, Hewlitt Packard, and Westinghouse. In a market where all firms are free to compete along the price and quality dimensions, this viable threat of self-supply will have the dual effect of increasing the price elasticity of demand and encouraging prices that accurately reflect incremental costs.

Finally, the phased-in implementation of the equal access provisions of the Modification of Final Judgment (MFJ) ensures that all inter-LATA telecommunications firms will be provided access to the local exchange that is "equal in type, quality and price." Given the ever more similar nature of the technical quality of long-distance telecommunications, it is almost certain that market shares will increasingly be determined by price. Accordingly, the effects of the MFJ will be to increase the price elasticity of demand for inter-LATA carriers.

Why Deregulation Has Not Materialized

In preceding sections of this paper, we have demonstrated why the current policy of asymmetric regulation is economically indefensible and why a policy of deregulation appears warranted. Given the rather compelling case against the current policy and the equally compelling case for deregulation, one might expect divestiture to have resulted in a rapid transition of the public policy that is applied to this industry. This transition, however, has not materialized.

At the federal level, deregulation dockets at the Federal Communications Commission have inched nominally forward with few or no substantive policy changes forthcoming. Meanwhile, efforts to deregulate intrastate long-distance telecommunications services have for the most part been similarly unsuccessful. Outright deregulation has occurred only in one state. In short, the widespread deregulation of this industry that had been anticipated at the time of divestiture simply has not materialized. Instead, asymmetric regulation has emerged as the prevalent policy toward the inter-LATA telecommunications industry.

In this section, we explore some of the principal reasons that policymakers have been reluctant to abandon the existing regulatory controls in the inter-LATA telecommunications market. These reasons are categorized into three major groups. First, public policy officials are uncertain about the likely outcome of deregulation along several dimensions. Second, current market participants who benefit from the present policy of asymmetric regulation are engaging in strategic behavior that plays upon the regulators' uncertainty.

And third, regulators themselves often have a vested interest in maintaining regulation.

Uncertainties of Divestiture and Deregulation

Three principal sources of uncertainty have lingered in the postdivestiture period and appear to have contributed to the delay in the deregulation of long-distance telecommunications. First, during a transitional period following divestiture AT&T will retain a unique and arguably superior form of technical interconnection with the local exchange companies. It is thought by some that this unique form of access by AT&T to the local exchanges affords AT&T a competitive advantage of sufficient magnitude that successful competition between long-distance rivals is not possible. Clearly, a unique technological advantage conferred upon any one carrier will permit that firm, *ceteris paribus,* to earn some monopoly rent.

Several points should be made, however, about this particular case. First, the different types of access that are currently provided long-distance firms are temporary. In fact, the MFJ provides explicit guidelines on the conversion of local exchange end offices to equal access status. For the vast majority of customers, the equal access conversion process will be completed by September 1986. Second, the rapid demand growth and low barriers to entry that we have already discussed will act to limit any ephemeral advantage of differential access. Third, it is important to note that successful competition does not require perfect homogeneity of either firm inputs or outputs. With low-cost access to the local networks, the OCCs have been able to successfully gain market share by offering a low-priced option for long-distance service. This sort of quality-price tradeoff is at the heart of other industries that are generally thought to support vigorous competition. Fourth, while differential access may confer some competitive advantage upon AT&T, other competitive advantages have befallen the OCCs.[31] It is not at all clear how these particular firm advantages net out. Finally, a reduced charge for access to the local exchange companies is currently granted to any carrier with less than "premium" access. The value of the discount, which was set to approximate the opportunity cost of premium access, is currently 55 percent on interstate calls. Having acounted for the competitive advantage of differential access through the carrier access charge, residual regulation to account for this technical difference is redundant.

A second fear of some policymakers is that, despite divestiture of AT&T from the Bell Operating Companies, AT&T remains a natural monopoly in the provision of long-distance telecommunication services. It is sometimes argued directly that the cost structure and demand conditions are such that only a single firm is efficiently able to supply telecommunications services.[32] At other times the allusions to natural monopoly are embedded in arguments that economies of scale and scope currently prohibit effective competition, but protection of new competitors through continued regulation of the "dominant" carrier will permit these smaller rivals to ultimately achieve the economies necessary to efficiently compete.[33]

While some policymakers continue to fear that the long-distance telecommunications industry remains a natural monopoly, our assessment of technology and demand conditions (reinforced by a modest amount of empirical support)[34] is that inter-LATA telecommunications is not a naturally monopolistic industry. Despite this view, the possibility that the industry remains a natural monopoly cannot be ruled out. Indeed, given existing data and tools of analysis it is highly unlikely that a definitive answer to the natural monopoly question can be resolved *ex ante*. However, regardless of whether the industry is or is not a natural monopoly, the appropriate public policy is not asymmetric regulation. If, as seems most likely, the industry is not a natural monopoly, then asymmetric regulation yields all of the costs that were previously identified but yields none of the benefits typically ascribed to regulation. On the other hand, if the industry is a natural monopoly, then the appropriate public policy is to ban entry and regulate the franchise monpolist. This is because entry into the naturally monopolistic industry generates forgone efficiencies from reduced economies of scale and scope from the incumbent firm. Again, asymmetric regulation, which allows free entry, exacts efficiency costs on society.

A third major source of uncertainty in the minds of public policy officials arises from a concern that AT&T, while facing signfiicant competition in urban markets, will retain substantial market power in lower density rural markets. Given the lower demand in these rural markets, competitive entry may not occur for some time. Moreover, these areas are the last to be accorded the equal access provisions of the MFJ. Thus a situation that may be described as quasi-monopoly (where a firm is perceived to hold monopoly power in some geographic markets while facing substantial competition in others) is thought by some to exist.

But the quasi-monopoly problem can be dealt with in two ways. First, based on an examination of prevailing technological, entry, and demand conditions, one can make a strong argument that the apparent monopoly power enjoyed by AT&T in rural markets is illusory.[35] Accordingly, it would appear that a policy of deregulation of the inter-LATA telecommunications industry would provide the benefits of competition to both urban and rural customers. This argument, however, has not yet carried the day with policymakers. As with the natural monopoly debate, it seems unlikely that *ex ante* arguments, in this case regarding the competitive influence of potential entrants, will prevail. As a result, any proposal to allow the invisible hand to allocate long-distance telecommunications resources in urban markets must, if it is to be adopted, incorporate some mechanism to defuse the quasi-monopoly problem in rural markets.

Thus, a second policy option, known as market-based regulation, has recently been proposed.[36] This proposal would allow both a competitive allocation of resources in urban markets and simultaneously ensure that the benefits of this competition are passed on to rural customers. In essence, this proposal requires the market prices in rural (quasi-monopoly) markets be set no higher than prices of inter-LATA services in urban (competitive) areas. While the proposal is described in detail elsewhere, it can easily be shown to have several desirable characteristics. Foremost among these is that it completely eliminates any need to apply traditional rate-based regulation to any firm in the industry. By utilizing the information generated in those markets that are competitive to establish fair and reasonable rates in those markets that may not be, there is no longer any need to conduct protracted and expensive hearings to establish a company's rate base and cost of capital. Also this policy eliminates any potential for the exercise of monopoly power in the rural markets. Since prices in the rural markets are set no higher than prices in urban markets, which in turn are competitive, the policy effectively spreads the benefits of competition to rural areas.[37]

Finally note that the market-based regulation proposal eliminates the host of miscellaneous impediments to relaxed regulation in the inter-LATA telecommunications industry. Since prices in urban and rural markets would be similar, the ability to exploit or extend any extant monopoly power through predatory pricing would be eliminated. When accompanied by a single "no abandonment" rule for AT&T, market-based regulation would ensure the continued provision of high quality long-distance services for all customers at competitive prices.[38]

Strategic Uses of the Regulatory Process

A second major impediment to deregulation evolves as a (predictable) twist of the economic theories of regulation literature. This literature suggests that regulation, or more generally the powers of the state, can be used to achieve cartel-like pricing when private cartelization is unattainable. That is, regulation can be viewed by the industry as an effective substitute for cartelization. Posner (1974) notes, however, that, similar to cartels, regulatory cartelization is not likely to eliminate incentives by individual industry members not to participate. In such cases, a subset of industry participants may seek the powers of the state in enforcing "appropriate" pricing and output on nonconforming industry members. In the case at hand, the asymmetrically regulated firm is seeking to avoid the de facto umbrella pricing scheme that regulation has created. Unregulated competitors who would remain financially solvent with industry prices approximating marginal costs are currently able to capture market share by simply underbidding the regulated price (which bears little resemblance to marginal cost). Accordingly, these unregulated industry participants, who stand to gain handsomely from a continued system of asymmetric regulation, are currently actively seeking to forestall the advent of relaxed regulatory controls.[39]

This strategic use of the regulatory process has generally been designed to highlight and magnify the real (but addressable) uncertainties that exist in the postdivestiture industry. By making these uncertainties appear bigger than life, alternative long-distance carriers have effectively conjured up certain ghosts that are portrayed as real threats to a deregulated long-distance industry. First, it is argued that predatory pricing will be used by the historically dominant supplier to drive competitors from the market. Second, it is alleged that the long-standing policy goal of universal service will be frustrated by both monopolistic pricing and the inability to sustain traditional systems of cross-subsidization. Third, it is warned that deregulation will result in a geographic deaveraging of long-distance rates. And fourth, it is prophesied that the less dense rural markets will remain subject to single firm supply in the future. It is then concluded that the current system in which one firm only is subjected to traditional rate-of-return controls must be maintained as an amulet against these dire visions of telephonic disaster.

Elsewhere we critically examine these economic spirits that presently haunt deregulation proposals.[40] Invariably, we find that the threatened ghoul is extremely unlikely to materialize in a deregulated environment. Moreover, we also find that none of these ghosts could justify a policy of continued rate-based regulation even if they were to arise. Less severe policies that provide adequate safeguards while still preserving the benefits of an actively competitive marketplace are available in each case. Regardless, however, of the logic of these warnings against deregulation, the entrenched regulatory apparatus with its lengthy adjudicatory process and ample opportunities for obfuscation is currently a significant source of delay in the deregulation of long-distance telecommunications.

Regulatory Inertia and Myopia

A third set of reasons why deregulation has not yet materialized arises from regulatory inertia and myopia. These appear to be the product of a combination of self-interested regulators and the inability (or unwillingness) of these regulators to consider novel policy prescriptions that break with historical regulatory options.

The economic theory of regulation indicates that regulators are more likely to be self-interested agents than public interest maximizers. This suggests that regulators are unlikely to be the most receptive body to hear arguments in favor of deregulation, which would limit their sphere of influence. A cursory examination of the major telecommunication policy changes over the past twenty-five years tends to bear out this point. The *Hush-a-Phone* decision, which opened the door (if only slightly) for competition in telecommunications equipment, was a reversal by a federal appeals court of an earlier FCC ruling. The *MCI* decision to permit entry into private microwave transmissions began in 1963 when MCI filed a request for authorization to build a private microwave system between St. Louis and Chicago. More than seven years later, in 1971, MCI was granted final approval by the FCC to begin construction. During those seven years MCI spent $10 million in legal and regulatory expenses for authorization to build a set of telecommunications facilities that cost less than $2 million. Also, the court of appeals, not the FCC, was the ultimate force behind competition in switched-message toll service when it ruled in the *Execunet* decision that AT&T had not been granted a monopoly over long-distance services. Further complicating the effort to deregulate is the fact that unlike airline deregulation, which was carried out mainly at the federal level, deregulation of inter-LATA telecommunications must be debated before not only the FCC but also fifty state public utility commissions.

Beyond historical inertia by regulatory bodies, there appears to be a strong proclivity by policymakers to consider only polar policy alternatives that have been considered or implemented in other industries. In the case at hand, the policy options are often painted as black-and-white: either maintain rate-based regulation or completely deregulate the industry. Given the uncertainty that accompanies deregulation and the unfamiliarity of policymakers with concepts central to deregulation (such as contestability and market power), regulators are driven to retreat to the safe (albeit costly) haven of rate-of-return regulation. Alternative policy options (such as market-based regulation) have only recently begun to surface. To date, however, regulators have continued to focus primarily on more familiar options.

Summary and Conclusions

The study of regulation and its economic consequences has increased greatly over the past two decades. As a result, major insights have been gained in the theory of natural monopoly, theories of regulation, and the costs of regulation. These developments shed substantial light on public policy in the telecommunications industry, which has undergone substantial technological and structural change over the past few years. In particular, we have seen that the current regulatory policy in this industry results in some very costly misallocations of society's resources, magnifies and prolongs existing uncertainties about the merits of past policy decisions, and denies consumers the benefits of an efficient supply of telecommunications services at the lowest possible prices.

While a strong case against asymmetric rate-based regulation can be made, an equally strong case can be made for deregulation of inter-LATA telecommunication services. Our examination of entry and exit conditions as well as prevailing demand conditions indicates that deregulation of the industry would yield significant benefits to society.

Despite the likely benefits of inter-LATA telecommunications deregulation, there are several reasons that deregulation has not yet materialized. Some of these reasons arise as legitimate concerns surrounding industry structure and the evolution of industry. Other factors that have materially delayed deregulation, however, are the product of intentional manipulation and magnification of these legitimate concerns of regulators. Finally, regulatory inertia and self-imposed restrictions by regulators have needlessly protracted the deregulation of inter-LATA telecommunications.

The telecommunications industry is technologically and structurally a very different industry than it was in the not-so-distant past. While public policy has in some ways stimulated these changes, it is currently withholding the substantial benefits to consumers of a more relaxed regulatory environment. While some headway toward a rational public policy in the long-distance telecommunications industry may be won through the unceasing presentation by economists of the costs of asymmetric regulation and the benefits of deregulation, the hope of rapid movement toward deregulated inter-LATA telecommunications appears to hinge on stimulus from the courts, the legislative arena, or broad-based public support.

Notes

1. For a more complete discussion of the appropriate boundaries of regulation see McKie (1970).
2. *Munn v. Illinois*, 94 U.S. 113 (1877).
3. See J. S. Mill (1926).
4. Formally, let y be an industry's output(s) and $C(y)$ be the cost of producing y. Then the industry producing y is a natural monopoly if

    $C(y) < C(y^1) + C(y^2) + \ldots C(y^N)$ for every $y, y^1 \ldots y^N$, where $\sum_i y^i = y$.

    For a thorough treatment of the recent developments along these lines see W. W. Sharkey (1982).
5. See Baumol (1977).
6. See Baumol (1982). Also, note that it has been known for some time that in a market with a single large producer with no cost advantages over a large number

of smaller firms, the large firm will be forced by the market to price competitively or face continually declining market share. For a review of this literature see Scherer (1980).
7. See Bailey and Panzar (1981); and Bailey (1982).
8. Some of the important contributions subsequent to Stigler's seminal paper are Posner (1974), Peltzman (1976) and Weingast and Moran (1983).
9. See Averch and Johnson (1962); and for a review of subsequent literature, see Baumol and Klevorick (1970).
10. See for instance Mayo (1984); and Primeaux (1977).
11. See Sweeney (1981); Caves and Roberts (1975); and White (1972).
12. In order to split the telephone industry between the supposed natural monopoly of local service and the competitive long-distance business, regulators have defined geographic areas known as LATAs, which is an abbreviation for "local access transport area." There are 161 LATAs in the United States, and they generally comprise a major city and the surrounding rural areas. The local telephone companies provide telephone service within LATAs, while the long-distance companies provide service between LATAs.
13. These firms include those with their own long-distance transmission capacity, collectively known as the OCCs (other common carriers); firms that lease transmission capacity for resale purposes (resellers); and firms that specialize in long-distance transmission of data.
14. Even if departures from marginal cost pricing were necessary, the extraordinarily high markup of (the relatively elastic) long-distance services compared to (the relatively price-inelastic) local service is directly contrary to the literature on quasi-optimal pricing. See Baumol and Bradford (1970).
15. MacAvoy and Robinson (1983) make this point more forcefully. Specifically, they argue that observed entry by OCCs is entirely motivated by the umbrella pricing created by regulation.
16. For more discussion on this point see Haring (1984).
17. For a similar argument in the antitrust arena, see Baumol and Ordover (1985).
18. *Notice of Inquiry*, CC Docket No. 83-1147, October 1983, p. 10, par. 16.
19. See Kaserman and Mayo (1984).
20. See Garfinkle (1983).
21. Sunk costs are those costs that a firm cannot recoup if it were to withdraw from a market. Accordingly, the presence and magnitude of sunk costs is a critical determinant of the height of barriers to entry into an industry. For a generic discussion of the relevance of sunk costs in the entry decision, see Baumol and Willig (1981).
22. See *Issues in Domestic Telecommunications: Directions for National Policy*, National Telecommunications and Information Administration, U.S. Department of Commerce (1985), 91.
23. We shall see momentarily that the combination of advances in technology and a broadening of the demand side of telecommunications has also increased the product market fungibility of telecommunications capital.
24. For an in-depth analysis of the economic characteristics of these technologies, see Katz and Willig (1983).
25. See Brock (1981).
26. Allocation of Frequencies in Bands Above 890 Mc. (Above 890) 27 F.C.C. 359 (1959), modified, 29 F.C.C. 825 (1960).

27. *The Dilemma of Telecommunications Policy,* Telecommunications Industry Task Force, 1977.
28. See, for example, "Telecommunications: Everybody's Favorite Growth Business," *Business Week,* 11 October 1982.
29. See Hause and DuRietz (1984).
30. Within the context of the dominant firm-competitive fringe model it has been firmly established that as the price elasticity of demand for an individual industry member increases, the market power of the firm decreases, *ceteris paribus.* See, for example, Landes and Posner (1981).
31. For instance, the OCCs may selectively enter or not enter particular market segments at will. AT&T, on the other hand, is obligated to serve all markets. This relative flexibility of entry and exit provided to the OCCs is clearly a competitive advantage. Similarly, the OCCs face little or no regulatory restraints on pricing flexibility. AT&T must undertake lengthy cumbersome and expensive rate hearings to justify price changes. Also, the OCCs are free to leave areas that prove unprofitable whenever they choose.
32. For example, see Charnes, Cooper, and Sueyoshi (1985).
33. See Johnson (1985, 9-22).
34. See Evans and Heckman (1983).
35. Katz and Willig (1983) make such a case.
36. See Kaserman and Mayo (in press).
37. The merits of this proposal rest upon the absence of any substantial geographic differences in the costs of providing the inter-LATA portion of an interexchange call. For discussion of this condition, see Kaserman and Mayo (in press).
38. This should not be construed as a general endorsement of restrictions on firm exit. Indeed, restrictions of that nature generally produce the undesirable consequence of raising barriers to entry. In the case at hand, however, the rule would not apply to potential or new entrants but only to AT&T, whose service offerings are universal. Moreover, this recommendation, which fosters the continuation of asymmetric regulation, should be phased out as the ability of competitive firms to provide service where demand exists is demonstrated.
39. For example, see *Joint Petition for Expedited Rulemaking,* GTE Sprint Communications Corporation, et al. before the Federal Communications Commission, 17 June 1985, 21.
40. See Kaserman and Mayo (1986).

References

Averch, H. A., and Johnson, L. L. 1962. Behavior of the firm under regulatory constraint. *American Economic Review* 52 (December): 1052-69.
Bailey, E. E. 1982. Deregulation of contestable markets: Application of theory to public policy. In *Deregulation: Appraisal before the fact,* edited by T. G. Gies and W. Sichel. University of Michigan.
Bailey, E. E., and Panzar, J. C. 1981. The contestability of airline markets during the transition to deregulation. *Law and Contemporary Problems* 44 (Winter): 125-45.
Baumol, W. J. 1977. On the proper cost tests for natural monopoly in a multiproduct industry. *American Economic Review* 67 (December): 809-22.
———. 1982. Contestable markets: An uprising in the theory of industry structure. *American Economic Review* 72 (March): 1-15.

Baumol, W. J., and Bradford, D. F. 1970. Optimal departures from marginal cost pricing. *American Economic Review* 60 (June): 265–83.
Baumol, W. J., and Klevorick, A. 1970. Input choices and rate-of-return regulation: An overview and discussion. *Bell Journal of Economics and Management Science* (Autumn): 163–90.
Baumol, W. J., and Ordover, J. 1985. Uses of antitrust to subvert competition. *Journal of Law and Economics* 28, no. 2 (May): 247–65.
Baumol, W. J., Panzar, J. C., and Willig, R. 1982. *Contestable markets and the theory of industry structure.* New York: Harcourt Brace Jovanovich.
Baumol, W. J., and Willig, R. D. 1981. Fixed costs, sunk costs, entry barriers and sustainability of monopoly. *The Quarterly Journal of Economics* (August): 405–31.
Bonbright, J. C. 1961. *Principles of public utility rates.* New York: Columbia University Press.
Brock, G. 1981. *The telecommunications industry.* Cambridge: Harvard University Press.
Caves, R., and Roberts, M., eds. 1975. *Regulating the product.* Cambridge, MA: Ballinger.
Charnes, A., Cooper, W. W., and Sueyoshi, T. 1985. A goal programming-constrained regression review of the Bell System breakup. College of Business Administration, University of Texas, Austin. May. Mimeo.
Cournot, Augustin. 1960. *Researches into the mathematical principles of the theory of wealth.* Translated by N. T. Bacon. New York: August M. Kelly. Originally published as *Recherches sur les principes mathématiques de la théorie des richesses.* Paris: Hachette, 1838.
Dupuit, Jules. 1844. De la mesure de l'utilité des travaux publics. *Annales des Ponts et Chausses.* Reprinted in *Readings in welfare economics,* edited by K. Arrow and T. Scitovsky. Homewood, IL: Irwin, 1969.
Evans, D. S., and Heckman, J. J. 1983. Natural monopoly. In *Breaking up Bell: Essays on industrial organization and regulation,* ed. D. S. Evans. New York: North Holland.
Garfinkle, L. 1983. Interexchange telecommunications markets in transition. *Public Utilities Fortnightly* 112 (21 July): 26–33.
Haring, J. 1984. Implications of asymmetric regulation for competition policy analysis. Federal Communications Commission. OPP Working Paper Series. December.
Hause, J. C., and G. DuRietz. 1984. Entry, industry growth, and microdynamics of industry supply. *Journal of Political Economy* 92 (August): 733–57.
Johnson, B. 1985. Direct Testimony, Docket 6095 Before the Texas Public Utility Commission, filed May 1985.
Kahn, A. E. 1984. The new steps in telecommunications regulation and research. *Public Utilities Fortnightly* (19 July): 13–18.
Kaserman, D. L., and Mayo, J. W. 1984. Issues and alternatives in the post-divestiture telecommunications industry. Department of Economics, University of Tennessee, Knoxville. January.
———. In press. Market based regulation of a quasi-monopoly: A transition policy for telecommunications. *Policy Studies Journal.*
———. 1986. The ghosts of deregulated telecommunications: An essay by exorcists. *Journal of Policy and Management* (Fall): 84–92.
Katz, M. L., and Willig, R. D. 1983. The case for freeing AT&T. *Regulation* (July/August): 43–49.

Landes, W., and Posner, R. 1981. Market power in antitrust cases. *Harvard Law Review* 94 (March): 937–95.
Leibenstein, H. 1966. Allocative efficiency vs. X-efficiency. *American Economic Review* 56 (June): 392–415.
MacAvoy, P. W., and Robinson, K. 1983. Winning by losing: The AT&T settlement and its impact on telecommunications. *Yale Journal on Regulation* 1, no. 1:1–43.
McKie, J. W. 1970. Regulation and the free market: The problem of boundaries. *Bell Journal of Economics and Management Science* 1, no. 1 (Spring).
Mayo, J. W. 1984. Multiproduct monopoly, regulation, and firm costs. *Southern Economic Journal* (July): 208–18.
Mill, J. S. 1926. *Principles of political economy*. London: Longmans.
Peltzman, S. 1976. Toward a more general theory of regulation. *Journal of Law and Economics* 19 (August): 211–40.
Posner, R. A. 1974. Theories of economic regulation. *Bell Journal of Economics and Management Science* 5 (Autumn): 335–58.
Primeaux, W. 1977. An assessment of X-efficiency gained through competition. *Review of Economics and Statistics* (February): 105–8.
Scherer, F. M. 1980. *Industry market structure and economic performance*. 2d ed. Chicago: Rand McNally.
Sharkey, W. W. 1982. *The theory of natural monopoly*. Cambridge: Cambridge University Press.
Stigler, G. 1971. The theory of economic regulation. *Bell Journal of Economics and Management Science* 2 (Spring): 3–21.
Sweeney, G. 1981. Adoption of cost saving innovations by a regulated firm. *American Economic Review* (June): 437–47.
Weingast, B. R., and Moran, M. J. 1983. Bureaucratic discretion or congressional control? Regulatory policymaking by the Federal Trade Commission. *Journal of Political Economy* 91, no. 5 (October): 765–800.
White, L. J. 1972. Quality variations when prices are regulated. *Bell Journal of Economics* (Autumn): 425–36.

9. Pricing Achievements in Large Companies

Kenneth G. Elzinga

THE RETAIL establishment of Lee's Sports & Hobbies in Kalamazoo, Michigan once had a very simple pricing objective. When new merchandise arrived, the invoice or packing slip revealed the unit cost of each item in the shipment. This amount was divided by 0.6 to derive the retail price of the product. Thus a fishing reel that had an invoice price of $12.00 would retail at $20.00 (its price tag would read $19.95). A model airplane with a wholesale cost of 60 cents would retail for a dollar. Lee's had a company objective to make a 40 percent markup. Any clerk or stock boy employed in that establishment in the 1950s and 1960s became acquainted with this pricing policy.

As a young employee of this store and one who spent several years implementing this cost-plus policy, one can imagine the attraction I had in graduate school to an article then being widely discussed about the objectives of large companies in the setting of their prices. This article appeared in the *American Economic Review* in 1958, was authored by Robert F. Lanzillotti, and was drawn from a larger study done by Lanzillotti with A. D. H. Kaplan and Joel B. Dirlam for the Brookings Institution.[1] The purpose of the article was to uncover the motives behind the pricing practices of large corporations.[2]

The theme of the article was that large companies selected a target rate of output and added a markup to their costs at this output such that the firm earned a target rate of return on investment. The administering of prices in big business, in other words, was done somewhat the way pricing was done at Lee's Sports & Hobbies, only in a more sophisticated way.

Paul Samuelson once wrote of the bliss of being young and studying macro-

Note: The author appreciates and wishes to acknowledge the input of Christopher P. Bolster, Keith J. Crocker, David E. Mills, and Derek A. Neal. The usual disclaimer applies.

economics in the late 1930s and early 1940s;[3] the parallel is only slightly stretched to say that bliss it was to be studying industrial organization at Michigan State University in the late 1960s. In my own course of study, I encountered, *par ordre alphabetique,* Walter Adams, Joel B. Dirlam, Robert F. Lanzillotti, Thomas G. Moore, Willard F. Mueller, Thomas Saving, and George Ward Stocking. This faculty listing does not include my teacher Abba Lerner, whose index of monopoly power continues to draw the attention of I.O. economists. No other university offered such a collection. The place was intellectually abuzz with ideas and controversy, of which Lanzillotti and Dirlam's work on pricing was an important part.

The methodology used in the Lanzillotti pricing paper was unusual at the time and would be even more unusual today. To find out the "specific objectives upon which business firms base pricing decisions,"[4] the author asked the executives responsible for corporate pricing. In particular, Lanzillotti interviewed corporate officials in twenty cooperating companies. The companies were Alcoa, American Can, A&P Tea Company, DuPont, General Electric, General Foods, General Motors, Goodyear, Gulf, International Harvester, Johns-Manville, Kennecott Cooper, Kroger, National Steel, Sears, Standard Oil of Indiana, Standard Oil of New Jersey, Swift, Union Carbide, and U.S. Steel. Each of these firms at the time was among the top two hundred corporations in the country and many were in the top one hundred.

The thesis of Lanzillotti's paper—that corporations did not have as their financial objective the maximization of profits—understandably attracted the attention of economists. Lanzillotti wrote that the most common pricing objective of these companies was instead to achieve a company-determined target return on investment. No more, no less. Some firms stressed the goal of stabilizing prices and margins. A few had objectives of maintaining a target market share or meeting the prices of their rivals.

Not only did most companies neglect to cite profit maximizing as their objective but they had no single *maximizing* objective. They claimed to be pursuing multiple goals. The article's findings did not seem to fit congenially with economic orthodoxy.

Lanzillotti conceded that what he was told may not have squared with economic reality. He knew that the business executives he interviewed might have been engaging in strategic misrepresentation; or possibly they may have been unable to translate what they were doing into the nomenclature of the professional economist; or they might have been confused by the inquiry itself. But Lanzillotti did not adopt any of these explanations. What made the Lanzillotti article notable and provocative was his conclusion that major U.S. corporations selected a standard volume of output and priced at a margin that would generate a company-selected target rate of return on investment for the enterprise.

This discretion to select their targets Lanzillotti elsewhere called the "plenary power to set prices within a considerable range." Understanding that corporations target their output and rate of return, he added, would focus attention directly "on the fact that our big corporations are interested *in and have the economic power to make administrative decisions that will fully utilize, or underutilize, industrial capacity as necessary to meet profit objectives"* (emphasis in original).[5]

The thesis of "Pricing Objectives In Large Companies" had tentacles that extended in several directions. It was viewed as an attack on the conventional theory of the firm, which held that firms, responding to market forces, are single-minded profit maximizers. If firms target their rates of return or have multiple goals, this places limits on the theory that firms unabashedly maximize profits.

At the microeconomic level, the article's implications questioned the value of demand and supply analysis. If firms shoot for volume targets and do not change their aim in the face of demand and cost fluctuations, market clearing prices do not emerge and their virtues are not secured.

At the macroeconomic level, the article was viewed as an attack on the usefulness of conventional economic tools to control aggregate economic activity. If firms are able to target their rates of return irrespective of demand and supply forces, fiscal and monetary forces would be handicapped in reducing inflation or inducing economic growth.

At the business school level, the article provided a new description of the pricing process. Lanzillotti argued for a revised sequence: the investment decision became a part of the pricing decision for the firm; the costing of a product became a function of price policy. Business schools would have to learn how to teach the selection and attainment of target rates of return or to instruct in strategies to maintain a firm's market share, at least in serving those students who would take jobs with *Fortune* 500 firms.

Because of these implications, the Lanzillotti article did not go unnoticed or without comment. A later issue of the *American Economic Review* contained responses to Lanzillotti by such industrial organization luminaries as M. A. Adelman and Alfred E. Kahn.[6]

Their objections need not be recounted at length. Adelman confined himself to Lanzillotti's observations on the A&P company. Kahn, whose comment was longer, offered his own exegesis of the responses given by management to Lanzillotti and his colleagues on the Brookings project. Kahn's interpretation was that the responses were consistent with that of "pricing to maximize profits, in a meaningful sense" and that the prices also reflected market forces.

Objectives versus Achievements

With the passage of almost three decades, it would be informative to replicate in its entirety the Kaplan-Dirlam-Lanzillotti study to learn of any changes in the pricing objectives of these companies. The objectives of this paper are more modest.

Since the Brookings study argued that the companies surveyed had control over their rates of return (as Lanzillotti put it, "If we are to speak of 'administered' decisions in the large firm, it is perhaps more accurate to speak of

Table 9.1. ROR on investment (after taxes)

Company	1947–55 Average	1947–55 Range	1960–84 Average	1960–84 Range	Designated target ROR
Alcoa	13.8	7.8–18.7	9.1	.3–21.7	10
American Can	11.6	9.6–14.7	8.8	−14.0–13.7	
A&P	13.0	9.7–18.8	.8	−65.3–13.0	
DuPont	25.9	19.6–34.1	14.3	7.2–24.3	
General Electric	21.4	18.4–26.6	16.6	11.1–20.5	20
General Foods[a]	12.2	8.9–15.7	16.1	11.2–18.6	
General Motors	26.0	19.9–37.0	16.2	−4.1–26.8	20
Goodyear	13.3	9.2–16.1	10.8	6.5–13.1	
Gulf	12.6	10.7–16.7	10.7	8.4–17.1	
International Harvester[b]	8.9	4.9–11.9	−17.3	−370.6–17.9	10
Johns-Manville[c]	14.9	10.7–19.6	8.8	−7.7–14.5	15
Kennecott[d]	16.0	9.3–20.9	8.5	−.4–16.0	
Kroger	12.1	9.7–16.1	12.2	6.6–17.5	
National Steel[e]	12.1	7.0–17.4	5.4	−36.7–15.6	
Sears Roebuck	5.4	1.6–10.7	13.0	8.0–15.7	
Std. Oil/Ind.[f]	10.4	7.9–14.4	12.6	6.6–21.3	
Std. Oil/NJ[g]	16.0	12.0–18.9	14.6	9.8–22.5	
Swift[h]	6.9	3.9–11.1	7.5	3.1–16.2	
Union Carbide	19.2	13.5–24.3	12.2	1.5–21.5	18
U.S. Steel	10.3	7.6–14.8	5.3	−18.5–17.9	8

[a] Data available for only twenty-three years.
[b] Now Navistar.
[c] Now the Manville Corp.
[d] Now owned by Standard Oil of Ohio. Data available through 1979.
[e] Now National Intergroup.
[f] Now Amoco.
[g] Now Exxon.
[h] Now Swift Independent. Swift & Company was acquired by Esmark in 1973. The meatpacking line of business was spun-off and reorganized as Swift Independent in 1983. Data on Swift available only through 1972.

administered *profits* rather than administered *prices"*),[7] it would be appropriate to examine the rates of return of the same companies since the study ended. From this one might ascertain: (1) the extent to which the twenty companies in the sample continued to "administer" or "target" the rates of return that Kaplan-Dirlam-Lanzillotti observed, and (2) whether those among the twenty that specifically designated a target rate of return as the foundation of their pricing policies have been able to meet that target. Lanzillotti's interest was in the pricing *objectives* of large companies. The passage of time permits us to examine the pricing *achievements* of the same companies. A convincing portrayal of the plenary power of these firms and the seriousness of their targeting efforts would be the twenty firms continuing over time to meet the objectives they purported to set for themselves.

Table 9.1 is a partial replication of data from table 1 in the Lanzillotti study. Columns (1) and (2) portray the rate of return on stockholder investment (after taxes) for the companies during the period 1947–55, the time frame of the original study. The table also depicts an updating of the figures, where available, for the same firms. Columns (3) and (4) list their rates of return for the twenty-five years of the period 1960–84.[8]

A perusal of table 9.1 indicates that most of the twenty companies received a lower rate of return in later years as compared to the profits they targeted or endeavored to administer during the 1947–55 period. The average rate of return for the twenty firms in the Lanzillotti study was 14.1 percent; the average rate of return for the same firms revisited was only 9.3 percent. In the period 1947–55, not one firm in Lanzillotti's sample had a fiscal year with negative returns. Eight of the twenty sustained losses at some point during more recent years. If companies were targeting or administering their rates of return, then either something happened in more recent years to provoke them to target lower rates or their plenary power has been inadequate for the task of realizing their aspirations.

Several companies in the original Lanzillotti study indicated that they pursued designated target rates of return as their principal pricing goal. The companies are: Alcoa, General Electric, General Motors, International Harvester, Johns-Manville, Union Carbide and United States Steel. Their target rates are recorded in the last column of table 9.1.

Note that no company among this group met its target during the period 1960–84. Alcoa had a designated target of 10 percent; it narrowly fell short. General Elecric and General Motors, the most avid targeters in the group at 20 percent, failed to average 17 percent during this period. International Harvester, with a target of 10 percent, lost money in such huge amounts that its average profit rate was negative for the interval examined. Johns-Manville, with a goal of at least 15 percent, did not achieve a 10 percent rate of return.

Union Carbide fell considerably short of its target, earning 12 percent instead of its objective of 18 percent. Even the firm with the most modest target was unsuccessful: U.S. Steel averaged a rate of return of 5.3 percent during the period although its goal was 8 percent. These target-return firms had an average objective of over 14 percent. Their collective effort of less than 8 percent is well short of the target.

Some goals change over time. A professor may aspire to become a dean. A housewife may decide to become a CPA. An entertainer may seek political office. Type A personalities may opt for more leisure. And conceivably a corporation could change its target, choosing to make lower profits. Perhaps a detailed study of these firms would reveal that they strategically and willfully lowered their target rates of return to levels below their original objectives. But why?

For a corporation to fail to meet an objective and then to settle for less also is consistent with the hypothesis that prices and profits are so powerfully influenced by market forces that firms cannot always systematically determine their own fate.

It requires imagination to think of either International Harvester or Johns-Manville (as of 1981, Manville Corporation) as masters of their fate. Due to litigation involving asbestos liabilities, Manville and twenty of its subsidiaries filed for Chapter 11 bankruptcy reorganization in August 1982. International-Harvester flirted with bankruptcy, a far cry from any corporation's objective, and has now shed the line of commerce that once was its forte: farm equipment. Shortly after the Lanzillotti study was completed, the firm's misdirected programs left it with enormous debt. In one four-year period, International-Harvester lost approximately $3 billion. With its farm equipment business now sold to Tenneco, the firm founded by Cyrus McCormick was reborn in January 1986 under the name Navistar.

Even in the case of General Motors from the 1970s on, to cast it as a firm boldly setting its own course on pricing, profits, and market share policy is to unfairly portray its role in the automobile industry. GM is disciplined by demand and supply forces that it no longer controls.

The General Motors that Lanzillotti ably studied and described using his administered profits framework in an earlier version of Walter Adams's *Structure of American Industry* is not the GM of today.[9] Parenthetically, Lanzillotti's description of GM squares with another, recently provided by General Motors' board member H. Ross Perot:

> General Motors and the entire American automobile industry had a big respite from competition . . . it got so bad that they tried to get divisions to compete with one another—Chevrolet compete with Pontiac, Olds-

mobile with Buick, and so on and so forth. Now we've got a whole generation of people who think that's what competition is. And I don't like that, and I say "Fellows, that's intramural sports." I said "You don't even tackle there, you just touch the guy. . . . Now the Japanese have showed up, and they're competing professionally. We've got to compete professionally with them."[10]

Competing professionally for GM, of course, now entails rent-seeking activity through the pursuit of government import protection and government imposed fuel economy and safety regulations. But without voluntary import agreements and given unfettered market competition, General Motors' ability to "target" its course would seem to be small indeed. Likewise, to attribute significant pricing power to either of the two steel companies in Lanzillotti's sample, sans import protection, is unwarranted (at least in today's market).

In the summary table of the Lanzillotti paper, A&P was listed as having its principal goal that of increasing market share. If this was A&P's goal, its aspirations fell short of reality. Indeed, few companies could show such a disparity between objectives and achievements. Ironically, the year the Lanzillotti paper appeared saw A&P's postwar share of the grocery business peak. In 1958, the company had 11.1 percent of the U.S. grocery business. By 1982, that figure had dropped to 1.7 percent.[11]

Kroger, the other grocery retailer among the twenty firms sampled by Lanzillotti, listed its primary goal as maintaining its market share. But in many areas it has expanded its market share, ranking first or second in eleven of the thirteen food-marketing territories in which it operates. Kroger has been more successful than A&P in expanding market share. But because of competitive pressures, even it withdrew in the 1970s from several metropolitan market areas.[12] And, as one student of the firm has described, Kroger has been bested by regional chains in markets in which it invested heavily to enter.[13]

Swift listed its principal goal as the maintenance of its market share in livestock buying and meat packing. It was hardly successful. On the heels of Swift's stated objective, meat packing was transformed by the westward-moving location of new plants that put them closer to cattle feeding operations, the innovation of boxed beef (a cost-saving technique where the packer produced primal and subprimal cuts, sealed the cuts in vacuum-pack bags, and shipped the beef in boxes), and the move to nonunion labor. Swift initially was largely bypassed on each of these fronts by several other packing houses, notably Iowa Beef Packing Co. Swift was acquired by Esmark and then spun-off. In its reconstituted form as Swift Independent it has returned to the ranks of the leading beef packers. In pork slaughtering and processing, the Swift

Pricing Achievements in Large Companies 173

story was much the same as in beef. Until the firm was reorganized, its master labor contract and less efficient plants made it a laggard in this subsector of meat packaging. Even now Swift Independent faces keen competition in the commodity cuts of pork packaging from Iowa Beef's planned entry into pork, from Con Agra's entry through the acquisition of several Armour plants, and from efficient regional sellers.[14]

Kennecott listed as its primary goal the "stabilization of prices." The company's track record in the copper industry indicates that if it ever had the plenary power to determine copper prices, it does not today. Copper prices are subject to worldwide forces of supply and demand that have a volatility Kennecott is unable to contain. Standard Oil of Ohio, now owned by British Petroleum, has fared no better with Kennecott after acquiring its assets. Hindsight reveals the acquisition of Kennecott—purchased in 1981 for $1.77 billion—to have been a major management blunder. It has yielded its corporate parent $700 million in operating losses.

In short, the track records of these companies cast doubt on their long-run ability to sustain target rates of return—unless of course the targets have been changed by management or corporate boards since the time of the Kaplan-Dirlam-Lanzillotti study. The evidence in table 9.1 suggests that these firms' achievements seldom square with their originally stated objectives.

Accounting Data and Administered Prices

It has been claimed that a franchisee may keep four different sets of books: one for viewing by the IRS; one for viewing by the franchiser; one for viewing by the partner; and one for running the business. There is very little discussion of this phenomenon by the manufacturing and retailing respondents in the Lanzillotti survey data. It is not clear whether the accounting targets and goals that the respondents claimed were influential in the operation of their firms are those reflected in the published accounting data of their firms or in other sources of operating data.

Economists have long harbored suspicions about the work of accountants (colleagues in accounting inform me that the wariness is reciprocated). Kenneth Boulding referred to economic profits and accounting profits as "uncongenial twins,"[15] and recent research in economics has further underscored the uncongeniality.[16] Since the Lanzillotti article appeared, economists have become increasingly skeptical of the economic content of published accounting records of the sort on which the firms in the study apparently base their targets.

This update of the Lanzillotti data entailed dividing each company's annual net income by its average stockholder investment for every year in the twenty-five-year interval. Most of the data were taken from *Moody's Industrial Reports*. By taking the average of stockholder investment at the end of a current year and the end of the year preceding (from 31 December 1964 to 31 December 1965, for example), the corporation's rate of return is less affected should there have been a significant difference in stockholder investment at the start or close of a fiscal year. Stockholder investment can rise or fall during the year, and the presumption is that any income the firm receives is earned over the course of the year, not on the first day or the last.

This definition of rate of return was chosen to replicate the Lanzillotti taxonomy, which itself was drawn in large part from data collected by the Federal Trade Commission (FTC).[17] The FTC defined "net income" as "the profits of the companies after provisions for Federal income and all other income taxes. In some cases, however, the reported net income was adjusted in order to reflect more accurately the results of operations during the years under study and to achieve statistical comparability between companies." "Stockholders' investment" was defined as "The rates of return in this report were computed on the average of the investment at the beginning and end of each year. The stockholders' investment as used in computing the rates of return in this report consists of the capital stock outstanding, paid-in or other capital surplus, earned surplus, surplus reserves, and minority interest in capital stock and surplus, less any reported appreciation."

A spot check of the FTC data showed that some of its figures did not square with the company source data, although the discrepancies generally seemed to be small. Some of the differences may involve judgment calls on the handling of certain nonrecurring or extraordinary financial items or adjustments made in one source but not picked up in later years by the other. The resulting data, no matter how refined, are only crude indicators of the rates of return of the sample firms.

There are other rate-of-return measures that could be tabulated and compared intertemporally for the twenty firms. Rates of return on assets, rates of return on sales, or rates of return to equity plus long-term debt are alternative measures of profitability. Possibly by these definitions one might demonstrate "plenary power" or a greater measure of "destiny control" than the returns to stockholders' investment that the 1960–84 figures in table 9.1 portray.

But as intertemporal measures of corporate profits all of these have their flaws. To learn more accurately how stockholders fared one should examine a company's dividends and share appreciation (if any) over time. A track record based on the combination of these two variables is more informative of a company's profitability than the accounting records shown in table 9.1. But such figures would deviate from the targets and objectives about which Lanzillotti heard. If managers of the twenty firms were targeting their performance on the basis of published accounting data, they were using an elastic yardstick.

Profit Maximizing versus Environmental Adaptation

In one sense, Lanzillotti's finding that business firms reject profit maximization as their motivator accords with economic theory. As Armen Alchian explained almost four decades ago, profit maximization is *"meaningless* as a guide to specifiable action."[18] Only realized positive profits determine the success, indeed the survival, of a business enterprise. The success of a company, Alchian argued, is a function of two phenomena: chance and the ability of the firm to adapt itself to its environment.

In this context, setting targets either for market shares or for rates of return might not conflict with profit maximizing. Targets may be the code words business managers use in specifying adaptive behavior. Business firms that set target rates of return, buy their advertising to achieve a fixed ratio of expected sales, derive their resale price through a set markup, woodenly follow the prices of rivals, or follow various other rules of thumb are adapting, for better or for worse, to their business environment. As I have shown, both in terms of accounting returns and actual business survival, some of the firms in the Lanzillotti sample of twenty adapted better than others.

It is not surprising that targeting became a popular business strategy in the 1950s and 1960s; the pricing and output decision calculus of prosperous firms will be copied by others who seek to emulate their success.[19] Nothing succeeds like success, at least until the business conditions and the attendant rules of thumb that enabled that success change. Imitative behavior is consistent with the orthodox theory of the business firm. However, when or if a firm selects targets (or objectives or rules of thumb) that no longer square with its economic environment, the firm's achievements will vary from its objectives. In some cases, firms that fail to change their "targets" will fail. Others survive and prosper by rejecting the targets, conventions, and rules of thumb that may have been trustworthy in an earlier environment.

Lee's Sports & Hobbies found that in the face of competition from discount stores it could no longer target its prices at the old markup. Its objective of a 40 percent markup led to the achievement of unsold inventory. Lee's, like those in the Lanzillotti sample who have survived and prospered, changed by abandoning its target.

In this sense, the experience of Lee's may be a microcosm of a broader phenomenon in retailing. Scherer reports a study of a simple wholesale cost markup rule that once enabled Cyert and March to predict (to the penny) the retail prices (albeit not necessarily the final transaction prices) of 188 out of

197 randomly selected pieces of merchandise sold by a prominent department store. Scherer adds that a followup study was less successful in predicting retail prices.[20] This further suggests that if a firm is going to operate by targets, moving market forces will require them to move their targets. In fact, one of the greatest pricing success stories in retailing involves a twist on the target pricing studied by Kaplan, Dirlam and Lanzillotti. In a story on Charles Lazarus, the founder of Toys "R" Us, a former colleague described Lazarus's pricing strategy:

> From the start, he approached retailing differently from most of his competitors, especially when buying and pricing merchandise. For example, many retailers set their selling price based on what they must pay wholesale. Charles never did that. . . . He would first say, "I can sell this product in great volumes at a certain price." He would *then* decide at what price he had to buy it.[21]

What Kaplan-Dirlam-Lanzillotti were describing as the mechanics of targeting is consistent with the orthodox economizing behavior of the firm. The differences in interfirm behavior Lanzillotti recorded in his sample reveal not so much differences in objectives or goals as variations in adaptive behavior to differing market circumstances. The company that selected the lower rate of return as its target may have the same motivation as the one proclaiming a loftier rate-of-return objective. All that may differ is the competitiveness of the particular market environment or, it appears from the Lanzillotti sample of firms, some businesses' faulty perception of that environment and their ability to shape it.

Much as students adopt different study habits to improve their grades in a class, businesses follow different methods in trying to improve their economic performance. Some students find over time that their study methods were faulty. Some of Lanzillotti's twenty firms found their targeting objectives to be unattainable in their economic environment.

Pricing in Theory and Pricing in Practice

Just as consumer preferences change, so do the tastes of economists. The economist's interest in the corporate pricing process, which was at the root of studies by Kaplan, Dirlam and Lanzillotti, as well as by Hall and Hitch, John Blair, and others who participated at that time in the discussion of price formation, yielded the spotlight to a new act that first opened in 1951. I refer of course to Joe Bain's statistical linkage of market structure and profit performance that sought to skirt the internal process of corporate pricing policies.[22] In the 1960s, what Scherer has called a "torrent" of articles on market structure-performance correlations was produced and studied by industrial organization economists. For a while, it appeared to be the only show in town.[23]

What remained of the economist's focus on pricing conduct was redirected primarily to discussions of limit pricing (here again the intellectual debt to Bain is significant). Limit pricing fit more comfortably within the maximizing paradigm that seemed to have been threatened by the administered pricing/administered profits literature. For this reason, economic theorists could be relieved. Moreover, the potential of limit pricing models to yield market failure situations seemed to satisfy many antitrusters. Interest in the pricing process itself and the pricing objectives of corporations had peaked.

Today a keen interest in business pricing has returned, but in a form scarcely recognizable by those who earlier had worried about the mechanics and objectives of corporate pricing. As structure-performance studies began to ebb in popularity, tastes shifted toward price as a strategic variable; in a sense modern I.O. returned to its roots in the Bertrand and Cournot duopoly models. The mechanics of how General Motors prices is out; what is in is the pricing strategy of unnamed duopolists with countable strategies operating in a world of instantaneous regime changes.

One may hope that scholars who read and participate in the contemporary oligopoly pricing literature will inquire: What does this have to do with understanding adaptive behavior in a modern market economy? And as tastes change the richness and diversity that inheres in the study of corporate pricing may be rediscovered.

The legacy of the Lanzillotti study is that it acquainted economists with an important variation in the pricing strategy of a corporation's adaptive behavior. Economists who work with the conventional theory of markets where profit-maximizing firms are assumed would be otherwise unaware of the richness and diversity in the pricing decision. Economists who work in the pure theory of oligopoly pricing also may overlook the empirical intricacies of the pricing decision. It is the patient digging of the institutionalist that informs and keeps oligopoly theory on track. If what Scherer calls the Tycho Brahe approach to industrial organization studies resumes a place of stature in industrial organization,[24] scholars again will turn to studies such as *Pricing In Big Business,* will learn from them, and will extend them in new directions.

Notes

1. Robert F. Lanzillotti, "Pricing Objectives in Large Companies," *American Economic Review* 48 (December 1958): 921–40; and *Pricing in Big Business* (Washington, D.C.: Brookings Institution, 1958).

2. Secondarily, the mechanics of how such firms priced their products was described.
3. As recorded in William Breit and Roger L. Ransom, *The Academic Scribblers,* rev. ed. (Chicago: Dryden Press, 1982), 109.
4. Lanzillotti, "Pricing Objectives," 921.
5. Robert F. Lanzillotti, "Why Corporations Find It Necessary to 'Administer' Prices," *Challenge* (January 1960): 48.
6. M. A. Adelman, "Pricing Objectives in Large Companies: Comment," *American Economic Review* 49 (September 1959): 669–70; Alfred E. Kahn, "Pricing Objectives in Large Companies: Comment," *American Economic Review* 49 (September 1959): 670–78. Lanzillotti's reply appears at 679–87.
7. Lanzillotti, "Pricing Objectives," 938; emphasis in original.
8. The data were gathered from *Report of the FTC on Rates of Return in Selected Manufacturing Industries* (various issues) and *Moody's Handbook of Common Stocks.* Further details on the calculation methodology follow later in the paper.
9. See Robert F. Lanzillotti, "The Automobile Industry," in *The Structure of American Industry,* edited by W. Adams, 4th ed. (New York: Macmillan, 1971), 256–301, esp. 279–80.
10. "H. Ross Perot Sees EDS Evolving into GM's Brain, Nervous System," *Washington Post,* 7 July 1985, K7.
11. Bruce W. Marion, *The Organization and Performance of the U.S. Food System* (Lexington, MA: Lexington Books, 1986), 332.
12. Ibid., 340.
13. Bill Saporito, "Kroger, The King of Supermarketing," *Fortune,* 21 February 1983, 78, 80.
14. Marion, *U.S. Food System,* 127, 135–36.
15. Kenneth E. Boulding, "Economics and Accounting: The Uncongenial Twins," *Studies in Accounting Theory,* edited by W. T. Baxter and Sidney Davidson (Homewood: R. D. Irwin, 1962), 44.
16. George J. Benston, "Accounting Numbers and Economic Values," *The Antitrust Bulletin* 37 (Spring 1982): 161–215 and "The Validity of Profits-Structure With Particular Reference to the FTC's Line of Business Data," *American Economic Review* 75 (March 1985): 37–68; Yale Brozen, "Significance of Profit Data for Antitrust Policy," in *Public Policy Toward Mergers,* edited by J. F. Weston and Sam Peltzman (Pacific Palisades: Goodyear, 1969), 110–27; William Breit and Kenneth G. Elzinga, "Information for Antitrust and Business Activity: Line-of-Business Reporting," in *The Federal Trade Commission Since 1970,* edited by Kenneth W. Clarkson and Timothy J. Muris (Cambridge: Cambridge University Press 1981), 98–120; Kenneth W. Clarkson, *Intangible Capital and Rates of Return* (Washington, D.C.: American Enterprise Institute, 1977), and the foreword by Yale Brozen; Franklin M. Fisher and John J. McGowan, "On the Misuse of Accounting Rates-of-Return to Infer Monopoly Profits," *American Economic Review* 73 (March 1983): 82–97, and the later commentary.
17. *Report of the FTC on Rates of Return in Selected Manufacturing Industries* (various issues).
18. Armen A. Alchian, "Uncertainty, Evolution, and Economic Theory," *Journal of Political Economy* 58 (June 1950): 211.
19. Alchian explained in some detail the reason for imitation. It "affords relief from the necessity of really making decisions and conscious innovations, which, if wrong, become 'inexcusable.' Unfortunately, failure or success often reflects the

willingness to depart from rules when conditions have changed; what counts, then, is not only imitative behavior but the willingness to abandon it at the 'right' time and circumstances. Those who are different and successful 'become' innovators, while those who fail become reckless violators of tried and true rules. Although one may deny the absolute appropriateness of such rules, one cannot doubt the existence of a strong urge to create conventions and rules (based on observed success) and a willingness to use them for action as well as for rationalization of inaction" (Ibid., 218).

20. See Scherer, *Industrial Market Structure and Economic Performance*, 2d ed., (Chicago: Rand McNally, 1980), 186–87, and the studies cited therein.
21. "Retail Genius: Charles Lazarus is A Reason for Toys 'R' Us Success," *Wall Street Journal*, 21 November 1985, 26; emphasis in original.
22. Joe S. Bain, "Relation of Profit Rate to Industry Concentration: American Manufacturing, 1936–1940," *Quarterly Journal of Economics* 65 (August 1951): 293–324.
23. F. M. Scherer, *Industrial Market Structure*, p. 267.
24. F. M. Scherer, "On The Current State of Knowledge In Industrial Organization," 1985, photocopy.

10. The Goal of the Firm: Revisited

Haim Levy

Abstract

A SEPARATION of ownership and management of large corporations may be a source of conflict of interest between the agent and his principal. It is shown that in an imperfect market with asymmetrical information, chief executives would tend to reject risky projects with a positive net present value. This result stems from the fact that in case of inferior performance, the manager may be replaced, which would cause him severe financial losses. This result is valid even if the agent and the principals have the same preference and the same initial wealth. Bonus incentive schemes tend to decrease this discrepancy between the goals of the stockholder and the manager.

Introduction and Background

The theoretical arguments that appear in the financial and economic literature virtually always conclude that the goal of the firm should be to maximize its market value or, alternatively, to maximize the market value of the stockholders' equity.[1] Based on this value-maximization goal, economists have developed some economic models by which they investigate important economic issues, e.g., optimal production, optimal financial structure, etc.

Accepting these classical economic models of the behavior of the firm im-

Note: The author acknowledges the helpful comments of Simon Benninga, Yoram Kroll, and Meir Scheneler.

plicitly assumes that no separation exists between the owner of the firm and its manager, or between the decision maker and the security holder. If indeed there is no such separation, then it is reasonable to assume that the decision maker operates the firm to maximize profit or, to be more precise (taking risk into account), to maximize the market value of the firm.

Empirical evidence, however, does not support this hypothesis. Lanzillotti (1958), who investigated twenty-five large corporations, reports on other declared goals, i.e., maintaining the firm market share, not falling below some minimum return, achieving a target return, etc. One way to interpret these findings is to claim that all these goals serve as proxies to value maximization. Another way, which seems more reasonable, is simply to accept these goals at their face value, hence the management goal does not necessarily coincide with the stockholders' goal. If this interpretation is valid, many of the well-accepted results of the theory of the firm that rely on value maximization do not hold and should be adjusted to reflect the discrepancy between the goal of the stockholders and that of the firm's management.

Since many modern corporations are managed by professional managers who are not the owners of the firm, economists have been concerned that the classical models of firm behavior may be inappropriate and other models that take into account the possible conflict of interest between managers and owners of the firm are called for.[2]

On the other hand, Fama (1980) claims that the separation between the ownership and management is an efficient form of organization. More specifically, Fama claims that the problems that arise due to the separation of ownership and management are resolved once we consider the opportunities provided by the labor market for the managers' service both within and outside the firm. The key factor in Fama's argument is that managers have a one-period contract that is revised every period. Hence, managers have no incentive to deviate from what they are supposed to deliver by their contract, since a deviation will cost them a wage reduction in the future. For example, managers may perceive that the present value of their future wages (human capital) changes by the same amount of wealth change experienced by other factors operating in the firm, and by the stockholders in particular. In this case, the managers have no motive to deviate from the stockholders' goal, which according to Fama resolves the potential problems induced by the separation of management and ownership characterizing most modern corporations.

In the model developed in this paper, I assume, like Fama, periodical revisions in the managers' compensation. However, I assume an imperfect labor market for executives. The stockholders evaluate an executive's performance by looking at the financial outcomes, but the executive has more information regarding the selected projects. Also, the labor market is not perfect since not all information regarding the performance of a given manager is available to all firms. As a result, it is no longer true that all factors operating within the firm are exposed to the same change in future wealth. For example, a 20 percent reduction in the stock price (owner's factor) may be followed by a greater than 20 percent reduction in the manager's wage (their human capital). Namely, the penalties resulting from bad performance are not identical for managers and stockholders. Indeed, inferior performance by a manager may cost him his job, even though the firm does not go bankrupt. Before this issue is elaborated, a few examples of actual executive layoffs are provided. The model established in the section "N-Period Model" is in line with these examples.

Establishing the precise reasons for a chief executive losing his job is not a simple task. Normally, the firm announces a "resignation" (rather than a layoff) of the chief executive. Although the reason for the layoff is almost never released, a careful analysis of the recent developments in the firm under consideration as well as an analysis of the income statements may reveal the economic reasons for the layoff. While a thorough empirical analysis of board of directors' decisions regarding this issue is beyond the scope of this paper, a few examples will demonstrate what is considered to be management failure leading to a layoff.

The *Wall Street Journal* of 31 August 1984 reports that Aetna's chief executive, John H. Filer, "will resign later this year." He was at that time fifty-nine years old and had joined the firm in 1958. Industry analysts praised Aetna's performance during most of Filer's tenure, but a recent drop in earnings caused the layoff. The earnings-per-share (EPS) of Aetna were as follows:

Year:	1979	1980	1981	1982	1983	1984
EPS: ($)	6.96	6.32	6.10	3.50	3.06	1.59

The earnings-per-share figure reveals a sharp drop since 1982. In August 1984, when it became clear that the earnings decline trend was continuing and even worsening, the company announced the layoff. In this example, three years in a row of a decline in earnings was a clear-cut signal to the board of directors that the decline in earnings was a result of mismanagement and not caused by random deviations from the mean earnings. The layoff followed a 20 percent reduction in the chief executive's salary in 1983 after a few years of a stable wage and bonuses of about $670,000 a year.

The second case has to do with the resignation of Wheeling-Pittsburgh's chief executive, Dennis J. Carney. This case is probably more famous than Filer's resignation because of the sixty-one-day labor strike and the specific demand by the employees that Carney be fired. In September 1985 Mr. Carney agreed to resign. On the surface it seems that the resignation was induced by the mishandling of the labor strike. However, another careful look at the earnings figures reveals that this company had suffered losses for three consecutive years:

Year:	1979	1980	1981	1982	1983	1984
EPS: ($)	12.16	2.85	7.03	d 21.05	d 15.74	d 14.12

(d denotes a deficit)

The board of directors probably made their decision based not only on the labor strike but also on the last few years' performance. Once again, three years in a row of bad performance indicated to the board of directors that these were *not* random deviations (which have nothing to do with the chief executive's talent), and he was therefore laid off. As in the previous case, the salary and bonus of the chief executive had dropped in the last few years. It was $355,000 in 1979, $265,000 in 1980, and $413,000 in 1981. From 1981 the drop in compensation was quite sharp: $280,000 in 1982 and $265,000 in 1983. These salary and bonus figures clearly reflect the board of directors' dissatisfaction with the management since 1982, which culminated in Carney's layoff in 1985.

A third and last case given in this paper is the resignation of the chairman and chief executive of BancTexas Group Inc., Edward C. Nash, which took place in August 1985. Unlike the chief executives of the two previous cases, who were close to retirement when they resigned, Nash resigned at age forty-four.[3] Though no official reason was given for the resignation, the firm's earnings-per-share given below provide sufficient explanation for the layoff.

Year:	1981	1982	1983	1984	1985
EPS: ($)	0.47	0.55	0.08	d 0.40	d (–)

(d denotes a deficit; "–" denotes that the precise figure is unknown)

In the second quarter of 1985 the loss was $13.5 million, compared with a loss of $6.5 million in the whole previous year (1984) and a profit of $3.6 million in 1983.

Thus, once again we obtain the same reaction from the board of directors: earnings dropped sharply in 1983, a deficit was recorded in 1984 that continued in 1985. In the third year, after the board of directors saw the 1985 results, a decision to lay off the chief executive was made.

Though our three cases are for illustrative purposes only, it is interesting to note that in each case the board of directors used three years in a row of "failure" as an indication that the decline was not caused merely by random deviations. According to the board of directors, such an event reflects mismanagement (or poor management talent) rather than random macroeconomic factors (e.g., a recession in the industry) that have nothing to do with the manager's talent. A second interesting point is that in each of the three cases the board of directors made the decision to lay off the chief executive in August-September, thus guaranteeing a fresh start with a new chief executive in the following year.

In a competitive labor market for managers one may claim that the fired manager could find a job in another firm and that his human capital should not be reduced by more than the reduction in his marginal product, even if he were fired. Theoretically this claim is valid. In practice, however, the "noise" is so large that the fired manager either would suffer a much higher reduction in wages or would not find a job at all. I believe that in practice the announcement that the manager of a given firm is fired induces an underestimation of the manager's talent that would cause him difficulty finding a job even at a lower wage. After all, what firms would choose to hire a name associated with failure?

Though it is obvious that one can find examples to counter this claim, we believe that for most managers being fired causes them to be underpaid in subsequent jobs. To be more specific, the market estimates the manager's talent T at time t (and determines his compensation accordingly) based on the past performance, $\psi\,(T_t/X_{t-1}, X_{t-2}, \ldots)$ when ψ is some estimation function and X_{t-1}, X_{t-2} are the past financial outcomes. There is no reason to assume that this estimate is biased. However, if it is announced that the manager is fired, a new market estimate is established $\psi\,(T_t/X_{t-1}, X_{t-2} \ldots, F)$, where F stands for the event "the manager has been fired." A basic ingredient in this paper is that there is asymmetrical information in the market. The other firms do not know what caused the manager's dismissal; hence the announcement of the event F causes other firms to offer the fired manager compensations below what he may deserve according to his talent (i.e., market overshooting to the new information). It may be that even if the expected value $E\psi(T_t/X_{t-1}, X_{t-2}, \ldots F)$ is unbiased, the variance of this estimate increases with the layoff information, so that risk-averse firms will offer the manager wages below his true and unobserved talent. Thus, this paper hinges on the assumption that the market is imperfect and the fired manager's opportunities in the labor market fall short of his talent.

The issue on which I focus in this paper falls into the well-known category of the agent-principal relationship. This category covers the relationships between the professional and his client, between the insurer and the insured, between the shareholders and the management, and many more. Most studies published on this issue deal with risk sharing and the establishment of a one-period contract that is Pareto-optimal.[4] Attention in this paper is on the share-

The Goal of the Firm

holders-management relationship. Unlike most other studies, this work emphasizes the multiperiod relationship that greatly affects an agent-principal relationship.

It is shown in this paper that under certain conditions management tends to take less risk than stockholders would be willing to take. A risky project deemed desirable by the stockholders may be rejected by the management. This is not because managers are risk-averse, but because of the multiperiod wage and compensation scheme that managers face.

The Model and Assumption

The economic literature that deals with principal-agent issues assumes that the agent has a utility function $U(C_1, C_2, e)$ (in the two-period case) with

$$\partial U/\partial C_1 > 0, \ \partial U/\partial C_2 > 0, \text{ and } \partial U/\partial e < 0,$$

where C_1, C_2 stand for the consumption in the two periods and e is the agent's effort (see Eaton and Rosen [1983]).

In this model, it is assumed that the firm's executive is giving his best effort on the job, hence e does not appear. However, there is one unknown variable, the manager's talent. The stockholders observe the past financial outcomes from which he can draw a conclusion about the manager's talent. I assume that the daily management is efficient and concentrate on the project's selection by the manager. We further assume asymmetrical information. The manager knows (or thinks he knows) the profitability of the projects that he selects, but the stockholders can evaluate the profitability level (adjusted for risk) just by looking at the ex post facto performance. The stockholders compensate the manager according to his talent, which is being estimated based on the ex post facto financial results. In case of severe reduction in earnings, the stockholders may want to replace the manager. Thus, as in testing a hypothesis in statistics, the stockholders develop a decision rule based on sample data (ex post facto returns), which will be like

$X \in R$: replace the manager
$X \in A$: do not replace the manager,

where R and A stand for the "rejection" and "acceptance" areas and X is a vector of ex post facto returns. The manager who knows that his income will be reduced in case that $X \in R$ will select projects that will increase the probability that $X \in A$ even if these projects are not in the best interest of the stockholders. As explained in the introduction, I assume that if the manager is fired due to imperfect information regarding his talent, the other firms overreact to this new piece of information and the manager's future income will be below his marginal productivity (his talent). Thus, the manager has a strong incentive to avoid the event $X \in R$.

Under this general framework, I show that the manager will not select projects that constitute the best interest of the stockholders. Thus, a conflict of interest between the stockholders and the manager arises.

It is simple to demonstrate a possible conflict of interest between stockholders and the firm's managers even without the need to assume asymmetrical information. For example, it is sufficient to assume that stockholders and the managers reveal different degrees of risk aversion (i.e., are characterized by different types of utility functions). Furthermore, even if all are characterized by the same preference it is sufficient that the managers and the owners will have different levels of initial wealth to explain a possible conflict of interest. These possible differences do not induce a systematic deviation in the management action from those desired by stockholders. The manager may be more risk-averse than some stockholders, but it would be absurd to claim that managers of all firms are systematically less (or more) risk-averse than all the stockholders. Thus, the fact that management and the stockholders are characterized by different preferences may lead to a random deviation of the manager's action from the one desired by the stockholders, but it does not lead to any systematic and predictable deviation. In my model I make some assumptions that neutralize this random deviation, hence concentrating on a possible systemic deviation.

Let U be the utility function of the manager and the representative stockholder. To avoid the "random" conflict of interest, assume that both also have the same initial wealth W_0 and that they hold the same number of shares in the firm. The manager gets in a year t a wage of W_t for the firm management, and the stockholder income from wages and other sources not related to the firm is also W_t. I further assume: (1) In each period t the consumption C_t is equal to the available cash flow; (2) When we deal with multiperiod decisions we assume an additive utility function:[5]

$$U(C_1, C_2 \ldots C_n) = \sum_{t=0}^{n} (1+r)^{-t} U(C_t),$$

where r is the discount rate; we assume that the manager as well as the stockholder act to maximize their expected utility; and (3) The returns induced by a given project are identical and independent random variables across years. (This assumption is not necessary but it simplifies the discussion.)

The Goal of the Firm 187

Before we turn to the analysis, once again recall that the random deviation of the manager's actions from those desired by the owner of the firm have been neutralized by assuming that stockholders and managers have identical preferences, identical initial incomes, face the same discount rate r, etc. Even in this case we show that the manager would tend to reject risky projects whose net present value is positive. When we relax some of these assumptions, the deviation will consist of a systematic deviation and a random deviation. Since the random deviation is nonpredictable, we concentrate in this paper on the possible systematic deviation.

The Results

One-Period Analysis

Suppose that the manager considers adopting a project whose initial outlay is I (all figures are proportional to the number of shares held by the manager and the stockholder) and the resulting cash flow one period hence is $X_1(I)$. If the project is not undertaken, the manager's current cash flow is W_0+X_0 when W_0 is his initial wealth including the wage received at time t_0, and X_0 is the cash flow he obtains at time t_0 (dividends) from the firm's currently employed assets. Note that the decision is made at period t_0, hence X_0 is already known and is not a random variable. Similarly, in period 1 his cash flow is given by $W_1 + X_1$. If the investment is carried out his cash flow in period t_0 is $W_0 - I + X_0$, namely the current dividends are reduced by the investment amount, and the future income is $W_1 + X_1 + X_1(I)$ where X_1 is the cash flow in t_1 from the currently employed assets, $W_1 -$ his wage income in t_1 and $X_1(I)$ is the additional cash flow due to the new investment. Obviously X_1 and $X_1(I)$ are random variables. Having this framework the manager would implement the project if and only if the following inequality holds:

(1) $\quad U(W_0 + X_0 - I) + (1 + r)^{-1}EU(W_1 + X_1 + X_1(I))$
$> U(W_0 + X_0) + (1 + r)^{-1}EU(W_1 + X_1)$

Note that the left-hand side of equation (1) is the expected utility if the project is executed, while the right-hand side is the expected utility if it is rejected. On both sides the first term (($W_0 + X_0 - I$), and ($W_0 + X_0$), respectively) is certain, while the second term is a random variable (X_1 and $X_1(I)$). However, W_1 is also certain since X_0 is already known; hence the manager's salary, which depends on X_0, is known.

The stockholder who is assumed to have the same utility function U, the same income from other sources (his wage) W_t, and hold the same number of shares as the manager does also would be better off with the project executed only if equation (1) holds. Thus, in this simple one-period model, there is no conflict of interest between stockholders and management. Obviously, if one of these assumptions is violated (e.g., the stockholders and the manager do not hold the same number of shares in the firm), equation (1) may hold for the manager but not for the stockholders or vice versa, but we cannot say which of the two situations occurs. Thus, under this set of assumptions, in the one-period model there is no conflict of interest between the managers and the owners of the firm.

Two-Period Model

All assumptions of the one-period case hold. However, the return on the investment is X_1 at t_1 and X_2 at t_2. The board of directors (or the compensation committee) examines the management performance at the end of the first period. They adopt the following rule: if X (or the equivalent earnings-per-share figure) is smaller than some minimum level D (D stands for a "disastrous level"), the manager is fired. The information that the manager is fired spreads out very quickly in the business community, and as a result he cannot get another job as manager. His income for holding the shares of the firm is unaffected, but his management income, W_2, in the second period, t_2, is drastically reduced. For simplicity and without loss of generality, let us assume first that $W_2 = 0$ in the case that the manager is fired (this assumption is later relaxed).

Table 10.1 summarizes the stockholder and the manager cash flows in the two-period model. Once again, note that the event in t_0 already occurred, and so all variables in the column t_0 are certain. For simplicity we also assume that $X_0 > D$, hence the manager is not fired at t_1. The stockholder income and the manager income in t_1 are identical and given by $W_1 + X_1$ if the investment is not executed and by $W_1 + X_1 + X_1(I)$ if it is executed. The two-period model differs from the one-period model with respect to the cash flow at t_2. It is $W_2 + X_2$ for both the manager and the stockholder if the investment is not executed.[6] It is $W_2 + X_2 + X_2(I)$ for the stockholder if the investment is executed. However, for the manager, it is $W_2 + X_2 + X_2(I)$ with probability $1-P$ and only $X_2 + X_2(I)$ with probability P, when P is given by

$$P = Pr(X_1 + X_1(I) < D).$$

In the two-period model, unlike the one-period case, the manager's compensation in the second period is a function of his performance in the first period. A conflict of interest between stockholder and the manager may therefore arise even when both have the same preference, U. Let us elaborate on this point.

The stockholder would be better off with the project executed if and only if inequality (2) holds:

The Goal of the Firm

Table 10.1.

	Period		
	t_0	t_1	t_2
Stockholder			
Without Investment I	$W_0 + X_0$	$W_1 + X_1$	$W_2 + X_2$
With Investment I	$W_0 + X_0 - I$	$W_1 + X_1 + X_1(I)$ $(= W_1 + Y_1)$	$W_2 + X_2 + X_2(I)$
Manager			
Without Investment I	$W_0 + X_0$	$W_1 + X_1$	$W_2 + X_2$
With Investment I	$W_0 + X_0 - I$	$W_1 + X_1 + X_1(I)$ $(= W_1 + Y_1)$	$X_2 + X_2(I)$ if $Y_1 \leq D$ with probability P $W_2 + X_2 + X_2(I)$ if $Y_1 > D$ with probability $1-P$

(2) $U(W_0 + X_0 - I) + (1 + r)^{-1}EU(W_1 + X_1 + X_1(I))$
$+ (1 + r)^{-2}EU(W_2 + X_2 + X_2(I))$
$> U(W_0+X_0)+(1 + r)^{-1}EU(W_1 + X_1)$
$+ (1+r)^{-2}EU(W_2+X_2)$.

The manager, on the other hand, will accept the project if equation (3) holds:

(3) $U(W_0 + X_0 - I) + (1 + r)^{-1}EU(W_1 + X_1 + X_1(I))$
$+ (1 + r)^{-2}[PEU(X_2 + X_2(I)) + (1 - P)EU(W_2 + X_2 + X_2(I))]$
$> U(W_0+X_0)+(1 + r)^{-1}EU(W_1 + X_1) + (1+r)^{-2}EU(W_2+X_2)$.

Comparing equations (2) and (3) reveals that all terms are identical apart from the second-year cash flow in a case where the project is executed. Ignoring the term $(1 + r)^{-2}$, it is

(4) $PEU(X_2 + X_2(I)) + (1 - P)EU(W_2 + X_2 + X_2(I))$

for the manager and

(5) $EU(W_2 + X_2 + X_2(I))$

for the stockholder. Since $W_2 > 0$, equation (5) is greater than equation (4)[7] which implies that equation (2) may hold but that equation (3) does not.

Hence, a project desired by the stockholder may be rejected by the decision maker, the manager.

Figure 10.1 illustrates a case where a project that is desired by the stockholder is rejected by the manager. Since the cash flows in t_0 and t_1 are identical for both parties, they are ignored in the graphic illustration, analysis being focused on the cash flows obtained at t_2.

Assume that X_1 (and X_2) obtains two values d_1 and d_2 with probability P and $1-P$, respectively. Define the variables $Y_1 = X_1 + X_1(I)$ and $Y_2 = X_2 + X_2(I)$. Assume that Y_1 (and Y_2) obtains two values h_1 and h_2 with probabilities q and $1-q$, respectively. Thus, if the project is taken in the second period, the stockholder obtains either $W_2 + h_1$ or $W_2 + h_2$. Since by construction point b is above point a, the project is desired by the stockholder.[8] Let us turn to the manager's cash flows. If $h_1 > D$ and $h_2 > D$, it is identical to the stockholder's cash flows, and no conflict of interest arises. However, in the most general case assume that $h_1 < D$ and $h_2 > D$. If h_1 occurs $W_2 = 0$; hence the manager obtains in the second period h_1 and h_2 with probabilities q and $1-q$, respectively. Since point c is below point a, the manager may reject the project. To be more specific, the manager gets expected utility c with probability P (where $P = Pr(Y_1 \leq D)$) and expected utility b with probability $1-P$. Thus, though $b > a$ (from the stockholder's point of view the project should be accepted), it might be that the project would be rejected, since for the decision maker the following may hold:

$$Pc + (1 - P)b < a.$$

Namely, from the manager's point of view the expected utility with the project is lower than the expected utility without the project.

This graphic analysis emphasizes the role of risk or the dispersion of outcomes in the decision-making process. If the dispersion of income is not very large, namely h_1 and h_2 are greater than D, or alternatively if $Pr(Y_1 < D)$ is very small, the manager will take the risky project. However, if $h_1 < D$, the project's cash flow dispersion is large enough so that the manager would reject the project. Note that from the stockholder's point of view the expected return outweighs the risk involved (see point b is above point a), yet the project is rejected by the manager.

Thus, managers tend to reject risky projects even though the expected return justifies taking the risk. In the capital asset pricing model (CAPM) analogy, projects with large beta would be rejected even though the estimated expected return ER_i is larger than μ_i—the equilibrium return as stated by the CAPM. Namely, projects that lie above the security market line may be rejected because of their relatively large risk.

The Goal of the Firm

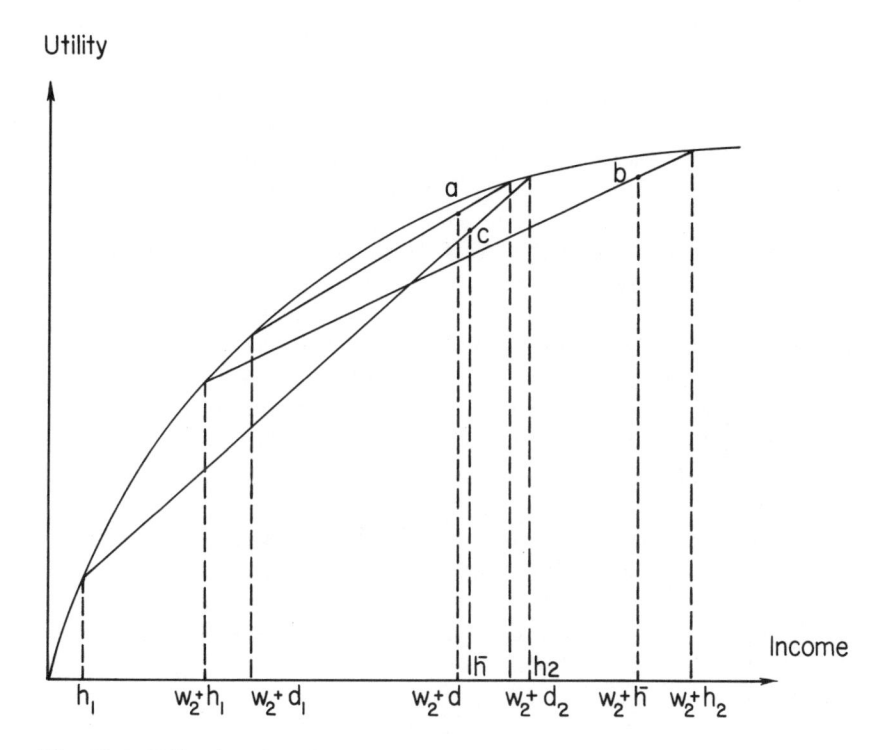

Utility

Fig. 10.1. Utility function of management.

Supportive evidence for this discrepancy between stockholder and manager attitudes can be found in a survey conducted by Blume, Friend, and Westerfield (1980). They have found that even though the industry cost of capital is 12.4 percent, managers (on average) set a cutoff rate of 16.2 percent. Thus, the managers require extra premium of about 3.8 percent above and beyond what is required by the stockholders.[9] In terms of figure 10.1, the manager requires that point b will be well above point a such that the weighted average $Pc + (1 - P)b$ would be higher than point a (see figure 10.1). Stockholders, on the other hand, simply require that $b>a$, and the stronger requirement by the managers reflects the extra 3.8 percent required premium.

Two-Period Model with Bonus and Penalty

So far we have assumed that whenever the first-year cash flow is below a certain level the manager is fired and his income is $W_2 = 0$. In this section we make the model more realistic by assuming that the second-year income from wage W_2 is a function of the first-year cash flow. This function is given as follows:

$$W_2(Y_1) = \begin{bmatrix} W_2 - \phi(Y_1) & Y_1 < D \\ W_2 & D \leq Y_1 \leq S. \\ W_2 + \psi(Y_1) & Y_1 > S \end{bmatrix}$$

When Y_1 is the first-year cash flow if the investment is executed, namely, $Y_1 = X_1 + X_1(I)$. Also $\psi'(Y_1)$ and $\phi'(Y_1)$ are positive, D denotes a "disaster" level of income, S denotes a "success," and W_2 is the second-year income if no bonus is received and no penalty is imposed. Namely, if the income Y_1 is below a certain level D the manager is penalized, and the penalty is a function of the deviation from D. If the income Y_1 is abnormally high, $Y_1 > S$, the manager obtains a bonus that is a function of the magnitude of the success. Any income in the range $D \leq Y_1 \leq S$ is considered as a normal income; hence the manager is neither penalized nor rewarded.

This model is quite general, and it includes the previous case $W_2 = 0$ when $\phi(Y_1) = W_2$ whenever $Y_1 < D$ as a special case.

It is simple to show that when a bonus incentive scheme does not exist our previous result (see (b) above) holds also with a continuous penalty function $W_2 - \phi(Y_1)$. However, with bonus as well as penalty schemes, unlike the previous result, it is not clear that the manager would tend to take less risk than the stockholder wishes. We turn now to investigate this issue.

Once again, since the cash flow in t_0 and t_1 are identical to both parties (see table 10.1), we focus our attention on the second-year cash flow. Denote the cash flow induced by holding the stock by Y_2, where $Y_2 = X_2 + X_2(I)$. The stockholder second-year expected utility if the risky project is executed is given by:

(6) $$E_s U(\cdot) = \int_{-\infty}^{\infty} U(W_2 + Y_2) f(Y_2) dY_2,$$

which also can be written as:

(6') $$E_s U(\cdot) = \int_{-\infty}^{\infty} U(W_2 + Y_2) f(Y_2) dY_2 \int_{-\infty}^{\infty} f(Y_1) dY_1$$

(recall $\int_{-\infty}^{\infty} f(Y_1) dY_1 = 1$)

The Goal of the Firm 193

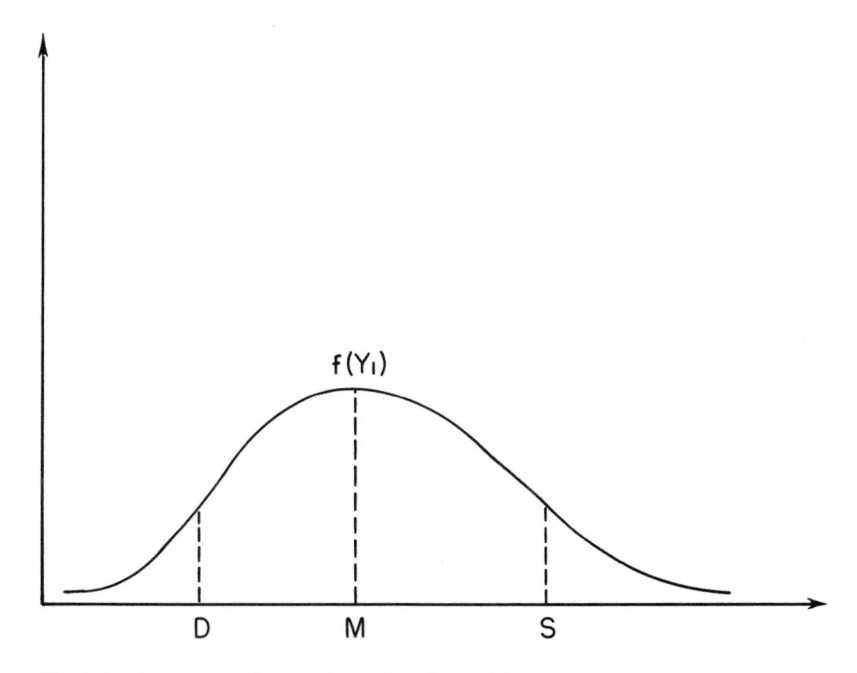

Fig. 10.2. Management reward-penalty relationship.

where the subscript s denotes the "stockholder."
Given the above reward penalty function, the manager's expected utility is given by $E_m(\cdot)$ (where the subscript m denotes the "manager"),

(7) $$E_m U(\cdot) = \int_{-\infty}^{\infty} f(Y_2) \int_{D}^{S} U(W_2 + Y_2) f(Y_1) dY_1 dY_2$$

$$+ \int_{-\infty}^{\infty} f(Y_2) (\int_{-\infty}^{D} U(W_2 - \phi(Y_1) + Y_2) f(Y_1) dY_1) dY_2 dY_2$$

$$+ \int_{-\infty}^{\infty} f(Y_2) (\int_{S}^{\infty} U(W_2 + \psi(Y_1) + Y_2) f(Y_1) dY_1) dY_2$$

A comparison of equations (6) and (7) does not reveal a clear-cut relationship, namely $E_s U(\cdot) \gtreqless E_m U(\cdot)$ is possible. Thus, unlike the previous results, the manager may execute a risky project even though it should be rejected from the stockholder's point of view. The explanation of this scenario is quite obvious: it is possible that $\psi(Y_1)$ is greater than $\phi(Y_1)$ and also that

$Pr(Y_1<D)$ is smaller relative to $Pr(Y_1>S)$, which provide the manager an incentive to take the risky project. Obviously, these parameters as well as $\phi(Y_2)$ and $\psi(Y_1)$ are indirectly determined by the firm's compensation committee.

However, in case of a symmetrical reward-penalty scheme as described by figure 10.2, and when $\psi(Y_1) = \phi(Y_1)$, the manager would be inclined to reject a risky project that is desired by the stockholders, a result similar to the one discussed in the previous section. To see this we have to show that $E_s U(\ ) > E_m U(\ )$. Subtract equation (7) from equation (6') to obtain:

$$(8) \quad \Delta \equiv E_s U(\cdot) - E_m U(\cdot) = \int_{-\infty}^{\infty} f(Y_2) \int_{-\infty}^{D} [U(W_2 + Y_2) - U(W_2 - \phi(Y_1) + Y_2)] f(Y_1) dY_1 dY_2$$

$$- \int_{-\infty}^{\infty} f(Y_2) \int_{S}^{\infty} ([U(W_2 + \psi(Y_1) + Y_2) - U(W_2 + Y_2)] f(Y_1) dY_1) dY_2$$

(the integral in the range (D,S) is cancelled out).

Since the integral with respect to Y_2 is identical for both terms, the difference, Δ, is positive if and only if equation (9) holds,

$$(9) \quad \int_{-\infty}^{D} [U(W_2 + Y_2) - U(W_2 - \phi(Y_1) + Y_2)] f(Y_1) dY_1 >$$

$$\int_{S}^{\infty} [U(W_2 + \psi(Y_1) + Y_2) - U(W_2 + Y_2)] f(Y_1) dY_1.$$

However, assuming risk aversion, a symmetrical distribution of Y_1 (and of Y_2), and that $\psi(Y_1) = \phi(Y_1)$ (see figure 10.2) implies that Δ is positive since the utility difference

$$[U(W_2 + Y_2) - U(W_2 - \phi(Y_1) + Y_2)]$$

is larger than the utility difference

$$[U(W_2 + \psi(Y) + Y_2) - U(W_2 + Y_2)].$$

The above analysis leads to the following conclusions:

1. With a bonus-penalty scheme, the manager may take a project that from the stockholder's point of view should be rejected, and vice versa. The de-

cision in this case is a function of $\phi(Y_1)$, $\psi(Y_1)$, and the determined levels D and S.
2. With continuous penalty $\phi(Y_1)$ but with no bonus scheme, management will tend to reject projects that from the stockholder's point of view (i.e., with a positive net present value) should be accepted.
3. With a symmetrical bonus-penalty scheme and risk aversion, the manager will tend to reject risky projects that from the stockholder's point of view should be accepted. With risk neutrality, however, there is no conflict if interest exists.
4. Regarding relatively safe projects, namely when

$$Pr(D < Y_1 < S) = 1$$

no conflict of interest between stockholders and manager arises, even with risk aversion.

Thus, in order to avoid the rejection of projects with positive net present value, the compensation committee that penalized a manager with a bad ex post facto performance must also include a bonus scheme to avoid a rejection of projects whose net present value is positive.[10] While the bonus scheme works in the desired direction, hence reducing the conflict of interest, finding a bonus scheme that guarantees that all projects with positive NPV will be accepted is not an easy task.

N-Period Model

In the two-period model I assume that if the income in the first year falls below a certain level the manager is fired. This is a very unrealistic assumption (see the three examples given in the introduction), since the compensation committee understands that a low income in one year may reflect a random deviation of the risky cash flow and has nothing to do with the manager's talent, just as buying a stock with a high variance may yield a negative income in a given year. Thus a multiperiod decision model is called for. I construct below a model that conforms with the cases of the "resignation" of the chief executives given in the introduction.

Suppose that the manager takes an investment whose mean is μ and standard deviation is σ. There is a probability P that the random variable will be below a critical level D. However, if the cash flow is less than D for n years in a row, an event with a relatively low probability, the compensation committee would decide that the true mean cash flow is not μ but μ_1 when $\mu_1 < \mu$ (the same analysis can be conducted regarding the project's risk). Thus the manager was wrong in taking this project and the negative cash flows reflect his poor judgment rather than random deviations from the mean; hence the manager should be fired. Such a policy if adopted by the board of directors is very similar to the classical process of hypothesis testing. Suppose that the manager thinks that the mean profit is μ. The board of directors estimates (subjectively) that $P(X < D/\mu) = P$, when P is some probability, say, .10. If the compensation committee observed, for example, that the cash flow was less than D for three years in a row, an event whose probability under the null hypothesis is relatively small ($P^3 = (0.1)^3 = 0.001$), they reject the null hypothesis and conclude that the manager executed a project with relatively low mean (for the given risk) and the deviations are not random, hence the manager should be replaced. Namely, the stockholders do not have information on μ of the selected projects but infer this mean return simply by looking at the ex post facto return.

Suppose that a manager considers taking a risky investment I. For simplicity also assume that if the investment is not taken the probability of having cash flow less than D in n years in a row is zero. The board of directors would fire the manager if the cash flow were less than D for n years in a row. Both the stockholder and the manager have N years planning horizon ($n < N$). Under these assumptions the stockholder would be better off if the investment were executed if the following holds:

(10) $$U(W_0 + X_0 - I) + \sum_{t=1}^{N} (1 + r)^{-t} EU(W_t + Y_t)$$
$$\geq U(W_0 + X_0) + \sum_{t=1}^{N} (1 + r)^{-t} EU(W_t + X_t),$$

where $Y_t = X_t + X_t(I)$, i.e., the cash flow in year t without the investment (X_t) plus the additional cash flow due to the new investment $X_t(I)$.

The manager's cash flow if the project is not undertaken is given by the right-hand side of (10). But if the project is executed, the manager's cash flow would differ from the stockholder's cash flow due to the possibility of an event that would induce his replacement.

Assuming independence over time and that $Pr(Y_t < D) = P$, the manager will be fired in the $(n + 1)^{th}$ period with probability P_n when

$$P^n = Pr(Y_1 < D \cap Y_2 < D \ldots \cap Y_n < D).$$

(Note that if $Y_t < D$ less than n years in a row he is not fired.)

The Goal of the Firm 197

The manager will be fired in the $(n + 2)^{th}$ period in the case that event B occurs when

$$B = (Y_1 > D \cap Y_2 < D \cap Y_3 < D \ldots \cap Y_{n+1} < D) \text{ and}$$
$$P_r(B) = (1-P)P^n.$$

Namely, this event is like having a "success" ($Y_1 > D$) in the first period and a "failure" in the next n periods. By similar argument, there is a positive probability P_t that the manager will be fired in year t when $t = n + 1$, $n + 2 \ldots N$. (Recall that $n < N$.)

Assuming no bonus in the case that there is an exceptionally high income (this assumption can be relaxed; see the two-period case), the manager will accept the project if and only if

(11) $$U(W_0 + X_0 - I) + \sum_{t=1}^{n} (1 + r)^{-t} EU(W_t + Y_t)$$

$$+ (1 + r)^{-(n+1)}[P_n EU(Y_{n+1}) + (1 - P_n)EU(W_{n+1} + Y_{n+1})]$$
$$+ (1 + r)^{-(n+2)}[P_{n+1} EU(Y_{n+2}) + (1 - P_{n+1})EU(W_{n+2} + Y_{n+2})]$$
$$\vdots \qquad\qquad \vdots$$
$$+ (1 + r)^N[P_{N-1} EU(Y_N) + (1 - P_{N-1})EU(W_N + Y_N)]$$
$$> U(W_0 + X_0) + \sum_{t=1}^{N} (1 + r)^{-t} EU(W_t + X_t)$$

when P_t is the probability of being fired on year t.

The right-hand sides of (10) and (11) are identical. Also, all terms up to $t = n$ on the left-hand side of both equations are identical. However, all other terms on the left-hand side of (11) are smaller (or equal) to the corresponding terms of (10); hence (10) may hold yet (11) does not hold. To be more specific, take for example the $n + 1$ term. We have (ignoring the discount rate):

$$P_n EU(Y_{n+1}) + (1 - P_n)EU(W_{n+1} + Y_{n+1}) < EU(W_{n+1} + Y_{n+1}).$$

Since $P_n > 0$, $W_{n+1} > 0$ and the utility function is nonotonic.

Thus, a project with positive net present value (from the stockholder's point of view) may be rejected by the manager. This discrepancy increases with the project's risk, since in general the higher the risk the higher the probability P_t. Thus, the manager would be inclined to reject risky projects even if they are characterized by positive NPV.

Concluding Remarks

Assuming either risk neutrality of the manager or risk aversion, the economic literature of the agent-principal issue investigates contract schemes that constitute a Pareto-optimal solution (see Shavell [1979]).

In this paper the manager-stockholder relationship is analyzed in a multiperiod context. Though the manager's contract is revised every year, his decisions are multiperiod by their nature. For example, the manager may prefer a nonprofitable project with a relatively large cash flow in early years, in the interest of establishing his reputation (and perhaps moving to another job; see Narayanan [1983]).[11] He may prefer to avoid risky projects characterized by a positive net present value, since the risky project may involve a sequence of negative (or low) cash flows that with asymmetrical information may cost him his job, even if there is no justification for his replacement.

In a perfect market with symmetrical information there is no conflict of interest between the manager and the stockholder, since the manager can find another job that pays him exactly his marginal productivity. I believe that the labor market for chief executives is far from being perfect. The announcement of the dismissal of a chief executive spreads quickly in the business community, and as a result the chief executive will be paid a salary much lower than his marginal productivity in any future positions. Namely, his estimated talent, given that he was fired, is smaller than his true and unobserved talent.

Thus, the chief executive's monetary loss is much greater than that of the stockholder if the risky project reveals a low outcome in a given sequence of years. Hence, the chief executive will prefer low-risk projects even though their net present value is smaller than the net present value of high-risk projects.

One way to induce the manager to take more risk is to provide an incentive scheme. Indeed, over 90 percent of firms in the United States have management incentive schemes (see Johnson [1984]). Moreover, about a quarter of the executives' compensation is in the form of bonuses. Under this incentive scheme the manager may lose more than the stockholder if a "bad" outcome occurs; but he is rewarded more than the stockholder if an exceptionally "good" outcome occurs. Thus he may be willing to take risky projects that would be rejected without the bonus scheme. In spite of these incentive schemes, I still believe that the "loss" outweighs the gain for many executives, since the loss if the executive is fired leaves its mark for many years to come. This may explain the seemingly paradoxical result of Blume, Friend and Westerfield (1980) who found that on average the manager in U.S. industry sets a cutoff of 16.2 percent for project evaluation despite the fact that the weighted average cost of capital is only 12.4 percent. In other words, the owners of the firms (for the given risk) require 12.4 percent return while the managers require 16.2 percent; and the 3.8 percent difference represents extra risk premium required by the manager but not by the owners of the firm. Thus, a risky project is taken only if its mean is relatively high, namely the probability that the outcome will be below a certain level for a few years in a row is relatively small.

Notes

1. It can be shown that whether one maximizes the total value of the firm, the value of the equity, or the stock price he obtains the same results, since all these three goals coincide if carefully analyzed and compared. For more details, see Levy & Sarnat (1977).
2. See, for example, Baumol (1959); Simon (1959); Cyert and March (1963); Alchain and Demsetz (1972); and Jensen and Meckling (1976).
3. On the relationship between experience on the job and the number of years remaining in the labor market, see Harris and Holmstrom (1982); and Narayanan (1983).
4. See Ross (1973); Spence and Zeckhauser (1971); Harris and Raviv (1982); and Shavell (1979).
5. In their theoretical model, Eaton and Rosen (1983) deal with a general two-period utility $U(C_1, C_2...)$ function. However, they admit that in this general framework the analysis of the firm-executive relationship is very complicated, and they therefore provide a qualitative rather than a quantitative discussion.
6. In order to emphasize the role of the new investment we assume that $Pr(X_1 < D) = 0$. Hence, a "disaster" may occur only if the new investment I is executed.
7. Subtracting (4) from (5) we obtain

$$P[EU(W_2 + X_2 + X_2(I)) - EU(W_2 + X_2(I))] > 0,$$

since $P>0$, $W_2>0$ and U is a nonotonic nondecreasing utility function. Thus, (5) is greater than (4), which implies that (2) may hold but (3) does not.
8. Recall that the cash flows are ignored in periods t_0 and t_1. Alternatively, assume that the expected utility derived in t_0 and t_1 is the same no matter if the investment is taken or not. This does not diminish the generality of the results but simplifies the graphic illustration.
9. They claim that the higher cutoff value in comparison to the cost of capital can be attributed to the following factors: greater risk aversion of management in comparison to common stock investors "generally who are better able to diversify their risk." It also may reflect in part capital rationing.
10. One way to decrease the conflict between stockholders and the managers of the firm is to pay the managers in the firm's stocks. Indeed, Lewellen (1969) claims that the stockholding of the senior executives of large publicly held corporations constitutes a significant proportion of their reward. Thus, the decision maker would try to maximize the share price, which coincides with the shareholder's

goal. However, even this type of incentive scheme does not eliminate the "layoff risk" that the manager should take into account in his decision making.

11. Narayanan (1983), by making some simplifying assumptions regarding the preference of the decision makers, has shown that managers may prefer to execute projects with short-term cash flow (profit) at the expense of the long-term interest of the firm. Thus, a short-term project may be preferred to a long-term one even though the latter has a higher net present value. The explanation for this behavior is that short-term profit improves the board of directors' perception of the manager's ability, which is followed by an early increase in his wage. Obviously, this model is possible only if the manager possesses some information that is *not* common knowledge.

References

Alchain, A., and Demsetz, H. 1972. Production, information costs, and economic organization. *American Economic Review* 62 (December):777–95.
Baumol, W. J. 1959. *Business behavior, value and growth*. New York: Macmillan.
Blume, M. E., Friend, I., and Westerfield, R. 1980. *Impediments to capital formation*. Rodney L. White Center for Financial Research. December.
Cyert, M., and March, J. 1963. *A behavioral theory of the firm*. Englewood Cliffs, NJ: Prentice-Hall.
Eaton, Jonathan, and Rosen, Harvey S. 1983. Agency, delayed compensation, and the structure of executive remuneration. *Journal of Finance* 38, no. 5 (December): 1489–1505.
Fama, E. F. 1980. Agency problems and the theory of the firm. *Journal of Political Economy* 88 (April): 288–307.
Harris, M., and Holmstrom, B. 1982. A theory of wage dynamics. *Review of Economic Studies* 49 (July): 315–33.
Harris, M., and Raviv, A. 1978. Some results on incentive contracts with applications to education and employment, health insurance, and law enforcement. *American Economic Review* 68 (March): 20–30.
Jensen, M. C., and Meckling, W. H. 1976. Theory of the firm: Managerial behavior, agency costs and ownership structure. *Journal of Financial Economics* 3 (October): 305–60.
Johnson, A. 1984. Executive pay: Reflecting the economy's healthy glow. *Nation's Business* (December): 46–48.
Lanzillotti, R. 1958. Pricing objectivess in large companies. *American Economic Review* 48 (December): 921–40.
Levy, H., and Sarnat, M. 1977. A pedagogic note on alternative formulation of the goal of the firm. *Journal of Business* 50 (October):526–28.
Lewellen, Wilbur G. 1969. Management ownership in the large firm. *Journal of Finance* 24, no. 2 (May): 299–320.
Narayanan, M. P. 1983. Managerial incentives for short-term results. *Journal of Finance* (December):380–87.
Ross, S. 1973. The economic theory of agency: The principal's problem. *The American Economic Review* 63, no. 2 (May): 134–39.
Shavell, S. 1979. Risk sharing and incentives in the principal and agent relationship. *Bell Journal of Economics* 10 (Spring): 55–73.

Simon, H. A. 1959. Theories of decision making in economic and behavioral science. *American Economic Review* 49 (June): 253–83.
Spence, M., and Zeckhauser, R. 1971. Insurance, information and individual action. *American Economic Review* 61 (May): 380–87.
Stiglitz, J. 1974. Risk sharing and incentives in sharecropping. *Review of Economic Studies* 61, no. 2 (April): 219–56.